Operational Security Management in Violent Environments

A Field Manual for Aid Agencies
by Koenraad Van Brabant

Good Practice Review 8

Humanitarian Practice Network (HPN)
Overseas Development Institute, London

CONTENTS

PART I INTRODUCTION

1 The Scope of This Good Practice Review   2

2 A Management Approach to Security   8

PART II SITUATIONAL ANALYSIS

3 Assessment and Analysis   16

PART VI PERSONAL AND PERSONNEL DIMENSIONS OF SECURITY MANAGEMENT

PART VII **SECURITY MANAGEMENT**

ANNEXES

List of Diagrams

Disclaimer

Security management is about reducing risk. It does not offer any guarantee that incidents will not occur. It is also about contextual adaptation and situational judgement. This Good Practice Review offers guidance of a general nature and does not cover all situations. The appropriateness of a specific measure will often depend on the context, and in some situations following the tips and guidelines mentioned here may not be the best course of action and could actually increase the risk. The author, the Humanitarian Practice Network and the Overseas Development Institute decline responsibility for incidents, and for loss of assets or injury or death.

Several case examples refer to specific countries and actors. They are invariably simplified and often no longer 'current'. Their purpose is to illustrate a point. They should not be taken as an adequate or currently valid statement about threat patterns in a particular country or as a statement about the security management of one or more agencies.

Glossary

Acceptance strategy: the attempt to remove the threat or have local actors control the threat on your behalf by getting their more or less formal consent and acceptance for your presence and your work.

Battlefield survival: measures to lessen the risk of death or injury when under fire, or in an area which is under fire from any sort of weapon.

Booby trap: an improvised or custom-made explosive usually attached to or concealed under ordinary objects that acts as a mine to deter or harm people approaching the booby trap area.

Car-jacking: the stealing of a car at gun-point, ie, while the driver is in the car.

Communications tree: an arrangement to spread information rapidly such as a security alert, whereby one person/agency informs eg, three others, who each in turn then inform three pre-identified others, and so on.

Compound mentality: a tendency of aid agencies, and especially their international staff, to discuss and analyse their environment among themselves with little reference to or interaction with non-aid actors in that environment.

Counter-surveillance: watching whether you are being watched and studied by people with malicious intent, here used in the context of a threat of kidnapping or armed robbery.

Critical incident: a security incident in which life was threatened and which led to an experience of mortal danger; either of the aid worker, or of someone emotionally dear or physically close to him/her.

Danger habituation: a usually unconscious adjustment of one's threshold of acceptable risk resulting from constant exposure to danger; the result is a reduction of one's objective assessment of risk, leading possibly to increased risk-taking behaviour.

Deterrence strategy: a strategy to try and deter someone from posing or effecting a threat against you by posing a counter-threat, in its most extreme form through the use of armed protection.

Evacuation: the withdrawal of staff across an international border.

Hibernation: choosing, or being forced to stay, in the middle of a crisis and danger zone often because evacuation could not yet/no longer be effected.

Incident analysis: deeper and more critical inquiry into the structural and contextual factors that allowed a security incident to happen; questioning the effectiveness of the various dimensions and steps in the security management, and asking whether or to what degree the agency or one or more of its staff members could have been perceived to be 'provoking' anger or aggression.

Incident inquiry: the collection of situational and circumstantial information about an incident that took place beyond the basic facts stated in the incident report.

Incident mapping: the visualisation, usually on a map but potentially also in a timeframe, of when and where and what type of incidents happened in an attempt to find patterns and identify high-risk areas and high-risk times.

Incident survival: what was done and/or avoided by those caught up in a security incident to minimise the harm that could be done to them.

Neighbourhood watch: a more or less formalised scheme among neighbours to keep an eye open for suspicious people and crime.

Personal sense of security: a subjective and therefore potentially misleading form of threat and risk assessment relying on one's personal impressions of a situation.

Post-traumatic stress disorder (PTSD): a psychological condition that may affect people who have suffered severe emotional trauma, and may cause sleep disturbances, flashbacks, anxiety, tiredness and depression.

Prodding: a key technique used in extraction from a (suspected) minefield whereby the soil is very carefully examined for possible mines before a foot is set on it.

Protection: used here as distinct from 'safety' and 'security' to refer to the 'protection' of civilians and non-combatants who are not aid agency staff.

Protection strategy: the use of protective procedures and devices to reduce your vulnerability; the strategy does not affect the level of threat.

Risk assessment/analysis: an attempt to consider risk more systematically in terms of the threats in your environment, your particular vulnerabilities, and your security measures to reduce the threat and/or reduce your vulnerability.

Risk reduction: the purpose of your security management, by reducing the threat and/or reducing your vulnerability.

Rules of engagement: guidelines to soldiers or armed guards regarding the conditions under which they can use force, and stipulating how much force may be used.

Safety: used here as distinct from 'protection' and 'security' to refer to 'accidents' caused by nature (eg, avalanche) or non-violent circumstances (eg, fire, road accidents) and to illness, injury and death resulting from medical conditions not brought about by violence, or due to lax safety guidelines and procedures in the workplace.

Scenario thinking: thinking 'forward' about how the situation may evolve in the near and medium-term future, and how the threats in your environment might develop; reviewing the assumptions in your plans and thinking about what you would do if they do not hold.

Security: used here to indicate the protection of aid personnel and aid agency assets from violence.

Security (alert) phases: a summary classification of various possible levels of risk and insecurity in your environment, each of which requires a specific set of mandatory security procedures.

Security strategies: used here to describe the three ideal-type strategies of acceptance, protection and deterrence.

Social reference: a recommendation or personal 'guarantee' about a potential recruit from someone who has not necessarily had any professional involvement with the recruit but knows his/her standing and reputation within a community.

Standard operating procedures: formally established procedures for carrying out particular operations or dealing with particular situations, here specifically to prevent an incident happening, to survive an incident, or to follow as part of the agency's incident/crisis management.

Terrain awareness: being attentive to the physical and social environment in which you are moving, where potential dangers may come from, and where you might find help or cover.

Threat: a danger in your operating environment.

Threat assessment/analysis: the attempt to examine more systematically the nature, origin, frequency and geographical concentration of threats.

Threat mapping: visualising and illustrating threats on a geographical map.

Threshold of acceptable risk: the point beyond which you consider the risk too high to continue operating so that you must withdraw yourself from the danger zone; influenced by the probability that an incident will occur, and the seriousness of the impact if it occurs.

Triangulation: cross-checking information or details by comparing the opinion or version from different sources.

Tripwire: a wire connected to the fuse of a mine or a booby trap; touching, cutting or displacing it will detonate the explosive.

Unacceptable risk: an assessment that even your security measures are not able to sufficiently reduce the likelihood and/or the impact of an incident occurring, to justify continued operations and exposure to the threat.

Unexploded ordnance (UXO): any type of munition (bullet, hand grenade, mortar shell, etc) that has been fused (prepared for firing) but not used, or that has been fired but has not gone off and is considered unstable and dangerous.

Warden/warden system: one or more focal points for security with typically a responsibility for a set of people in a defined geographical area; the warden is an important node in the communications tree and will also ensure that all those under his/her responsibility follow agreed security procedures.

Dedication

This Good Practice Review is dedicated to Smruti and Medinah, life-long friends through security.

Acknowledgements

The list of people who one way or another have contributed to this GPR is very long. Among them special mention should be made of Lucy Brown, Jan Davis, Philippe Dind, Jonathan Dworken, David Dyck, Rob Lowe, Michael O'Neill and Lisa Schirsch, with whom I had the immense pleasure of developing and pilot testing a training curriculum on operational security management. The role of Jane Swan, who brought us together and transformed us into a 'well-bonded' and effective team, was crucial. Others who need mentioning include Mark Bowden, Nan Buzard, Bob Churcher, Kateri Clement, John Cosgrave, Jean Philippe Debus, Veronique de Geoffroy, Jayne Docherty, Enrique Eguren, Sue Emmott, John Fawcett, Pierre Gallien, Max Glaser, Sean Greenaway, Francois Grunewald, Andy Harriss, Melissa Himes, Chris Horwood, Bernard Jacquemart, Tajma Kurt, Toby Lanzer, Nick Leader, John Logan, Sarah Longford, Richard Manlove, Randy Martin, Rae McGrath, Paul Meijs, Anita Menghetti, Jonathan Napier, Sydia Nelo, Nick Nobbs, Annemarie O'Reilly, Smruti Patel, Mike Penrose, Noël Philip, Eric Pitois, Marc Powe, Steve Penny, Moira Reddick, George Somerwill, Arne Strand, Eric Westdorp and Jim White. I thank all of them for their input and for their patience while I was pestering them for documents or feedback. In addition, case studies and feedback from participants and resource people in several training and workshops in the US, the UK and France and in Albania, Kosovo and Indonesia, and from students at the universities of Geneva, York and Oxford Brookes, were invariably useful. I hope the participants in the workshops got as much out of them as I did as a co-facilitator. The merits of this Good Practice Review I share with them, the weaknesses and mistakes are mine. Finally I need to mention my first 'mentors' in appropriate security management; Philippe, Etebori and Ehsan in Afghanistan, and Mohammed Hussain, Mohammed Jibreel, Daher and Abebaw Zelleke in the Ethiopian Ogaden. Their advice in critical situations often proved invaluable.

Special thanks are due to Rachel Houghton for the challenging task of editing this GPR, to Margaret Cornell for assistance with copy-editing, and to Olivia Cheasty for patiently making on-screen changes. Also to Rebecca Lovelace for her tremendous assistance in preparing the document for publication, and to the team at DS Print & Redesign.

Invitation

This GPR should be regarded as 'work-in-progress'. Feedback, comments and additional case material to make further editions and training more complete, relevant and appropriate are therefore very welcome.

PART I
INTRODUCTION

1 The Scope of This Good Practice Review

1 ▶ The Scope of This Good Practice Review

1.1 Target Audience

This Good Practice Review (GPR) is targeted at those individuals who are responsible for the management of an agency's staff and assets at field level. The question of whom to vest with this responsibility is discussed in Annex 4. The review does not constitute a personal compendium of guidance to be distributed to each individual staff member. Although some recommendations and guidelines are formulated as if addressed to individual staff members, they are meant as guidance for managers. The review has been written in this way so that managers can easily copy sections for their staff.

On the other hand the GPR strongly recommends that security management should be a team exercise. A clear indication from the review of good practice at field level is that security in crisis situations cannot be managed adequately at field level alone but requires the support of policies, expertise and capacity at the overall organisational level: security management requires a division of responsibilities, an allocation of tasks, and communications and decision making between an agency headquarters and the field office. How this is practically framed will differ among agencies and is beyond the scope of the present GPR, which is written for individual agency managers at field level. The GPR also strongly advocates better interagency exchange of information and collaboration around security management; in that sense it is also targeted at focal points for security in interagency fora.

Note: This GPR does not contain secrets and is not confidential. However, it does discuss sensitive issues and gives tips and suggestions on how to manage threats and risks. It could be misused and therefore should be handled with care.

1.2 Terminology

This GPR focuses on security. The meaning of security as used here differs from safety and protection. By security we refer to risks to staff and assets from violence; by safety we refer to accidental hazards, such as car accidents, fire or medical risks. While these are causes of injury and death among aid workers, there is existing literature available on them. Protection is used to refer to the risk of violence against civilian populations that are not members of aid organisations. To a certain degree there is a correlation between risk control (security) and protection of civilians and aid workers, although the risks, and the measures to control them, are not always the same. Those interested in protection can refer to RRN/HPN Network Paper 30, *Protection in Practice,* by Diane Paul.

1.3 Risk Reduction

Security management has, or can have, different functions. It can:

- help you assess the dangers and risks which will inform the decision as to whether or not to go into a country;
- reduce the risk so that you can enter and remain in a dangerous environment;
- help you decide when the risk becomes too high so that you withdraw.

Aid work in violent environments will always carry a degree of risk. Having an appropriate security management policy and appropriate security procedures does not guarantee total security. Security management is about controlling, or rather 'reducing', risk to a level considered acceptable.

1.4 Security Management is More Than a Security Plan

This GPR does not provide a ready-made security plan with detailed procedures and checklists. This is deliberate, for three reasons:

1. Safety and security management are, partially, a matter of procedure. Procedures are only effective, however, if they are an appropriate response to the risks in the environment. The challenge, therefore, is to identify correctly the threats and vulnerabilities in any given environment. Procedures need to be underpinned by ongoing contextual or situational analysis.

2. Procedures are a preventive measure. An incident may still occur. Those directly involved in an incident will have to draw on their own skills and situational judgement to survive it, while those at the field-base will need to manage the incident and its aftermath. Appropriate responses can be partially prescribed as procedures, but beyond that situational judgement, interpretation and common sense are required.

3. This GPR is written as a generic reference tool that is out of context. What is good practice in one context may not be good practice in another and it is therefore difficult and sometimes misleading to provide generic procedural guidelines or prescriptions.

The need for situational adaptation means that there are few 'global recipe' procedures and recommendations that can be universally prescribed. Beyond tips and suggestions this GPR develops question sheets and guidelines and tries to list issues to consider rather than provide answers.

The aim of this GPR is to help field managers think through risk, risk control and incident and crisis management in their specific situation. This will allow them to develop an appropriate security plan, but also to manage risk in a wider sense.

This GPR is therefore a starting point, not an end point. But it is clear on what in general constitutes good practice. It offers:

1. A structured management approach to security.
2. A holistic approach.
3. A language with which to talk about security management.

The need to be alert and to analyse the situation is an ongoing daily requirement. In a violent environment, threats and vulnerabilities can evolve and change. This means that nothing can be quite so dangerous as no longer scanning your environment because you have developed a security plan and are adhering to it! Procedures and checklists should never stop agencies from monitoring and analysing their situation and using their judgement.

1.5 Implementing Good Practice

When exploring this GPR you may feel that its suggestions make sense but that you simply do not have the time to spend on them because you are too busy implementing your agency's programmes. Lack of time is the single most consistently invoked reason for not adopting good practice in humanitarian aid work. You need to question this for a number of reasons:

- As a professional, you should in general not accept that you cannot implement good practice for lack of time.
- With regard to security, it should not be acceptable that somebody can get seriously injured or killed because your agency has failed to take time to implement good practice.
- Is time really that scarce? Are workloads so heavy or is there an issue about how the 'emergency culture' and 'mind-set' shapes the way you work and organise your time?
- If you are in a high-risk environment, security management has to be a priority. Tasks should be allocated across the agency to make time for this. If that is impossible, then the agency needs to obtain extra staff capacity.

More importantly, good practice in security management is closely linked with, builds on and reinforces good practice in programme and personnel management. These are not separate tasks and workloads; there is an important positive multiplier effect. Good programme management also requires an understanding of your operating environment and the impact of your presence and work, building good relationships, managing your international and national staff well, and collaborating with other agencies.

Security management, like gender and the environment, can be regarded as a specialist area. It definitely needs expertise. But it is also a crosscutting dimension of all the work you do, and therefore can and must be integrated.

1.6 The Perspective of this GPR

This GPR is written from the perspective of international aid agencies operating in violent environments, where the agency is providing humanitarian assistance and/or helping with reconstruction. The general principles of good practice in security management, however, also hold for other types of organisation such as national service deliverers, human rights activists, election monitors, etc. The author is also conscious of the fact that the GPR is written from the perspective of international staff, whereas often the majority of staff, and perhaps staff most at risk, are nationally recruited. Attention is drawn to national staff concerns and perspectives in various chapters, but admittedly this manual does not capture a full national staff perspective on security.

At least three factors complicate the articulation of security management guidelines for national staff: the relative lack of policy and analysed practice in many aid agencies, the even greater importance of contextual factors, and the fact that national staff cannot be looked at as one, monolithic category. Risks and vulnerabilities may differ significantly for individual national staff members, especially in countries experiencing internal conflict. It is hoped that national organisations, or programmes of international organisations staffed completely or managed by national staff, can usefully adapt guidance of this GPR. Otherwise internationally recruited managers in international organisations are advised to discuss the security concerns and various security management measures with their national staff.

An issue not covered is the responsibility of an agency that acts as a donor/partner to a local organisation for the security of the latter. Although the responsibility for the security of its own staff lies formally with the local organisation, one can argue that a donor/partner should not push the implementing agency to take risks and that it could, perhaps, offer capacity building support in security management.

1.7 How to Use this Manual

While this GPR is structured in a logical way it is not meant to be read from cover to cover. It is recommended that Part I (Chapters 1 & 2) is read fully as this defines the scope of the manual and spells out a management approach to security. Part II (Chapters 3 & 4) and the next chapter (5) on security strategies should also be read in full as they highlight the importance of context analysis and risk assessment to underpin security management, and clarify major types of security strategy which in current practice remain largely implicit and unarticulated. Chapter 21 on security plans and security management makes more explicit the case for a refocusing, away from the 'security plan document' to ongoing security management as a daily practice. Annex 4 asks the question of who carries the responsibility for security management at field level. Chapter 22 raises dilemmas that agency managers need to consider. These chapters together form the 'foundation' for good practice in security management and can be considered 'core reading'.

Part V on information and communication management constitute their own domain in security management. They can be used to check and perhaps improve already existing practice. A particular emphasis is put on improving the exchange of security-related information between agencies, and on analysis rather than just reporting. Chapter 17 on telecommunications is not a technical manual, which agencies often have developed, but addresses the topic from a management and planning point of view – sometimes a weaker practice.

Part VI on personal and personnel dimensions of security management also constitutes its own domain. It is sometimes but not always recognised as relevant to security management in current practice.

Part IV is about the management of specific threats. It discusses many common threats, but not every possible threat. For example, it does not address risks related to aviation or navigation in violent environments, arson, death threats related (or not) to an extortion racket, or additional risks from operating in very cold or desert-like environments. Chapter 6 on armed protection can be referred to selectively as the need arises. The same holds for the Annexes 1, 2, 3, 5 and 6, which concentrate on some topics of relevance in security management.

2 A Management Approach to Security

2 A Management Approach to Security

'**Organisational failure cannot be a disproportionately contributing factor to injury or death.'**

2.1 Room for Improvement

Although many agencies operate in violent environments, few have a strong organisational culture of safety and security. There is an excessive confidence in the immunity of humanitarian workers and foreigners. A perceived increase in risk (Annex 1) is gradually changing that. But there remains a gap between rhetoric and practice and great scope for improvement at both field and headquarters level.

Regularly encountered weaknesses in practice include a total absence of and/or inappropriate/incomplete security guidelines at field level; reactive rather than proactive thinking about security; reliance on a 'personal sense of security' rather than proper risk assessment; the allocation of responsibility for security management to managers who lack the requisite skill or competence; insufficient preparedness, briefing and training for all staff; security measures undermined by poor discipline; and security considerations overridden by the interests of programme expansion and implementation.

2.2 Managing Security

What is also missing is a 'management approach' to security – something that this GPR attempts to offer. Diagram 1 illustrates this approach. The vertical core of the diagram shows the main components of project-cycle management: assessment (who are you, where are you), strategy development, planning, monitoring of implementation, and critical review when problems arise. The different sections of this GPR will take you through these steps in some detail. Here we offer a first rapid overview.

Diagram 1: The Security Management Framework

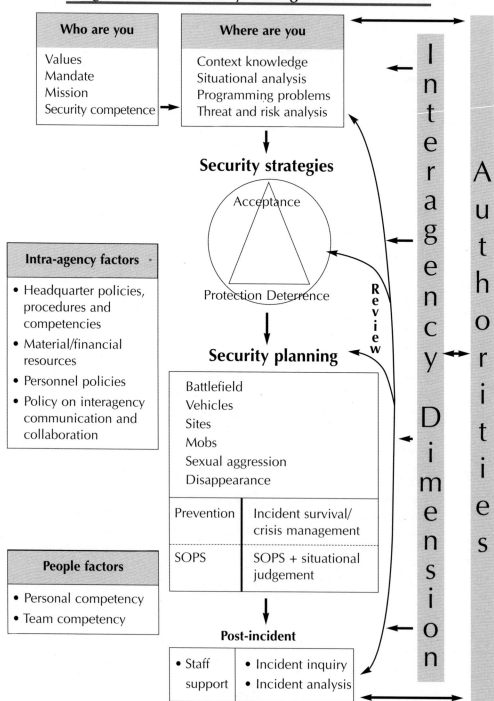

Who are you
Values
Mandate
Mission
Security competence

Where are you
Context knowledge
Situational analysis
Programming problems
Threat and risk analysis

Security strategies

Acceptance

Protection Deterrence

Intra-agency factors
• Headquarter policies, procedures and competencies
• Material/financial resources
• Personnel policies
• Policy on interagency communication and collaboration

Security planning

Battlefield
Vehicles
Sites
Mobs
Sexual aggression
Disappearance

Prevention	Incident survival/ crisis management
SOPS	SOPS + situational judgement

People factors
• Personal competency
• Team competency

Post-incident

• Staff support	• Incident inquiry
	• Incident analysis

Review

Interagency Dimension

Authorities

The first step in security management in a violent environment is the consideration of two external realities: the nature and mission of your agency and the nature of your operating environment (Chapter 3). The nature of your agency and its particular mission in a region, country or part of a country will influence whether you enter a violent environment or stay in it, what types of programmes you may choose to implement, and probably what security strategies you will have a preference for. Next to that, you need to acquire a good understanding of the risks in your operating environment: what are the threats and what are your particular vulnerabilities (Chapter 4).

Rather than jumping immediately into security planning you should first consider (a mix of) different security strategies to try and control the risk. There are three ideal types (Chapter 5): reducing the risk by increasing the overall acceptance of your presence and work, reducing the vulnerability with protective measures, and deterring the threat with a counter-threat (Chapter 6).

The next step is security planning. Typically, agency guidelines articulate what this GPR calls 'standard operating procedures' (SOPs) of do's and don'ts. These, however, are only half the 'plan'; they are meant to prevent an incident from happening. Proper planning also implies contingency planning, ie, being prepared when an incident or security crisis happens. Two types of preparedness are required here: that of those who are caught up in the incident or crisis (incident survival) and those who manage it (crisis management). Too many security plans are fairly generic, ie, they do not differentiate very much between different types of threats or possible types of incident. This GPR offers more detail on the most common threats, ie, related to battle related dangers (Chapter 7), vehicle movements (Chapter 8), site security (Chapter 9), crowds and mob disturbances (Chapter 10), cash security (Chapter 11), sexual aggression (Chapter 12), disappearance of staff (Chapter 13) and finally withdrawal or hibernation (Chapter 14).

Security management does not stop when the incident is over. The aftermath of an incident also needs to be managed: it must be reported and analysed, and that analysis should lead to a review of the agency's threat and risk assessment and of its security strategy and planning (Chapter 16). Staff involved in a security incident may need support, as well as their family and friends and other staff members.

Whereas this 'model' coincides with a project cycle management approach, it should not be understood and followed as a planning process! Good security management, certainly in volatile and dangerous environments, keeps all components or 'steps' constantly alive – ie, they are all practised on a daily basis. This requires that security management is not embodied in a piece of paper, the 'security plan', but in all staff, as constant awareness and as an acquired skill (Chapter 21).

Crosscutting issues also come into play at each stage of the security management cycle. These include:

• general organisational policies and capacities regarding safety and security (Chapter 21);
• policies and practices specifically related to staff management and team functioning (Chapters 18, 20);
• the competencies (awareness, knowledge, skill, self-control) of individuals (Chapters 18, 19);
• material resources for security;
• policies and practices regarding interagency communication and collaboration surrounding security (Chapter 16, 21).

Security management therefore is not simply a matter of hard measures and material resources, such as high walls and radio equipment. It is also a question of wider organisational culture, as expressed in organisational policies and capabilities. And there are a substantial number of 'soft' skills involved that have to do with building relationships, managing agency image, managing people and self-management.

2.3 The Interagency Aspect of Security Management

Current security management in the aid world is very agency-centred. There tends to be confusion about the need for, and limits of, interagency collaboration on security management. The following rules of thumb may help to create some clarity:

• As an employer your agency must assume responsibility for the safety and security of its personnel, just as it is responsible for any assets that have been donated.
• Different agencies have different mandates or missions in a specific context and may therefore establish different thresholds of what they consider 'acceptable risk': one agency may want to stay while another pulls out.
• You may be pursuing security strategies that are more effective than those of another agency, and may even feel that another agency is foolishly creating problems for itself.

These are arguments for security management on an individual agency basis. However, there is ample evidence from case analysis that security incidents causing injury and death to aid workers would have been perfectly avoidable if agencies had shared security information better. This is unacceptable.

There are a number of good reasons why agencies in the same violent environment should cooperate:

- **Collective alert:** If one agency suffers, or only narrowly avoids, an incident, it must be assumed, until there is proof that it was a targeted attack, that other agencies are at risk from the same perpetrators or the same type of incident, in the same location or elsewhere. Rapid reporting to alert everyone is a collective responsibility. Agencies involved in curative medicine should consider what their case statistics indicate about patterns of violence and routinely share this information.
- **Direct interdependence:** There can be straightforward interdependence between organisations. If one agency has the capacity to bring in a plane or ship to evacuate staff and others do not, then they should meet in advance to agree on evacuation criteria and procedures.
- **Indirect interdependence:** The security strategies of one agency can have repercussions for others. If one agency pays bribes at checkpoints this will create problems for those that do not. If a number of agencies operate in a district and the majority of them decide to adopt armed guards, this will increase the vulnerability of the remainders who have now become a comparatively 'soft' target. If an agency decides to 'suspend' aid to a certain district because one of its vehicles has been stolen at gunpoint, this may affect the relationships and security of other agencies working there.

There is further scope for collaboration:

- **Analysis and monitoring:** Every agency has to do this, and will normally contact others informally to obtain information and insights. Where there is trust and confidentiality is respected, it is possible to collaborate in a more structural way to maintain an understanding of the evolving situation.
- **Centralising security incident information:** Incident mapping and pattern analysis are not possible unless incident information is centralised (Chapters 4 and 16).
- **Common emergency channel:** A radio channel for emergency purposes can be shared, with collaboration to ensure 24-hour monitoring.

- **Specialist expertise:** Rather than each agency bringing in or hiring skills, for example, in telecommunications or training on mines or in how to construct a bomb shelter or a blast wall – specialists can be brought in on a collective basis.
- **Liaison with the authorities:** Rather than negotiating individually, agencies can make a stronger and more consistent case together.

This is an argument not for handing over and centralising the security management of all agencies to one lead agency but for responsible information sharing, interagency discussion, and collaboration around security.

One special type of situation needs mention: that of 'seconded staff'. There needs to be clarity from the outset between the 'recruitment' and the 'deployment' agency in terms of who is responsible for the safety and security of the staff member. This needs to be spelled out in legal and financial terms, covering both management of the crisis and post-incident support.

2.4 The National Authorities and Security Management

Often overlooked is the role that national authorities can, want to, or should, play with regard to the security of aid agencies. In highly politicised and politically sensitive environments agencies have tended to rely on their own competence and resources. But the issue cannot be ignored even if sometimes it creates real dilemmas with no best possible option (Chapter 22).

PART II
SITUATIONAL ANALYSIS

3 Assessment and Analysis

3 ▶ Assessment and Analysis

Good security management, like good programming, requires that you develop a solid understanding of your environment and of the (perceived) role that your agency, and (international/aid) agencies in general, play in that environment. This will help you to manage your image and constantly position yourself in a conflictual and probably dynamic – ie, constantly changing – arena.

3.1 Know Who You Are

Field managers and indeed all field staff should have a clear understanding of the nature and the intended role of their agency in a given environment. This includes national staff who communicate most with local outsiders. The benefits of this are:

• You can clearly and consistently explain who you are and what you are doing in a particular environment.
• It will give you guidance on how to 'position' yourself in the face of moral and political challenges or dilemmas.
• It will help you to determine a threshold of risk, beyond which you should not enter a situation or stay in it.

Key questions to ask are:

• What are your values and principles?
• What is your global/general mandate?
• What is your mission in a specific context?
• What is your capacity to manage the security risks in that context?

The following considerations apply not only at regional or country level. They may also be pursued in the light of the question as to whether to start up operations in a new province or district of a country.

3.1.1 Values and Principles

On the surface aid agencies appear to have clear values and principles, some of which are expressed in the Code of Conduct of the Red Cross Movement and International NGOs. These often include belief in:

- 'humanity', 'universality', 'impartiality', 'neutrality';
- the right of people in need to humanitarian assistance;
- that aid should be sensitive to culture;
- that aid should not be used as an instrument of foreign policy or to promote a particular religious view.

Moreover, aid agencies will often implicitly or explicitly subscribe to human rights, gender equality, working with local partners, peace and non-violence, and social justice.

In reality, matters are more complicated.

Understanding concepts

Staff may be familiar with these concepts and may use them in their own speech. However, they do not necessarily have a common and precise understanding of them. You need to clarify the precise meanings.

Tensions between values

There are inherent tensions between certain of these values, particularly when they are applied to a context of armed violence. The tension is clearest between neutrality and social justice, even if neutrality is pursued not as an ethical but as a pragmatic, operational principle in the belief that in the long run it is the best method of safeguarding access to victims of conflict. Neutrality implies that you do not express yourself, for example, on the causes of conflict or the legitimacy or 'justness' of certain groups taking up arms. From a social justice point of view, however, there may be circumstances in which armed struggle has become inevitable, for example, in a colonial liberation war, or to oppose a small and oppressive elite. Another area of potential tension is that of commitment to human rights, gender equality, and respect for culture: how do you position yourself, for example, with regard to the policies of the Taliban in Afghanistan, which they claim to be Islamic and in line with 'Afghan' tradition but which violate human rights and women's rights?

Practical dilemmas

Practical dilemmas arise when trying to put these principles into operation: can you work with local partners if they are not, or cannot be, 'neutral', or if they pursue policies with which you disagree? Can you continue to deliver humanitarian assistance to people in need if a certain amount of it is diverted by warring parties? Will you withhold life-saving humanitarian aid unless these diversions stop? And how do you define 'life-saving'? Can you claim to be providing aid on an impartial basis, if in practice your aid allocations are determined less by need than by access considerations?

These dilemmas are real. You will therefore have to reflect on your own practices and decide where you draw the boundaries between principle, practicality, and complicity. And not only because you want to be able to maintain a value-based position in your own eyes, but also because you will be challenged by outsiders over perceived inconsistency of practice and you will have to argue your position convincingly.

Clarifying 'Neutrality' and 'Impartiality'

You can test your own insight and that of your staff by asking questions that outsiders might challenge you with:

- What do you mean by 'neutrality' and 'impartiality' (and perhaps 'independence')?
- How does your claim of 'neutrality' reconcile with your professed support for democracy, social justice and civil society development, with statements of solidarity with the poor and displaced, and with peacebuilding initiatives?
- Is your professed 'neutrality' compatible with the monitoring and analysis of the political dynamics? Is it compatible with advocacy for protection and for human rights?
- Is your professed 'neutrality' compatible with working with local partners who are not perceived as 'neutral' or who do not want to be 'strictly neutral'? Will you only use them as implementers, also build their capacity, or not work through/with them at all?
- What relationship and what degree of interaction with the police, the military and non-state armed forces does a position of neutrality allow?
- How can you claim to be impartial if it is obvious that aid is not allocated strictly on the basis of need only but driven by considerations of access, visibility, cost-effectiveness, agency interests and expertise, etc?

One possible position you could develop would go as follows:

- We value the basic rights and freedoms of all individuals; we proclaim solidarity with the poor and those suffering from violence; we believe in political democracy and in non-violent ways of solving conflict.

Continued...

> * We practice 'neutrality' as an operational principle. This means that:
>   * we will not take sides and work in the areas of all groups;
>   * we will not comment on the reasons for taking up arms;
>   * but we have an opinion about how this conflict can best be resolved (even if we choose not to express it);
>   * and we will take a position when it comes to the treatment of civilians and non-combatants and the tactics of war in that regard, which we will express.
> * The provision of assistance is in response to unmet needs, but it is also shaped by our mandate, our mission in this context, our expertise and our capacity and by agreed policies, as well as by the access and acceptance we obtain. Within these parameters assistance is provided to all non-combatants irrespective of identity, age, gender, political affiliation, religious conviction, etc.

3.1.2   Mandate and Mission

The decision to enter, stay in, or withdraw from a high-risk environment, and what role you adopt in that environment, will also be influenced by your mandate and mission. In practice reasons of finance (availability of donor funds) and of visibility (high-profile situations with much media attention) also play a major role, which can lead to a distorted assessment of the security risks.

Many aid agencies do not refer to a 'mission' only to a mandate. The advantage of articulating a mission concept is that it makes you consider more closely:

* the context, its opportunities, constraints and risks;
* the roles already being played and the functions already being fulfilled by other organisations;
* the core skills and resources required to achieve your mission;
* the requirements for mission-specific training/briefing/preparedness of staff;
* whether or not you can achieve, and are achieving, your specific objectives.

The mandate

The mandate is the general raison d'être of the agency's existence, and sets the global focus of its work. For instance:

- your core mandate might be emergency response, development, human rights and democratisation and/or conflict-resolution and peace building;
- it could involve service delivery, training and capacity-building, protection and/or advocacy;
- you might have a specific target group such as refugees, children, or women, or you could have a sectoral focus such as food aid, health, water, etc;
- you could be primarily an operational agency or a donor working with and through local counterparts.

The advantage of a broad or expanding mandate is that it allows for flexibility and the possibility of addressing all sorts of unmet needs. But it also creates problems of skill and capacity, makes it difficult to decide when to exit from a situation, and can create practical dilemmas, for example, protesting over human rights abuses to an armed group may lead to your being denied further access.

The mission

A mission concept is more time-bound than a mandate. It can be reviewed. The challenge is to articulate and review it consciously, and to establish an institutional memory of these articulations and decisions.

The mission sets out the more precise focus of what you want to address and achieve in a particular context. This may be less than is allowed by your mandate, for internal reasons (eg, lack of funding) and/or for external reasons (eg, key issues that fall within your mandate are already being covered by other organisations). The mission concept sets clearer boundaries. Your mandate may very well allow you to get involved in developmental work, for example, but in a specific place you can decide that you will limit yourself to emergency relief and leave when the emergency is considered to be over.

How does this relate to security? It helps you to answer two of the questions mentioned earlier: what role you have come to play, and whether you have reached a threshold of risk beyond which you should not enter a situation, or stay in it.

> ## Operationalising Your Mandate
>
> If your mandate is essentially developmental, and/or working through national and local governmental structures, you are likely to suspend operations or withdraw if the situation becomes more violent. Faced with the same situation you are likely to decide to stay if your mandate is emergency response and is refugee-oriented. This is why, for example, not all UN agencies respond in the same way to a deteriorating and violent situation: UNHCR, for example, may be expanding, while FAO and WHO are reducing staff. Similarly, if your mission is to provide emergency health services in a conflict zone or vocational training in an unstable area you may decide to suspend operations or withdraw when the circumstances become such that you can no longer fulfil your mission: too much medicine and health equipment is being looted, or the situation has deteriorated to a point where the jobs for which you are offering training can no longer be pursued.

3.1.3 Capability

The key point to consider is: do you have the capability – the resources and the skills – to manage risk and insecurity? Effective and responsible management would hold that if you do not have the skills and capacity, and you cannot quickly recruit or sustain them, then you should not be operating in a violent environment.

3.2 Know Where You Are

3.2.1 Knowledge of the Context is Essential

Analyses and evaluations of policy and practice and anecdotal testimony from aid workers time and again highlight the crucial importance of in-depth knowledge of the context.

In-depth understanding of the context in which you are operating benefits programming and security management. It will also win you respect among local people and those with whom you might have to negotiate.

Recognising the importance of this has practical implications. For example, it means investing staff time in initial analysis and ongoing monitoring, documenting the analysis to maintain institutional memory, and building it into the initial briefing of newcomers and the handover to one's successor. Lack of time during an acute emergency and continuous staff turnover are constraints to be overcome, not excuses.

In practice, developing inside knowledge is an ongoing and iterative process, but in this exposition it is presented step by step.

3.2.2 General Situational Analysis

The history and current dynamics of a conflict
Key areas to consider are:

- **Social struggle:** Struggles over resources, control of the state, long-standing discrimination and exclusion (structural violence), individuals who mobilise social or identity groups, and the use of ideology, myths and symbols in that mobilisation.
- **The political economy of elites:** Who controls the state, and how is that authority exercised in terms of the allocation of resources, privileges and opportunities? What is the historical origin of the elites and what has been and is currently their economic powerbase? What is their 'security' powerbase: what has been the role of the armed forces (army, police, paramilitary)? What is their composition; what sections of society do they come from; what privileges do they enjoy; how did/do they exercise violence?
- **External players:** What has been and is currently the role, overt and covert, of regional and international players? Is the conflict really a national one or a regional or even international one?
- **The reasons for conflict:** What are the historical and the current reasons for conflict? Conflicts may have root causes but their dynamics over time also change and the reasons for their continuance may be quite different from why they initially started.

Understanding the 'bigger picture' will help you understand:

- who the main protagonists are, and what they seem to be struggling over;
- what historical grievances and more recent events shape and influence the experiences, attitudes and perceptions of the main protagonists, and also the different local populations;
- how international actors, of whom you may be one, are (likely to be) perceived, and what 'hidden agendas' people may suspect that you have.

Case Study: History and Current Dynamics of a Conflict

The Afghan conflict has multiple layers. In the 1980s it had Cold War overtones. In the 1990s it became a regional conflict. More recently (towards the end of the decade) it has acquired ethnic and religious dimensions, and awakened the old question of who controls the state. Underlying it is the long-standing struggle between 'tradition' and 'modernity', going back to the late nineteenth century and in which the position of women has always been a powerful symbol. Key issues are the nature of the state and the relationship between state and society. Western politicians and aid workers are perceived as representing particular concepts of state and society.

The conflict in Sri Lanka is ostensibly an ethnic one between a Sinhalese-dominated state and a Tamil minority. But there are additional conflicts within the Sinhalese body politic and the Tamil body politic, and between Tamils and Muslims – all of which have had violent expressions and at times have become entangled with each other. Underlying issues are the challenge of nation-building and the identity of the nation, control of the state, and the nature of party politics.

The situation in northern, mainly Kurdish, Iraq, cannot be understood solely in terms of the relationship between the Kurdish minority and Baghdad and the rivalry between the two main Kurdish parties, the PUK and the KDP. The role of Iran and Turkey and their sensitivities about, and armed actions against, their own Kurdish militants, is an equally important element. So is the geopolitical importance of Turkey and its membership in NATO. This influences the international attitude towards the Iraqi Kurds and their 'safe haven'.

Society and culture

Key areas to consider are:

- **Social norms and codes**, for example, related to group loyalties and solidarity, interactional styles of behaviour, interactions between men and women, definitions of 'private' and 'public'.
- **Social status** as accorded to different identity groups in a multi-ethnic or caste society, or to individuals on the basis of age, gender, wealth, education, etc.
- **Religion and social and political ideology** in terms of what are the key beliefs, key symbols, key areas of sensitivity and respect, etc.

Society and Culture

To operate and manage security in a Somali environment you need to familiarise yourself with the nature and dynamics of a segmentary lineage system. In east Afghanistan you need to understand something of the 'Pushtunwali' code and in northern Albania the 'kanun' code.

Clan or tribal dynamics should also be kept in perspective. There may be a big social and cultural divide between city and rural dwellers; 'clan' identification will not necessarily be present or be equally prominent in the population as a whole; and 'tribal identity' itself is subject to manipulation and emphasis or de-emphasis in different contexts and periods.

Crime

Key areas to consider are:

- The nature and prevalence of crime.
- Whether small arms are easily available.
- How problematic the economic situation is, in particular regarding unemployment.

Crime

It is not difficult to find out that San Salvador has become more violent and dangerous than it was during the civil war; that violent crime with firearms has risen rapidly in South Africa since the mid-1990s; or that armed robbery and car-jacking are a risk in many Nigerian towns.

A well-known situation of increasing risk of crime follows the rapid demobilisation of armed forces, particularly if there is incomplete disarmament, little retraining and few employment opportunities.

Infrastructure and climate

Key areas to consider – with the help of a map – are:

- The nature of the terrain.
- The impact of climate.
- The nature of the infrastructure.

Infrastructure and Climate

Mountains can make for more dangerous driving as well as problems with radio communications. They limit access and exit routes that can be used by cars. Snow and ice increase the risk of driving, can block vital passes, expose you to the danger of avalanches or of freezing if your car breaks down, and make minefield markings less visible. Autumn rains and spring thaw may cause mines to 'migrate'. Monsoon fog and low cloud may also complicate flying and disrupt plans for evacuation by air.

Economic crisis as well as economic boom can contribute to security risks. In Central Asia the economic changes after the break-up of the Soviet Union meant that local airlines could no longer maintain safety standards. Aid workers identified local flights as a major risk. In Albania, the rapid economic growth in the early 1990s led to a sudden influx of private cars into a country where virtually everyone had been using only bicycles. Road infrastructure and the overall level of driving skill lagged behind the rapid expansion in vehicle traffic.

3.2.3 Detailed Contextual Analysis

Over time, the general situational analysis has to become more detailed and refined. The relevant dimensions in situations of armed conflict are: analysis of actors; political and military developments; the political economy of the armed groups. The nature of crime can also be inquired into in more detail. Mapping violence is a useful exercise.

Analysis of actors
This is relevant for various reasons. It:

- focuses the inquiry and discussion and can yield insights that would otherwise be overlooked;
- provides a tentative picture of the relationships between various actors and their (temporary or more stable) alliances and antagonisms;
- helps, to a degree, to anticipate possible scenarios that may impact on your programmes and security;
- helps you to 'position' and 're-position' yourself in what may be a dynamic and shifting environment;
- gives you a handy tool for briefing newcomers and successors.

This exercise can proceed in two steps: first list all the relevant actors, then visualise their relationships. This is an exploratory exercise. It should be ongoing and will certainly initially raise more questions than it yields answers.

The relevant actors will include the various armed groups fighting each other, and the national and international participants formally trying to mitigate and mediate the conflict.

National or local participants could include the urban middle class, radical student groups, trade unions, large landowners, the churches or militant religious or nationalist radicals, the local media, local NGOs, traditional leaders, secret societies, etc. Potentially relevant regional and international actors might be the neighbouring powers, intergovernmental organisations, transnational corporations, diplomats, human rights and humanitarian organisations, as well as the diaspora populations of the country in turmoil.

To illustrate the interactional dynamics between the various actors different types of lines can be drawn between them to represent different types of relationships. Again, you may often not easily know the answers, but the first step is asking pertinent questions.

As the analysis deepens you may become aware that groups of allies, or single actors, are not as monolithic as first appeared. There may be factionalism and power struggles within the government or within a resistance movement; different UN organisations and NGOs may have different opinions and perspectives; international political actors may be jostling with each other to take the lead in the conflict management process. The more you know about where an organisation or individual stands within the rivalries and dynamics of what appears to be a common interest group, the better you will be able to fine-tune the relationships you cultivate.

Political and military developments

Keeping abreast of national and international political developments and military developments will enable you to monitor the dynamics of your environment, and to anticipate changes in the overall 'constellation' that may affect your programmes, your image, and your security.

For example, you could consider:

• Who is and who is not invited to important political meetings. Who shows up and who is conspicuous by their absence.

Diagram 2: Actor Mapping

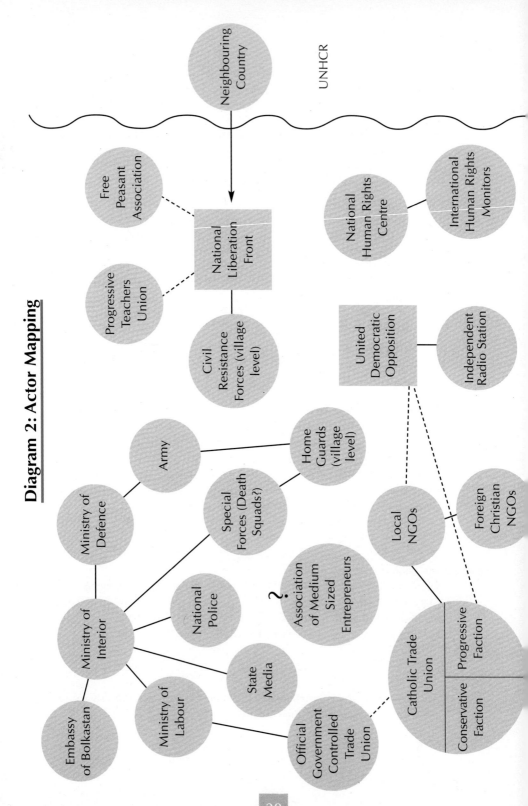

- If peace talks are progressing, identify who stands to lose from peace and who might therefore try to derail the process.
- Changes in leadership, the arrest, death or release from prison of an important leader, all have implications for the intensity and direction of the conflict or the political violence. Certain factions may want to obstruct or manipulate the voting process.
- The capture or loss of a strategic town can lead to an improvement in the security of an area, but also to retaliatory actions such as shelling and air raids.
- Climate can influence military campaigns so be prepared for the annual 'spring offensive', but check whether major offensives in the past started in the spring!
- Recently routed and retreating troops are prone to looting, as are soldiers who have not been paid for months.

The political economy of armed groups

This is a difficult and highly sensitive subject but one that it is important for you to understand in terms of how and why your presence and programmes might be manipulated or threatened. Again, insights will come only gradually and piecemeal, and may be speculative and hard to substantiate.

Key areas to consider are:

The organisation and structure of command and control

This is relevant in terms of whom to talk to and negotiate with, and the sort of practical outcomes you can expect from a formal agreement with a 'leader'/'commander'.

In this respect you might want to think about: how a certain group is organised; whether there is a clear hierarchy; whether the organisational logic is that of a separate structure or a traditional social entity (eg, kinship-based); who the leaders and decision makers are; what are their personal backgrounds; how centralised is the decision making; how good are the communications between the decision makers and the soldiers or militia members; how well trained are the fighters; are there factional divisions or alternative sources of authority in the area controlled by an armed group such as religious figures, drug barons, or wealthy merchants, etc.

The 'ideology'/mythology of a movement or organisation

This is important because it gives you a feel for the language and emotional symbols that are used within different groups and which may be of a totally different nature from the concepts and symbols that you use. Understanding something of the worldview and ideology of the 'other' will help you in your discussions and negotiations, and perhaps also help you to read and interpret public statements and communications from different groups which might include reading into them an implicit 'warning' to you and your activities.

In this area, think about what key actors in the conflict claim to be the reasons and justification for their struggle, how they mobilise support through a certain ideology or worldview and what symbols and myths are woven into this, and how aid agencies and international political actors appear in that perspective. An important element is whether an armed group has a 'state-project' or not. If it does, the leadership will, to a degree, be sensitive to international opinion, as one day it may have to obtain its approval and recognition. If, on the other hand, violence and war are simply 'economics by other means' – ie, a strategy of economic gain and enrichment with no real political dimension to it (any more) – then as an international organisation you are likely to be more vulnerable to outright violence.

The nature and structure of violence
This is relevant because it influences the degree to which you can more or less anticipate where violence will erupt, how restrained, or not, it is likely to be, and what the likelihood is that you as foreigners and/or aid workers will be involved in it. Note, however, that although these reflections are relevant they by no means amount to an exact science. The purpose again is to ask questions that will lead to a better understanding of the context, but will also go beyond a generalised impression of violence as always and everywhere the same.

For example, if you are dealing with relatively structured 'battle campaigns' such as those in Angola or the Balkans, the threats are by comparison somewhat easier to anticipate than in a guerrilla insurgency and counter-insurgency, as was the case in the Central American civil wars. The risk of an unexpected ambush, a hit-and-run attack, a mine planted on a road, or a massacre of civilians exists in both, but may be higher in the latter.

Another issue to consider is that paramilitary and militia-type operations may differ from guerrilla operations, with such groups often avoiding real battle and mainly looting and terrorising the civilian population. 'Home guards' can be a civilian self-defence force, but can also become a form of less well trained militia, who seek out 'softer' targets. Here your security may depend to a great extent on how you are perceived, especially at the local level.

'Raiding' is another slightly different form of violence, sometimes – in Sudan or in Mali – with roots in local culture and tradition from times when modern weaponry was not yet available. Its purpose is the capture of resources and sometimes of slaves, and your staff and assets may not be regarded as immune by the raiders.

Questions to consider include: Are terror tactics being used in your environment, and if so what is their nature? Are the attacks against political and military targets or against an 'illegal foreign presence' (eg, the attacks against 'illegally present' foreigners in northern Iraq in the early 1990s), or against civilians (such as those committed by Renamo, and also Frelimo, in the Mozambican war, or by the RUF in Sierra Leone)?

'Mob violence' in the streets can be an orchestrated means of pressure by political groups or individual power brokers. 'Communal violence', for example, between Hindus and Muslims and more recently against 'Christians' in India, also tends to be events portrayed as spontaneous but are more often than not politically orchestrated.

The relevance of this type of reflection can be illustrated with reference to rape. In the Balkans, rape has been used as a weapon of ethnic cleansing to demoralise the opponent. In general, international staff were less at risk than local staff. By contrast, in Sierra Leone rape has been widespread – less as a tactic of war but more to subjugate and terrorise civilian communities (another form of 'looting'), and to psychologically transform and brutalise the (child) soldiers committing it, to alter their values and self-perception and 'close the doors' on a return to normal life. In such a setting international staff will be just as much at risk as national staff, particularly if there is little regard for international political (Western) opinion.

The 'social contract' between an armed group and the civilian population
This is another important area because the greater the social contract the more likely it is that you will obtain secure access to provide services to civilians. The more abusive the armed groups are against civilians under their control, the more difficult and dangerous it will be for you. Finally, if your presence and programmes are perceived as threatening and/or undermining the control of an armed group over a civilian population, they may well intimidate or retaliate against you.

For example, the Khmer Rouge in Cambodia and the SPLA in south Sudan in the 1980s and the Liberian warlords in the early 1990s, all pursued exploitative relationships with the civilian populations with forced conscription, occasional looting, extortion of food produce and means of transport, and sometimes forced labour. By contrast, during the Ethiopian civil war against the Menghistu regime, the Tigray People's Liberation Front and the Eritrean People's Liberation Front very much assumed responsibility for the well-being of the civilians in their areas.

In Latin America, during the dictatorships and civil wars of the 1970s and 1980s, not only social activists and human rights monitors but also teachers and literacy educators became a target or repressive regimes because education and even literacy were perceived a first step in 'empowerment'.

The resource base and the war economy issue
Your presence and programmes can contribute to, or threaten and undermine, the resource base of an armed group. As an aid agency, you have many resources that can be looted and sold off. The armed group may try to manipulate you but also directly attack you to obtain your resources. You may also be threatened or attacked to stop you providing resources to the enemy, or to scare you away from an important area where the armed group obtains or trades some of its main resources.

Armed groups need ammunition, weapons and weapons training, transport and communications, food, medicine and other supplies for the fighters, and money to pursue the war. In most cases, war economies have external and internal dimensions. Weapons, fighters and funds may come from abroad, as a 'grant' from an external sponsor or from the diaspora. But resources may also have to be bought on the market in which case the armed group needs cash or other assets such as hardwoods, rubber or minerals, drugs, diamonds, oil or gold to export. This can involve transnational companies as well as 'middlemen' operations. The armed group therefore needs to establish and maintain control over the resource-rich areas, organise their exploitation, and secure export routes.

However, where there are few alternative resources those of aid agencies assume a greater importance in the war economy; this will make them more vulnerable. If your presence or activities take place in a sensitive area where natural resources that support the war economy are exploited, or along the export/import routes, you could be perceived as a hindrance or an undesirable witness. Your programmes may also complicate the recruitment drive directly, for example by introducing income generating programmes for ex-fighters, or indirectly, for example, by supporting schooling and agricultural rehabilitation and thereby offering alternative 'livelihoods' to young males.

A profile of crime

Crime, as much as warfare, is an increasing source of threat to aid agencies (Annex 1). In reality there may not be a neat distinction: fighters can commit criminal acts and become criminals, and criminal gangs may be involved in the war economy of the fighters. It may be much more difficult to obtain a profile.

This line of inquiry is relevant because it could be useful to try and anticipate what threats exist in your environment (Chapter 4) and also whether you as an agency could become a target, and if so why: because of the assets you possess, because of the larger 'wealth' and 'money' people think you can access, because of the contracts you offer, or because of the programme activities you carry out?

Some exploratory issues to consider include the following:

The nature of criminal activity

Is crime opportunistic on the part of one or a few individuals, or are you dealing with more organised crime? What type of organised crime? Is the criminal group linked to an armed group, for example, is it exporting drugs or diamonds and importing weapons in return? Is it linked to political interests, such as the 'thugs' that get used by political power-brokers to intimidate and attack their opponents or instigate 'mob violence'? Or is it a criminal group working on its own account, enriching itself through illegal activities? Are you dealing with international networks or with a local gang?

Case Study: The Political Economy of the Liberation Tigers of Tamil Eelam (LTTE) in Sri Lanka

- **Organisation and command**: hierarchical; different divisions with a political and military wing, and well organised tactical units in the military component; well-trained and disciplined 'cadres'; good communications; units in east Sri Lanka, however, less well organised, disciplined and controlled by LTTE command based in north Sri Lanka.
- **Ideology**: state project of independent Tamil Eelam; opposed to Sinhalese-dominated government and moderate Tamils; violently hegemonistic against other Tamil militant groups; authoritarian outlook; underlying caste issues; mythologising of Tamil past in Sri Lanka; martyr cult also operationalised in suicide commandos.

Continued ...

- **Nature of violence**: mainly frontal battle, guerrilla warfare and terrorist attacks, mostly targeted but some designed to terrorise to Sinhalese civilians by occasional massacres of rural civilians and bomb attacks in Colombo, also to discourage foreign investors.
- **Social contract**: LTTE understands the need to keep Tamil civilians 'on its side', although also maintains control over the civilian population and eliminates potential alternative Tamil leadership and political project; will increase pressure on civilians to contribute fighters and finance when the LTTE is put on the defensive and needs resourcing, but no flagrant exploitation; Tamils often ambiguous: may not feel comfortable with LTTE but lack of political compromise and violence on the part of the government create a sense that only the LTTE can effectively 'protect' Tamil rights.
- **Resource base**: LTTE in past armed by Indians, then by Sri Lankan government when fighting the Indian peacekeeping force, also by Pakistan as part of its rivalry with India; resources also obtained by capturing weapons from government troops and purchasing weapons on open market; diaspora funding, direct and indirectly through remittances to civilians in LTTE-controlled territory; certain level of taxation of civilians under their control; smuggling across frontline; wants foreign aid as support for civilians under its control, but prefers minimal foreign presence and aid channelled through Tamil NGOs which it can control better. Other resource bases?

Note that such a 'profile' should not be treated as static. All aspects of it may change over time.

Socially sanctioned brigandage or personal greed

There are a number of 'traditional' environments and societies where there exists a socially sanctioned 'brigandage' – ie, a traditional culture in which valuables and resources that do not pertain to a clearly demarcated 'in-group' are therefore considered 'common resources' and are 'up-for-grabs'. Examples include the mountain areas of east Afghanistan and northern Albania. The outsider whose possessions have been looted, or whose colleague or relative has been kidnapped, will perceive the perpetrators as criminals. Yet within their social group these 'criminals' obey and respect strong rules and codes of behaviour: the stolen goods will not simply serve their personal interests, but will be partly redistributed among the group.

The nature of their business and how they go about it

What is the nature of their business: for example, stealing cars, cash, household and/or office commodities, trafficking in people. How do they go about their business: for example, robbery, extortion, manipulation of contracts, bribery, blackmail, etc.

Frequent targets

Is there any person in the society in which you operate who seems to be a particular target or are there more specific targets such as sedentary communities, shop-keepers, members of low castes or low status groups, foreign businesspeople, non-corruptible policemen, rival gangs, etc?

Mapping violence

Visualising information on a map can be an enormous help and is in principle good practice – except where there is a high degree of suspicion about the reasons for your presence, in which case you may not want to feed that suspicion by being seen to be 'mapping' your environment. Again, you may not be able to come up with a complete map, but focusing a discussion around a map is likely to yield information and insights that would not emerge clearly in conversation or from a written document.

You can map areas known to be of high risk to crime – for example, certain urban neighbourhoods, roads or mountain passes. This may prevent you from locating an office or a residence somewhere that is only accessible through a high-risk area.

In a war-torn environment look at potential targets of attack: military installations, command buildings, police stations, fuel depots, the airfield, etc. You can also monitor military developments on a map. This may be possible using information from public sources, such as the local press.

3.3 Finding Out Information

The information for this sort of analysis is not normally at hand, though more is available than you might initially realise. Two changes are required: some staff time has to be allocated to learning in more depth about the context, and a change of culture is needed whereby aid agencies reduce their 'compound mentality' and engage more with outsiders.

The following 'public sources' are generally available:

- **Published expert analysis:** Conflict and conflict analysis has become an area of greater interest in recent years; the amount of literature and informed analysis, especially in English, tends therefore to be vast and increasingly relevant to the topics discussed here. This literature is produced by international and also national analysts, academics and investigative journalists, and increasingly by human rights and conflict-management and conflict-resolution organisations. Sometimes, for example, with regard to Angola or Somalia, it is easier to find this literature in Western countries, which is then a job for headquarters. In other cases you will find a great deal of material in the larger towns on location. Some of it is published commercially; some of it remains unpublished but may now be more accessible on a website.

- **Agency archives:** When aid agencies have been operating in an environment for a number of years there is often a wealth of information in their 'archives' at headquarters and in the field. Browsing through your own dusty archives and/or inquiring about good reports with fellow agencies may actually yield some very interesting material!

- **Local officials and authorities in your environment:** These will include embassy staff, government officials, the local head of police, an army commander, a 'rebel' commander, OSCE monitors, the commander of international peacekeeping forces, as well as 'village leaders' and 'elders' in the countryside. Some may be well-informed and willing to share their views, others may be poorly informed or will give you a deliberately distorted picture. You can also use this opportunity to inform others about who you are and what your aims and roles are in the particular context.

- **Local intelligentsia:** These will include local academics, journalists, teachers, missionaries, social activists, religious leaders, political activists, etc. They are usually better interviewed by human rights and conflict-resolution organisations than by humanitarian agencies whose emphasis is on supply and aid delivery. They may have a good analytical and critical perspective on their own living environment, and on past and current developments. Some of them may be among your own staff. Again, some will be better informed and will give a more insightful and objective analysis than others. They will probably be more informative with regard to the broader context analysis than the more precise identification of security risks.

- **Local 'risk assessors':** Some will share your concerns about risk and security. They probably 'monitor' the security of the neighbourhood on their own behalf, for example, taxi-drivers, local traders and merchants, local banks, local insurance companies. Again, some of your locally recruited staff who are well-connected and politically aware will have, or be able to obtain, a good current assessment of particular areas.

- **The press:** It is worthwhile monitoring the national media – not only the English, Spanish, Portuguese or French language ones, but especially those in the national language(s). The latter may or may not be objective and well-informed, but they are the ones that the population at large will listen to and are therefore very influential in shaping perceptions and attitudes. Sometimes the embassy or the local UN mission produces daily notes about how the national media comment on relevant events. If not, they are easy to set up on an interagency basis.

3.3.1 Quality of Information

A constant issue in this inquiry is the quality of the information you are given. Over time you will come to identify people and sources that are better informed and more reliable than others, but at the outset you will wonder who to believe. There are a number of reasons why a particular account may not be reliable. For example, it repeats a rumour that has not been verified; the informant has an interest in misrepresenting the security situation for you by either exaggerating or downplaying the risks; or s/he does not know you, does not (yet) trust you, and therefore does not want to give you his/her real assessment of the situation.

Different stories will not necessarily add up and may lead to confusion. However, they can still be interesting as they may come to reveal the positions and interests that shape them.

'Triangulation', or the cross-checking of information through different sources, may still not be decisive as it is possible that everybody repeats the same rumour that has circulated widely.

You can arrive at an assessment of the quality of the information and the reliability of a source by considering a number of questions:

- Is the lack of a relationship or trust a possible factor?
- What interest can someone have in misrepresenting the situation?

• Can the information be confirmed through another independent source?
• Does the source have first-hand direct knowledge of what is described?
• Does the source have in-depth knowledge of what is described, and can s/he answer your follow-up questions?
• Is the story analytically plausible? Does it hang together?

You can make a quick score of the possible answers to each question, and thus come to an overall judgement. When new to an environment it is recommended that you assess the contextual information and analysis you are given in a formal way. Over time, as your own knowledge develops and you get to know people, you will rely more on your 'sixth sense' about people. Do not forget to brief your successor about reliable sources of information.

4 ▸ Problem Anticipation, Threat Assessment and Risk Analysis

4 ▸ Problem Anticipation, Threat Assessment and Risk Analysis

4.1 The Security Dimensions of Presence and Programming: Problem Anticipation

The previous chapter on situational analysis highlighted the importance of asking how your presence, your programming and your positioning, as revealed through formal and informal statements, affect the (perceived) interests of other actors and what that means for your security. The following are some key points and questions to help you think this through and anticipate problems that can generate threats.

4.1.1 Danger Zones

- Do your programmes put you in the path of military operations? Are you locating your operations too close to potential political or military targets? Can your entry and exit routes be affected?
- Do your programmes put you in areas that are important to the war economy or the illegal trade transactions that are part of it?
- Do your programme activities take you into high crime areas?

4.1.2 Impact on the Political Economy

- Can the national origin of your agency, your sources of funding, or the way you operate (eg, in the areas of certain actors only or under the umbrella of a peacekeeping force that is not perceived as neutral) cause you to be perceived as being associated with certain political interests or certain groups (eg, specific ethnic groups) that are actors in the conflict? Can certain public statements of your agency be construed as indicating a hidden political agenda?
- Can your programmes be perceived as strengthening the war economy or the political economy of somebody's enemy, ie, as changing the balance of power?
- Are you undermining someone's power base (political, military, criminal)? If, for example, you organise your distribution system so that goods are handed out directly to the intended beneficiaries you may be 'cutting-out' the camp committee, the local 'commander' or the village council who would prefer to control the resources as a mechanism for patronage, and who may now create security problems for you.

- If abuses and atrocities are committed can you be seen as an undesirable witness?
- Do you have 'lootable' resources in residences, offices, warehouses, programmes, etc? For whom would they have value? Can you replace them with less lootable items, for example, distributing wet feeding instead of dry food; less desirable local maize rather than highly valued imported rice; cheap local building materials such as palm tree leaves (cadjan) rather than plastic sheeting or tents; using second-hand 2-wheel drive pickups or classic and less comfortable Landrovers rather than flashy new 4-wheel drive Nissans and Mitshubishis; typewriters rather than computers? Does the market value of your resources fluctuate in ways that can make them more of a target, for example, food aid during the hungry season or when the harvest has failed or been destroyed by the 'enemy'; shelter and building materials at a time of acute scarcity because of a new large-scale influx of displaced people; surgical equipment and supplies at times of intense fighting with heavy casualties; saleable commodities in the months after a large-scale demobilisation leading to many unemployed ex-fighters.

4.1.3 Controversial Programmes

Are your programmes controversial? Why and for whom?

- In a conflictual environment do your programmes touch on a source of conflict, such as the reconstruction of houses in ethnically divided and ethnically cleansed towns (the Balkans), agricultural rehabilitation where there are disputes about land ownership (north Iraq), or water supply in water scarce environments (the Sahel or Somalia)?
- Alternatively can your programmes become a new source of conflict in an already conflictual environment, eg, when you propose building a health centre on the territory controlled by one group or one authority, in a divided or factionalised environment with rival authorities or power brokers, or groups in conflict with each other?
- Can you find a solution which is acceptable to all such as 'coverage through mobility' (a mobile health or animal vaccination service reaching all groups); 'equitable alternation' (such as the reconstruction of 10 houses and irrigation canals first for one group, and then 10 for the other, or the children of the host population using the school in the morning and the refugee children in the afternoon); 'necessary duplication' (ie, a health post, school, etc, for each) if no compromise can be achieved.

Problem Anticipation, Threat Assessment & Risk Analysis

4

4.1.4 'Impartiality' in the Allocation of Limited Resources

Aid agency principles hold that resources are allocated on the basis of need only. In practice that is seldom the case. Other factors such as access, visibility and cost-effectiveness all come to play a role in allocation decisions. Resources also are limited, whereas needs often are not. In a fragmented environment, local power brokers and populations will often insist that impartiality be interpreted not in terms of 'degree of need' but of 'equal share' – namely, that if there are five groups they should each get the same (this may be the argument of the smaller groups; the bigger ones may argue for allocation on the basis of numerical size).

- What is your principle regarding the allocation of resources?
- Have you communicated clearly and in advance the practical constraints resulting from limited resources?
- What are the contesting criteria for the allocation of resources brought by actual and potential recipients?
- Have you diplomatically but firmly negotiated the criteria to be applied?
- Who is bypassed? It is now accepted that one cannot focus all aid and attention on refugees and neglect the host population. Less acknowledged is the old military principle of protecting your supply lines. What will be the perception of those in the areas that you transit with your resources? Will they not at some point start feeling resentment and try to force you to provide them with aid? Similarly, by running your own logistics operation you may be competing with local transport companies or depriving them of business they want. Will this lead to problems?

4.1.5 Transparency and Accountability of the 'Intermediary'

If you implement programmes through an intermediary (contractor/local partner) you may get into a dispute with your intermediary or be held responsible for their acts and omissions. Clear expectations from the outset can help to avoid problems or manage them as they arise and prevent them from escalating into violence. The clear allocation of tasks and responsibilities will also reduce the risk of your being challenged and perhaps threatened because of the actions and omissions of your collaborators. If you implement your programme through intermediaries, partner-NGOs or community organisations, councils, committees, the relief wing of an armed group, local authorities, etc, have you discussed in advance, and perhaps in an open forum with sufficient 'witnesses', what standards of transparency and accountability you will expect and what procedure will be followed if these are not met and/or malpractice or corruption is identified?

4.1.6 Provoking Anger and Resentment

Some of the common causes of anger and resentment that can flare up into violence, and which are partly or wholly provoked by aid agencies, are the:

- differing quality standards and programme criteria in the same operational zone, for example, different qualities of the houses reconstructed, different interest rates in credit programmes, different admission or eligibility criteria for programme benefits;
- perceived bias and partiality: a perceived concentration of resources or attention and care on one group which is resented for economic or political reasons by others; (reported) public statements that are perceived as biased and/or politically driven;
- assessment and inquiry fatigue: yet another agency assessment mission, asking the same questions but never followed up by tangible programmes or another new agency staff member asking the same questions that have already been answered for three of his predecessors;
- unaddressed offences: for example, an agency's vehicle killed a cow from the village on the road but never stopped or came back to sort the matter out;
- real or perceived broken promises: about a project that never materialised or not as quickly or on the scale that was promised or overheard.

Note that other people often fail to make distinctions between aid agencies and put them all 'in the same bag', so that you may experience a problem that was 'created' by another agency. This is an argument for an interagency forum on security matters (understanding security here in a wider sense than is typically the case!), and also a signal that you should not create or leave problems for other agencies.

4.2   Risk Analysis

Risk = threats x vulnerabilities

Risk analysis is always interpretative. It looks at risk through the lens of actual incidents and potential threats. The more complete and precise the data on accidents and incidents, the more precise your risk assessment can be. This is why some Western insurance companies offer different rates on, for example, car insurance and domestic valuables at risk from burglary because the statistics indicate that certain age groups of drivers and certain residential areas constitute a higher risk than others. There are also some private security companies that do 'risk assessments' of many countries, their main clientele are international companies and their information does not come cheap.

However, these are not the approaches that aid agencies can typically use. The approach spelled out here is less rigorous, but practically possible. Once again this is not an exact science, so keep your eyes and ears open.

The various steps to work through would be: retroactive threat assessment, threat and incident pattern analysis, proactive threat assessment, vulnerability analysis, and establishing a threshold of acceptable risk.

4.2.1 Retroactive Threat Assessment

A simple retroactive approach consists of listing the identified threats, prioritising them, mapping known incidents, and reflecting on/analysing trends. These various steps can be explored during in-house discussion with national staff, in an interagency forum, as well as in discussions and conversations with non-agency staff.

Listing threats

Brainstorm to list threats. For example, artillery fire, burglary, arson, theft from warehouses, mines, car-jacking at gunpoint.

Priority ranking

The first criterion in ranking threats would be frequency: which ones occur most regularly? Bear in mind that reporting bias may give a distorted impression: certain incidents, notably but perhaps not only rape, are notoriously under-reported, and the actual frequency may be much higher. As pointed out in Chapter 3, people may also have reasons to deliberately downplay security risks and therefore also the frequency of certain types of incidents. Ranking by frequency might yield the following: first, armed robbery (individuals, vehicles, offices and warehouses); second, car accidents; third, public disorder and riots; and fourth, cross-border shelling and sniper fire. This, in fact, was the ranking of threats produced during an interagency workshop on security in Albania in May 1999.

A second criterion might be geography. Different provinces/districts or urban neighbourhoods may produce a different ranking. During the meeting mentioned above, for example, Albanian national staff were able to indicate a few spots they considered as high risk because they 'remembered' that during the disturbances in 1991 and 1997 those were the places where a great many cars were hijacked.

A third criterion might be vulnerability. There is not necessarily a single 'risk profile' for everyone in the organisation. Different staff members may face different threats because of their origin, affiliation, age or gender.

Incident mapping

The perception of geographical differences in the relative priority of threats can be informed by and cross-checked against an 'incident map'. This illustrates the reported incidents. Obviously such a map is only as good as the information you have to work with: the more complete the record of incidents, the more representative and therefore useful the map will be. When there is no database or record you may be able to gain some information from people's memory, including local knowledge. However, this may not come to your attention unless you explicitly seek it out. Introducing a map into the discussion and asking specific questions is a technique worth trying.

Diagram 3 shows an example of an incident map overleaf.

Trend analysis

There is also a time dimension to the assessments described above. For example, ask yourself if there have been changes over time in the frequency of certain threats and what explains these changes.

Be cautious in about interpreting perceived or 'statistically proven' changes: a perceived change can indeed reflect the actual frequency of a certain type of threat, but it can also reflect a change in the information available or in the exposure/vulnerability to threat. For example, information related to car-jacking at gunpoint. It may appear that there are a lot more car-jackings now than in the past. But is this because there are indeed more armed robbers stealing cars or because:

- the international aid effort has brought many more cars on to the roads and although the absolute number of cars stolen has increased threefold (the numerator) there are probably six times as many cars around as before (the denominator). Objectively speaking then (number of cars stolen/thousand cars) the rise in car-jackings has not been as great as it as first appeared;
- car-jackings did occur frequently before, but the local people affected by this crime tended not to report it to the police whereas international personnel do. The perceived rise in car-jackings therefore reflects changes in reporting more than in actual incidents;
- any combination of the above.

Similarly, a decrease in reported mine accidents can reflect, for example, effective de-mining operations, or increased awareness of local people, or simply seasonal variatons such as reduced agricultural activity in winter.

Retroactive analysis can produce valuable insights. The more complete the information on security incidents, the better you can analyse them. To facilitate

Diagram 3: Incident Mapping

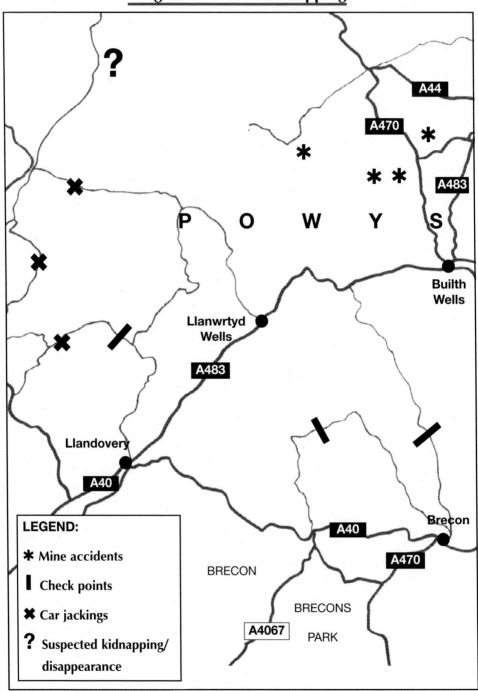

LEGEND:

✱ Mine accidents

❙ Check points

✖ Car jackings

? Suspected kidnapping/
disappearance

this you should identify or establish a central point for security incident reports and incident pattern analysis, and produce reports on incidents that you have experienced or narrowly avoided and feed these into a central security information centre (Chapter 16).

4.2.2 Threat and Incident Pattern Analysis

Incident pattern analysis means developing a more detailed profile of incidents, of the victims and their vulnerabilities and of the perpetrators of malicious acts. Proceed by looking for patterns or consistencies across various security incidents.

Pattern Analysis

Example 1

Car-jackings occur most frequently in two suburbs of the city and on three passes across the mountain range to the south of the city. New 4-wheel drive vehicles, especially the more comfortable Nissans, Toyotas and Mitsubishis, are more likely to be stolen than the older, less flashy and less comfortable Landrover Defender. In the city the perpetrators are believed to be unemployed young men organised into gangs; they take the cars to the port and ship them overseas. The car-jackings in the mountains, however, appear to be carried out by people from the economically marginalised villages in the area and although a few of them may be sold off to 'dealers' in the city, most are used by local strongmen for travelling over the rough terrain. The police tend to act against the gangs in the city, but court sentences are short and convicted thieves are released within a year. The police in the countryside tend not to take any action, either because they themselves come from the mountain area and are therefore related socially to the perpetrators, or in the case of outsiders because they run the risk of retaliation from the local people.

In both cases the threat is of the same type, but with clearly different patterns that may lead to somewhat different security strategies. In the city you may perhaps switch to less powerful secondhand cars; in the mountains try an 'acceptance' strategy (Chapter 5) – for example, through some modest support for water supply and irrigation – so that the mountain people no longer steal your vehicles or return them to you.

Example 2

In the past two years seven foreign females have been raped. One rape

Continued...

---

took place during a burglary at a residence and did not appear to be premeditated; it is the only known instance of a burglary also leading to a rape. Three other rapes occurred in the parking area underneath modern apartment blocks after 10pm when few residents enter or leave, and were clearly premeditated. Another three occurred in two medium-class hotels, somewhat away from the city centre and often used by tourists travelling on a low budget and occasionally by aid agencies. These, too, appeared to be premeditated. Aid agencies now use only two hotels where there is stricter supervision of those entering the premises.

This type of information, derived from pattern analysis, provides some clues about risk and risk reduction when providing accommodation for female staff.

Pattern analysis is not possible unless incidents are analysed in considerable detail and the various analyses can be centralised. Good practice requires you to carry out an inquiry and produce an analysis of every incident that occurs or is narrowly avoided, for the purpose of your own review and learning. But centralising the information at a field-level 'security information centre' (Chapter 16), or for analysis by researchers (Annex 1), is required for pattern analysis of a broader, and therefore possibly more representative, sample.

4.2.3 Proactive Threat Assessment

Given that your context is probably dynamic, with new threats and threat patterns arising, retroactive threat assessment needs to be complemented by proactive assessment. The art of risk reduction is about seeing the danger or risk coming in advance, in order to avoid it or be better prepared for it, and not just about analysing incidents that have taken place.

This requires good knowledge of the context and close monitoring of current events. The technique is one of scenario thinking. Three fundamental questions to guide you are:

1. On the basis of the available information, would you expect that the threats you have identified and prioritised on the basis of frequency will increase/decrease over the next three to six months? Why?
2. On the basis of your contextual analysis, would you expect that as yet unidentified threats might reveal themselves as a new source of security incidents? Why?

3. Could your agency become a target, and why? In general there are three main reasons why aid agencies are targeted: to drive out the agency, to influence the policy of humanitarian programming, or to extract recognition and concessions from actors other than the humanitarian agency on the ground.

Problem Anticipation, Threat Assessment & Risk Analysis

Case Study: Retroactive and Proactive Threat Assessment in Kosovo and Albania

During a workshop on security in Kosovo in November 1999, retroactive analysis identified accidents (in cars and at construction sites), problems arising from disputes over ownership of property, discontented beneficiaries and disgruntled staff, ethnic confrontation, problems of cash security, and mines and unexploded ordnance as current threats. Proactive analysis, however, suggested a potential rise in crime (burglary, car theft, armed robbery) because of unemployment, drug trafficking and criminal gangs moving back into Kosovo, increased driving risk on the roads in winter conditions, increased winter risk from fires (unsafe heating in buildings with damaged chimneys), sexual assault (given the practice of rape in the ethnic violence and the presence of small arms) as well as election violence between Serb and Albanian Kosovars and also between the major political groupings of Albanian Kosovars.

During an earlier workshop in Albania in May 1999, sexual assault and demands for protection money were identified not as a current, but as a potential, threat. A few months later these threats had indeed materialised in the form of real incidents.

Warning signs

Sometimes before an agency is (seriously) targeted, a warning is given. This may be explicit: a threatening letter or phone call, or some shots over your roof or in front of your car. Sometimes it may be much more subtle and therefore difficult to notice or interpret: a chance remark by someone, the guard dog poisoned, etc. Be on the alert.

4.2.4 Vulnerability Analysis

$$\text{Vulnerability} = \frac{\text{threats x your exposure}}{\text{your security measures}}$$

Threats to aid agency workers tend by and large to come from one of five sources (if we exclude the threat staff can be to themselves by indulging in risky behaviour such as drunken driving or unprotected sex):

i.   military and terrorist actions;
ii. politically motivated actions;
iii. criminal actions;
iv. actions by disaffected populations;
v.   actions by disgruntled staff.

We have already explored the first four of these. Actions by disgruntled staff can be prevented by good personnel management. Most of the good practice in this respect is contained in manuals on staff and personnel management, and is not repeated here. Aspects of staff management as it relates to security management, are addressed in Chapter 20.

Vulnerability analysis is closely related to threat analysis but goes one step further. Threat analysis is general, ie, it identifies dangers that exist in the wider environment for the population at large and for all aid agencies. Vulnerability analysis looks more closely at where and why your agency in particular might be at higher risk. The key question is: where is your particular exposure, and why?

You can derive more detailed questions from the preceding sections in this chapter and Chapter 3. More general questions would be:

• Are you at risk of military or terrorist activities – eg, because of the location of your programme sites and travel routes, the timing of your movements or the value, from a military or terrorist perspective, of your assets/programmes?
• Are you at risk of targeted political action – eg, because of the politics of your home government; the simple fact of your being foreigners/Westerners; the identity of your international or national staff (this would include ethnic and communal violence); the nature and balance of your relationships with different interest groups in a conflictual situation; or the public statements you have made?
• Are you at risk of criminal acts – eg, because of the (perceived) value of your assets; the location of your offices, residences, warehouses; the nature of your travel movements; the proximity or hindrance of your presence and programmes to criminal gang activity?
• Are you at risk of angry and aggressive actions by disgruntled populations – eg, because of the anarchic and uncoordinated nature of aid agency activities in a certain area, the controversial nature of your programme, the conflict-inducing way the programme is implemented, the provocative attitudes of your staff?

Second, vulnerability analysis looks at who in your agency might be most at risk, where, when and why? This may vary depending on nationality, ethnic identity, gender, etc, but also geographical location or tasks and responsibilities.

Vulnerability analysis, however, does not stop by looking at who is potentially exposed to different threats, and where. The degree of your vulnerability will also depend on the appropriateness and effectiveness of the security measures you take to reduce the risk. This leaves you with a last type of question to answer, ie, about the quality of your security measures:

- Are your current security measures appropriate to the types of threat and the specific vulnerabilities that you have identified?
- Are your staff competent and disciplined about complying with security measures?

4.2.5 The Threshold of Acceptable Risk

So far you have considered in mounting detail threats and vulnerabilities. In your threat analysis, you have also ranked threats in terms of their frequency and therefore likelihood, and in terms of their geographical/spatial variations. You need now to look at threats from the angle of impact.

The main purpose of this exercise is to avoid the 'frog-in-the-boiling-water syndrome': the frog feels the water heating up but does not jump out in time, and when the water reaches boiling point it is too late. 'Danger habituation' is something that frogs and some human beings, among them many aid workers, have in common. Although there is awareness that a situation is deteriorating, people do not withdraw from it or reinforce their security measures until after an incident has occurred. This is a costly and potentially tragic way of managing security. Rather, you should frankly assess in advance whether you can reduce the risk sufficiently. If not (or no longer) and you decide that the level of risk has become unacceptable, then you should withdraw from or stay out of the danger zone.

Risk-impact assessment

A simple tool to clarify your thinking and analysis is a graph that presents 'risk' along an X-axis of probability and a Y-axis of impact. Where you plot a point depends on your answers to two questions:

1. How likely is it that a certain threat/accident will happen to you?
2. If it happens, how serious is the impact on the individual(s) directly involved, and your agency's presence, programmes, general image, reputation, etc?

Diagram 4: The Threshold of Acceptable Risk

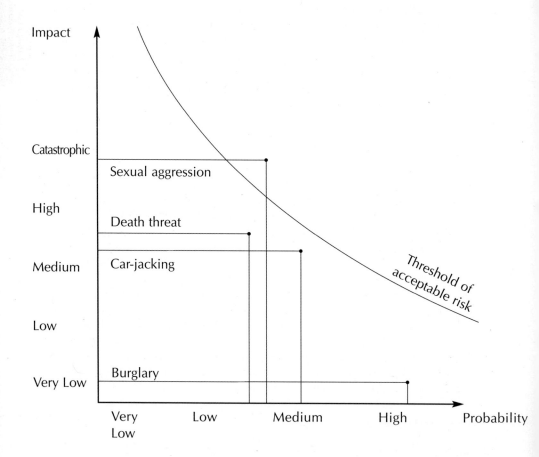

Diagram 4 illustrates the following conclusions of a team discussion:

- The risk of burglary in residences or of office equipment is fairly high, but its impact on staff and on the programme would be limited.
- The risk of car-jacking may be medium but the effect on the programme would be considerably higher as it is heavily dependent on the vehicles for implementation.
- By contrast, a serious death threat or the rape of a staff member would seriously impact on the person concerned but also more widely on the agency's readiness to continue working in that environment.

Risk-impact reduction assessment

The next step is to consider what security measures could reduce either the probability of an incident affecting you and/or the seriousness of its impact.

For example, if you have a field office in a war zone where air bombardment is a real risk, then building bomb shelters and blast walls would be measures to reduce the impact. Painting your logo in bright colours on the roof and giving the precise coordinates of your office premises to the air command are also measures to reduce the probability of being bombed. Both may be necessary.

You might run the risk of a robbery on the street and on individual staff member's valuables being stolen. Strengthening the capacity of the local police may be a medium-term approach to reducing this risk. In addition, never walking alone, driving rather than walking, or walking with body guards, are all measures to reduce the risk. Giving instructions that, in case of an attack, all valuables should be handed over as demanded and without resistance, is a measure to try to reduce the impact.

Defining the threshold of unacceptable risk

The third step would be to admit that, for reasons internal to the agency (eg, lack of resources/skills) or external (no influence/control), you may not be able to reduce the risk or its impact, and therefore that the risk is unacceptable. The decision then must be not to go into a danger area, or to withdraw from it.

You are already thinking creatively now about different, probably complementary, measures to reduce risk. Before we look at some specific frequent threats in more detail (Part 4), we first need to elaborate on risk-reducing strategies at a more strategic level (Chapters 5 and 6).

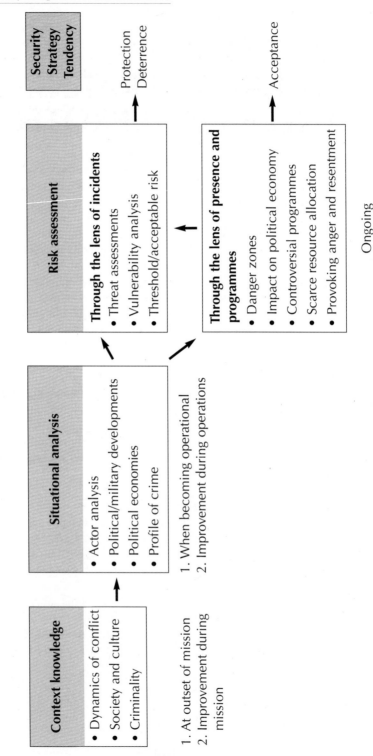

Diagram 5: Risk Assessment: from the General to the Specific

PART III
SECURITY STRATEGIES
AND ARMED PROTECTION

5 ▶ Security Strategies

5 Security Strategies

5.1 Ideal-type Strategies

A review of agency security guidelines and manuals suggests that the most common response to perceived threats and risks is to adopt protective devices and procedures. Understandable as this is, and necessary as it may be, it also reflects a reactive and besieged mentality. It begs the question of why agencies have become so besieged. It also ignores or obscures the fact that threats may be triggered by how the aid agency positions itself in a conflictual environment, how it designs and implements its programme, or how, in any other way, it acts in a way that could be considered provocative.

This chapter discusses three ideal-type security strategies: acceptance, protection and deterrence.

Diagram 6: Security Strategies

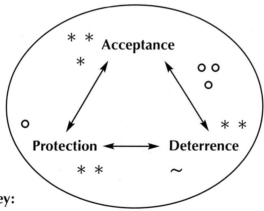

Key:

~ Different

* types of

o threat

An acceptance strategy tries to reduce or remove threats by increasing the acceptance (the political and social 'consent') for your presence and your work in a particular context (politicians and the military call this 'winning hearts and minds'). A protection strategy uses protective devices and procedures to reduce the vulnerability of the agency, but it does not address the threat. In technical jargon this is called 'hardening the target'. A third approach is to deter a threat by counter-threat. This ranges from legal, economic or political sanctions to, most prominently, a counter-threat of defensive or offensive use of force.

The three approaches constitute a range of options from 'soft' to 'hard': seeking acceptance and consent, adopting protective procedures and using protective devices, and threatening with sanctions or counter-violence. In other words, acceptance is about making more friends, protection about sheltering at a distance, and deterrence about intimidating your enemies.

The different strategies have different resource and operational implications. An acceptance strategy may imply that resources are allocated not strictly according to need, but in a way which may facilitate the overall operation. Protective devices carry a direct financial cost while protective procedures (for example, curfews, two-car rule) can restrict operational capacity. A deterrence strategy can have large resource implications and can, in the short term, facilitate operations. However, in the medium-term it can profoundly impair operations.

In the aid world, different agencies generally favour different strategies. The preferred strategy of the International Red Cross and a number of NGOs is to seek acceptance; that of the UN and a number of other NGOs is to reduce vulnerability through protective measures; that of military peace-support operations is to adopt measures of deterrence.

Security problems arise when the preferred security strategies fail to match the threats in the environment. NGOs which provide aid are accustomed to feeling accepted. There are two dangers here:

1. Acceptance cannot be assumed; it has to be won and actively maintained.
2. Acceptance may not be an effective security strategy against all threats. For example, if you are facing 'opportunistic' robbers who are still part of a social community, and in that sense can be influenced or controlled by that community, then enhanced 'acceptance' by that community is likely to increase your security. But if you are facing hardened criminals who are organised into gangs to which they shift their primary loyalty, then a protection and even deterrence strategy might be required. Most aid agencies

operating in the northern Caucasus in the mid-1990s, for example, underestimated the degree of suspicion about 'hidden agendas' and therefore the need for special efforts to build acceptance. They also underestimated the threats from conflict entrepreneurs and organised crime gangs.

A deterrence strategy could equally turn out to create more problems than it solves. The style of the US troop landing on the beaches of Mogadishu in late 1992 revealed the security strategy to be one of deterrence. Attempts to cultivate the initial goodwill and acceptance of the Somali population were not systematically pursued and the relationship soon became antagonistic and many Somalis turned hostile to the peacekeepers.

This seems to suggest that a protection strategy is most desirable. But while it may be necessary, it is not sufficient. Its two main weaknesses are that it focuses on you as the potential target, while in no way addressing those who pose the threat. It also tends to lead to a bunker mentality – ie, dig yourself in and isolate yourself from your environment. This complicates the development of relationships with others, and probably reduces their quantity and quality.

There are many actors in violent environments. Some pose a threat, others become allies. In practice, therefore, you will need a combination of strategies: you may, for example, want to cultivate acceptance and good relationships with local populations and their leadership, but also adopt protective measures against crime. The point is that in proactive security management you make more conscious choices about the strategy or mix of strategies you pursue in the light of the range of threats you identify.

Which Security Strategy in North Niger?

An aid agency involved in child vaccination and food distribution has security concerns in north Niger. The area of the Tobu people is difficult to access and vehicles are often attacked and stolen at gunpoint. Pastoralists are difficult to reach with the vaccination programme.

Discussions conclude that two major security strategies would be possible:

1. The first would institute convoys under the protection of army troops. However, the difficulties of the terrain and the practical arrangements required make this a problematic option. Moreover, the aid agency would be perceived to be associated with the government army, which is resented by the Tobu.

Continued...

2. The second would be to seek and build up acceptance by the Tobu. This would require the identification of places and times when they are reachable, such as at their annual autumn festival, the setting up of radio programmes in the Tobu language on topics of interest to them, and the combination of an animal and child vaccination programme.

In practice the emphasis of one strategy over the other may shift in the light of evolving circumstances.

5.2 The Acceptance Strategy

Key matters to consider in the context of an acceptance strategy are: broad-based relationships, meetings and stated messages, implicit messages, and programme impacts and perceptions. Key principles are to establish and maintain contacts; to try to maintain balance in your relationships; to manage your image; to show respect and to make yourself respected.

5.2.1 Broad-based Relationships

Developing relationships

The proactive positioning of an agency involves developing broad-based, inclusive contacts with the multiple authorities and powerbrokers. This is where your situational analysis and mapping come into use. In highly fragmented environments where groups enter into shifting alliances this poses a considerable challenge. It is easy to overlook one or more power broker who may then retaliate violently.

In a conflict situation where the belligerents have seemingly cohesive structures the perception of humanitarian agencies and their operations is not necessarily transmitted through the ranks and local commanders may have considerable discretion with regard to their response to aid agencies. This requires you to have sufficient competent staff with the time to develop and maintain a network of contacts. They also need to be clear about the values, mandate and mission of your agency (Chapter 3).

In the face of problems, intimidation or threat, temporarily suspending your work and reducing your presence should not be the automatic response. Analyse what the causes might be. If it seems to be a lack of contacts or poor relationships you may decide to reinforce your presence and so strengthen your relation-building capacity. This will enhance your acceptance.

Formal agreements

You may have to, or choose to, formalise the relationships you build. You will have to do so with governmental authorities, and could choose to do so with certain armed opposition groups.

Formal agreements are useful in that they provide formal recognition and explicit reference. They can also be problematic when they are valid for only a limited period of time: in protracted situations negotiations often become more difficult over time.

If you keep the terms fairly general this leaves flexibility for your operations. However, general and vague terms can work against you as they leave the other party room for the denial of responsibility. With regard to security, spell out and agree on fairly detailed terms. Your agreements on security should also spell out the procedures to be followed if security problems do arise.

Written agreements do not have the same value in every social environment. For example, the word of honour of the right person might be more important. The obligation implied is likely to be more strictly observed, if it is widely known that someone has given his word.

Socialising

Socialising to develop a more relaxed and personal relationship is a standard practice in diplomacy: government officials are invited to private dinners or parties at the residence of the agency representative; you accept the hospitality of the tribal leader who slaughters a goat or sheep in your honour, or invite the elders to 'tea'.

Building a relationship requires more than rare, brief, formal meetings. A formal agreement may turn into a mere piece of paper if there is no other contact to maintain the quality of the relationship. At the same time, socialising should not make you lose the critical distance that you need to be able to be firm and perhaps even to go public when real problems arise, while at the same time being sensitive to the potential host–guest relationship.

Be careful who you are seen to be socialising with. In an environment of radical antagonisms and high suspicion, socialising (too much) with a particular party can contribute to the threats against you.

Interactional and negotiating styles

Pay attention to the different interactional and negotiating styles of different social subgroups. Armies have their own organisational culture and language; so too do career civil servants and bureaucrats. Aid workers with a military

Security Strategies 5

background may therefore find it easier to negotiate with, for example, Russian officers in the Caucasus or Nigerian ECOMOG officers in West Africa. These same people, however, may find themselves very much out of place in a more tribal environment, for example, in Afghanistan or the Horn of Africa where an anthropological background could come in handy. People with a background in social work or trade unionism may in turn fit most easily into a Latin American environment with its strong tradition of community organisation and social mobilisation.

The above point is an argument in favour of involving competent national staff in important negotiations (Chapter 20), as they will understand the vernacular language, be able to read non-verbal messages, be familiar with the social codes of behaviour, and generally have a far deeper contextual knowledge than you have. Prepare important meetings together in advance: What do you know about your interlocutors? What positions and arguments do you expect them to use? What will be your position? What style and tactics will you adopt? Such a team approach to developing and maintaining relationships requires trust and respect between those involved (Chapter 18).

In many contexts it may be advisable that messages and decisions that are likely to displease your interlocutor come from an expatriate who is less susceptible to pressure, intimidation and possible retaliation than a national. Be clear in advance about the respective roles you will adopt in the negotiations.

5.2.2 Meetings and Stated Messages

Public statements

Critical public statements are seldom received with gratitude. It is important to consider:

- what the reasons are for going public rather than delivering the message more discreetly;
- whether to inform the recipient of the message in advance and/or deliver the message first before (also) going public;
- how to phrase your statement: what can you document/substantiate if challenged, what could be a less provocative way of phrasing it?
- if you can, control the final version that goes into the public domain: for example, the content of a written press release is easier to keep under control than a press conference that allows questioning, or a live interview;
- beware of 'leaked' statements: how much can you trust a statement 'off the record' to be kept confidential? (For some journalists nothing is 'off the record' if

it makes a good story.) How confidential will statements remain which are made in an open forum such as an interagency coordination meeting? There may be all sorts of reasons why a statement is leaked in a more or less distorted form.

Messages from meetings

Messages and images are conveyed not only in meetings but also through the type of meeting that takes place. Who calls the meeting, who is invited, where it takes place, what the seating arrangements are, are all well-known aspects of diplomacy; they also play a role in developing a certain type of relationship. Summoning local elders to your office, for example, conveys a different message from going to see them in their own environment. People may come to your office to make demands that you quickly know are unacceptable. But it may make tactical sense to spend more time with them than you need to convey your response, until the visitors conclude the meeting rather than you. You will have to balance the management of your time against the effects of appearing brusque and impolite.

Staff communication

Senior agency staff may handle the formal encounters with many groups and actors. But messages about your agency are not only communicated by senior staff and in formal meetings and encounters. It is the perhaps the more junior programme staff who are most likely to deal with local-level government officials, with fighters at roadblocks, with local counterparts and with representatives of the local population. Also drivers, logisticians and administrative staff interact with large numbers of outsiders. Make sure they have a clear view of the principles and role of the agency, and of its mission and position in that particular context, and that they are aware of the sensitivities about communications, messages and styles of interaction, and their impact on your overall image and relationships.

5.2.3 Implicit Messages

Implicit messages are conveyed through appearance, behaviour and male–female interactions, all of which may lead to misunderstandings that could negatively affect your image and your relationship.

Appearance

Appearance is important. Hair style, body decoration and dress code are not only a matter of fashion, but also carry social and political meanings. This includes earrings, tattoos, make-up and style of spectacles (the Khmer Rouge killed any Cambodian who wore spectacles because of the 'intellectual' class position it revealed), an 'Islamic' beard, choice of clothing and how much it covers or reveals, etc. Khaki-coloured trousers and jackets with many side-pockets may communicate a 'safari image' that is associated with the wealthy but ignorant tourist. T-shirts with the different aid agency logos can give the impression of a group of competitive outside interveners. Adopting local dress that may belong to one group in a divided and polarised context may be perceived as signalling an alliance.

Also consider the image that is projected by the use of mobile phones and VHF radios, the new 4-wheel drive vehicles with air-conditioning and tall radio antennae, uniformed guards at the compound gates, large desks of finished hardwood with two telephones and a secretary in attendance. Well organised, well protected, but well accepted?

Behaviour

It will be important to consider the following:

- While inappropriate behaviour by itself does not necessarily translate into a threat, it could aggravate existing suspicions and tensions and provide fertile ground for those whose objective is to stir up animosity towards you. A good briefing on, and monitoring of, interactional styles can help avoid many problems (Chapter 18).
- The kind of behaviour that is considered appropriate or inappropriate in your particular social/cultural environment, as well as your status, gender and age. For example, in certain social environments (certain categories of) men are expected to show highly assertive behaviour. Other social environments emphasise the need for composure and self-control.
- Many social environments have implicit norms about the consumption of stimulants such as alcohol. Even when this is not frowned upon, its acceptance tends to be limited to particular places, times and social occasions. The acceptance of alcohol consumption should not be confused with the acceptance of drunkenness, especially in public. Consuming alcohol with others can be an important ritual, but you will be expected to be able to 'hold your drink' and the risk of saying or doing something stupid increases as you lose your self-control.
- The public expression of anger or irritation is always resented and can be provocative. Firmness in saying 'no' will generally do you no harm when it is combined with a correct and polite attitude. But arrogance, real or perceived, tends to create resentment. A foreigner will have to pay extra attention, but this applies equally to national staff.

> **Case Study: Resentment Aggravated by Staff Behaviour**
>
> In 1996 the national staff of an agency working with refugees and the host population became the object of verbal and written death threats, and eventually were being shot at. These threats and violence were partly rooted in a broader context of tension between the host population and the refugees. Delays and uncertainties about services, in particular the delivery of food aid, also caused resentment, though the agency had undeniably brought many tangible benefits in difficult circumstances. Yet it was the behaviour of the national staff that triggered the violence. Speeding agency vehicles caused a significant increase in road accidents involving local people. Staff were criticised for being arrogant, abusive and unwilling to listen. Several of the well-paid staff members had also become involved in informal relationships with refugee and local women, sometimes leading to pregnancies outside marriage.

Female behaviour and male–female interactions

Many patriarchal societies articulate their moral and communal integrity in terms of the 'purity' of women, for which dress and behavioural codes provide a strong indicator. In times of conflict, when group identities are often redrawn or reaffirmed, such codes may apply even more strongly. Apart from signalling an urban origin in rural areas, the wearing of shorts, short skirts, and open-necked blouses and sleeveless shirts can be seen as socially provocative and religiously offensive. At one end of the spectrum the response may be one of disapproval. At the other end there may be sexual harassment or worse. In order to gain respect for their personal qualities as professionals or as women, female staff should be mindful of these issues rather than insisting on personal freedoms in ways that could be perceived as disrespectful to local codes and sensitivities. But men, too, need to consider whether the way they dress evokes respect or is perceived as disrespectful.

It is also important to be sensitive to, and careful about, the social norms regulating the behaviour between women and men outside the immediate family, as well as the different notions of 'public' and 'private'. Many social environments have more restrictive codes about the public display of 'intimate' behaviour such as holding hands, embracing and kissing.

5.2.4 The Messages and Politics of Staff Composition

The composition of your national staff in particular is important from a security point of view for two reasons:

1. It influences how you are perceived and therefore how people will relate to you.
2. It influences the breadth of the informal contacts and information channels you can establish and maintain.

Real or perceived divisions among staff

In an ethnically divided environment, for example in Bosnia, Kosovo, Liberia, Chechnya, Guatemala, etc, make sure that all major ethnic groups or clans are represented on your staff.

Another common 'divide' is that between people from urban and rural backgrounds. This can cause problems in places where the urban and rural environments constitute very different social worlds and where city-dwellers can be as much 'outsiders' as foreigners. For instance, in Albania a number of agencies went to the more traditional north with drivers and translators recruited from Tirana and were surprised to have their cars stolen.

In other places such as Karachi in Pakistan, tensions can exist between an older indigenous population and more recent 'immigrants'. Another possible divide can be that of political affiliation. You don't want, unknowingly, to end up with most of your staff being members of the same political party.

Ideally you want to strive perhaps not for 'proportional representation' but for a 'defendable mix' of members of various groups in a fragmented social environment. Where this is not possible – because one ethnic group, clan or political party etc. is dominant – you may want to strive for a 'balanced presence' among the territories of different 'segregated' groups and, if possible, have mixed staff in the central field office in the capital city.

A strategy of 'defendable mix' for the sake of acceptance (for programmatic and security reasons) may override a policy of recruitment on the basis of skill and equal opportunity only. In other words, you may deliberately seek out, or give preference to, people from a certain category, even if they are not the best qualified. Beware of a mix of staff belonging to different groups between which there are tensions or even open conflict which could potentially import 'conflict' into the organisation. It will be a challenge to develop an in-depth understanding of the conflict, clarify the position of your agency in that context, and exercise your 'conflict-mediating' skills vis-à-vis your own staff!

5.2.5 Programming

Chapter 4 discussed a number of ways in which how you and other agencies identify, design and implement your programmes can enhance or lead to the loss of acceptance.

Diagram 7: Different Images and Perceptions

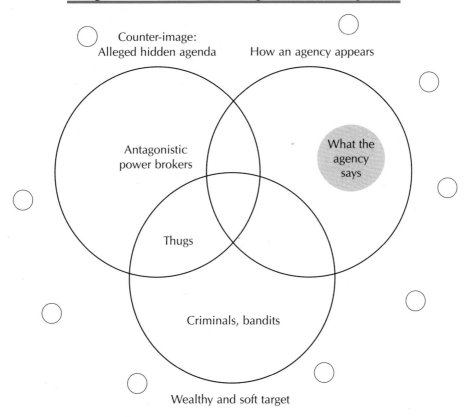

How an agency is perceived in general does not only depend on what it says about itself and its intentions and role. In the eyes of criminals and bandits, it may well be perceived as a wealthy and soft target. Powerbrokers who are antagonistic to one or more humanitarian agencies may also spread a different image of it, for example, as an actor with a hidden agenda. In doing so they may give a 'spin' to certain actions, sayings or appearances of the aid agency or its staff as 'evidence' for the perception that they suggest.

5.3 The Protection Strategy

There are many different facets to a protection strategy. These are often used in combination.

Reduce exposure

This includes reducing exposure for personnel, imposing no-go zones and no-go times (curfew), withdrawing female staff from areas with a high risk of rape, reducing staff numbers (to 'essential staff' only) or withdrawing/evacuating all staff members and suspending or closing the programme. With regard to assets, it may mean limiting the amount of cash (Chapter 11) and other valuables/assets that can constitute an attraction for robbers.

Reduce or increase visibility

In situations where aid agencies enjoy a high degree of acceptance the prominent display of the agency emblem or logo on staff shirts, compound entrances, vehicles and the rooftops of field offices can provide protection. In other situations, however, it may signal to unscrupulous criminals, politically motivated groups or resentful populations where the 'soft and wealthy target' – ie, the aid agency – is. A protective tactic may be to blend into the background by reducing your identification marks. For individuals living in a tense or risky environment, this translates into keeping a low profile with regard to your residence, means of transport, personal appearance and behaviour. During the NATO air campaign against Serbia in the spring of 1999, for example, the Macedonian population was divided. Its Albanian minority was generally in favour of NATO action; its Slav majority sympathised with the Serbs. An aid agency operating there used removable logos on its vehicles: in the Albanian-inhabited areas they were put on; elsewhere they were removed.

Strength in numbers

Driving in convoy (Chapter 8), the instruction that staff should never go out alone, moving agency compounds closer together (Chapter 9) and neighbourhood watch schemes are all attempts to reduce vulnerability by grouping together.

Protective devices

These include helmets and flakjackets for individuals; blast walls, bomb shelters and sniper walls near battlefields (Chapter 7); and compound protection measures such as high walls with barbed wire, barred windows, a burglar alarm and/or closed circuit television, increased lighting, and the use of unarmed guards and/or watchdogs (Chapter 9). Radios are often seen as protective devices because they allow you to maintain communications (Chapter 17). Note, however, that radios, just like 4-wheel drive vehicles, can actually increase the risk in certain contexts, because they mark you out as 'wealthy', or because armed groups want to capture the radios for their own use, etc.

Protective procedures

Announcing your movements to the warring parties in advance and perhaps seeking their explicit consent before you set out can be a protective procedure (Chapter 7). So too the practice of controlling who goes in and out of the compound, or searching visitors and cars (Chapter 9).

Protection money

Aid agencies are not known to pay cash directly as 'protection' money. However, accepting the levying of 'tax' in kind by all sorts of illegitimate authorities can be considered a variation on the theme. This includes the payment of bribes (in cash or more often in kind, for example, a number of food bags). This is a form of buying acceptance and is therefore not genuine acceptance. At the outset it might temporarily reduce your vulnerability, but beware of getting into an inflationary spiral where the 'cost of protection' may increase beyond what you deem acceptable.

Protect your life

Staff should be instructed not to resist armed attackers, in particular. While surrounding personal and agency valuables does not reduce the risk of being robbed at gunpoint, it does reduce the risk of a gun being turned on the victim. Similarly, not resisting a sexual assault may be the response if the victim becomes convinced that resistance could lead to greater harm or loss of life (Chapter 12).

5.4 The Deterrence Strategy

5.4.1 Legal, Political and Economic Sanctions

Field-level security management and frontline diplomacy may need to be backed up by additional pressure from the threat of sanctions. It is useful for your staff to know what legal protection they enjoy as aid workers, and under what conditions (Annex 2). Unfortunately, in most circumstances, referring to and threatening with legal, political or economic sanctions will not be a very effective deterrent.

- There may be no effective state security forces or they may be in collusion with criminals and/or insurgent forces, or the 'security forces' can themselves be a source of insecurity.
- Peace accords sometimes require the granting of an amnesty to those who have committed abuses and atrocities in order to persuade all parties to sign.
- International criminal tribunals are not for the time being much of a deterrent, as few indicted persons are ever apprehended.
- International sanctions are not very effective against authoritarian regimes, or against non-state actors without a 'state-project' or with 'alternative' sources of supply.

5.4.2 Suspension of Operations and/or Withdrawal

In the face of certain threats, and often after security incidents, agencies have at times 'threatened' the suspension of their aid programmes. The continuation or resumption of the programme is then made conditional upon the resolution of the problem and pledges from those targeted by the measure of greater efforts to maintain the security of the agency. Anecdotal evidence and more rigorous reviews of the effectiveness of aid conditionality suggest that in many cases the tactic does not work very well, and that after a while the aid agency resumes its programme although there has been no noticeable improvement in the contextual conditions of work. The threat may have signalled your disapproval, but its ineffectiveness also highlights your vulnerability, while resuming the programme without improvements in working conditions, leads to a certain loss of credibility. Next time your threatened suspension will not be taken so seriously. It is important therefore to consider the conditions and the chances of success in resorting to suspension.

The following are suggested circumstances under which the chances of effectiveness are increased:

- There is a sufficiently influential section of the population and/or local leadership that, for reasons of self-interest or more general acceptance, can be mobilised on your behalf.
- The local community or local authorities have influence over the offenders, or are prepared to act potentially with force to catch them.
- The suspension or withdrawal is not perceived as primarily punishing innocent civilians who have no involvement in the causes of insecurity and are not in a position to improve your security.

- There is a real preparedness to suspend operations and to maintain the suspension until the situation is satisfactorily resolved, and not to annul the decision too quickly because of internal agency pressures to resume activities.
- Unless the incident is very serious, a selective suspension and/or gradual reintroduction of services gives you more room for tactical manoeuvre. A total suspension tends to create a difficult all-or-nothing situation.
- Other agencies do not undercut your tactic of suspension by stepping in to fill the gap. You should therefore first build-up a common front.

Suspension as a tactic seems to work best when there is a high level of acceptance, and when it is adopted in a way that does not erode that acceptance. Where the offenders are not concerned about your aid programme or the impact of its suspension on the largely powerless population, they are unlikely to respond to your threat. You can still decide to suspend the programme to signal your protest at the insecure conditions in which you are working, but not with the intention or hope of exercising effective pressure.

5.4.3 Armed Protection

The strongest form of deterrence is the use of armed protection. Even when a force is small, lightly armed and under instructions to use its weapons only in self-defence, the potential use of fire power in the face of threat introduces a qualitative difference in your security strategy. It also profoundly affects the image and perception of aid agencies in general.

Case Study: Strategic Choices in Incident Resolution

Within the space of six months, two aid agency vehicles are stolen at gunpoint in a refugee camp close to the border. The car-jackers disappear across the border.

Agency 'Nice' runs a large supplementary feeding programme in the camp, and decides to try and pursue an acceptance strategy. The manager and some selected national agency staff have a low-profile meeting with camp 'elders', some of whom belong to the same social group as the bandits. The agency argues that it does not want to punish the vulnerable women and children in the camp, but now faces a practical problem. It cannot mobilise another vehicle, and has no means of taking the food and staff from the central store in the camp back and forth to the various outlying feeding centres. It asks the elders to try to get back the vehicle, and in the meantime to share in the responsibility for the well-being of their family and clan members. It asks the elders to mobilise a private vehicle, for which the agency will pay only for the fuel, until such time as the stolen one is returned. They do so.

Agency 'Tough', however, which provides the general ration to the camp population, pursues a deterrence strategy. It calls the camp elders to a high-profile public meeting where they are seated on school benches and accused by the agency representative of having harboured the bandits without preventing the car jacking taking place. The agency immediately plays its trump card: it will suspend general food distributions until the stolen vehicle is returned. It ignores the elders' protests that innocent people cannot be made to suffer for the misconduct of a few individuals.

Agency 'Nice' had its vehicle returned by the local people; agency 'Tough' did not and after a while, predictably, had to abandon its suspension of the general ration without having gained anything.

6 Armed Protection

6 ▶ Armed Protection

6.1 The Basic Question

Armed protection and humanitarian action remain uneasy bedfellows. Although in reality many agencies at one time or another have used some form of armed protection, the discussion about it quickly turns emotive. This chapter is an attempt to provide a more systematic framework for considering the matter, and to stimulate depth and clarity of reasoning in coming to an informed decision. It is not intended to be an argument for the use of armed protection. At every step in the line of reasoning it is possible to arrive at the conclusion that armed protection is not the option.

Before proceeding, however, consider that if you start actually thinking about armed protection you may have reached the threshold of acceptable risk and should withdraw or stay out. If you consider that this threshold has not yet been reached, or that the use of armed protection could perhaps reduce the risk to a more acceptable level, then three major areas come into play in thinking through the decision: principles, context and management.

6.2 Questions of Principle

The first stage in thinking this through concerns principle:

- Do you believe that the use of force can be justified under certain conditions or not?
- Do you believe that the use of force is compatible or not with humanitarian action?
- Do you believe that using armed protection would contribute to the local/global arms race?
- Do you believe that it can be justified to pay for armed protection?

6.2.1 Conditional Use of Force

Clarify your attitude, in principle, to the use of force and distinguish between absolute and conditional pacifism and non-violence. (Absolute non-violence is the rejection of force under any circumstances. Conditional non-violence can accept the limited and defensive use of force in the face of clear aggression or violent threat.)

Diagram 8: Thinking Through the Decision to get Armed Protection

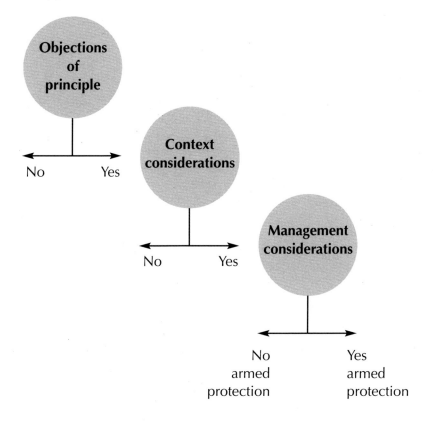

6.2.2 Force Compatible with Humanitarian Action

Is armed protection against the basic principles of what constitutes 'humanitarian action'? Or is it only a response to the conditions in which humanitarian action has to take place, and one that, when carefully and proportionately used, does not undermine its basic principles?

Arguments against the use of force

These tend to be inspired by ethical and/or long-term operational considerations. The ethical argument holds that humanitarian action is never compatible with the use of force. The long-term operational consideration is that, whereas in a specific context armed protection might be justifiable, it erodes the overall image of humanitarian action worldwide and may therefore lead to increased insecurity elsewhere or in the future. According to this line of reasoning, resorting too quickly or too often to armed protection undermines global efforts to restore respect for international humanitarian law and with it the immunity of aid workers.

Arguments in favour of the use of force

These might hold that force can be acceptable as a last option, and when people's lives and survival would be at risk if humanitarian and other assistance were not 'forced through' under armed protection. There is no dispute about the fact that 'moral authority' – a measure of acceptance – is the best way to obtain compliance. But there may be violent people who cannot be made to respect other people's rights and integrity by moral arguments only. Hence democratic and peaceful countries maintain a police force that, if necessary, can be used to apprehend dangerous criminals, serial rapists, armed robbers or violent hooligans.

Contradictory positions

Is the use of armed protection by an aid agency compatible with a policy of forbidding arms in agency vehicles and compounds? This requires a consideration of international humanitarian law (IHL) and the origins of the policy forbidding weapons in aid agency premises/vehicles. Strictly speaking, in terms of IHL, the purpose of humanitarian action is to insert 'humanity' into a situation of violent conflict, but not per se to halt that violence. IHL does not condemn the use of arms and is not an anti-war declaration. It tries to introduce restraint among combatants and measures of protection for civilians and non-combatants, and to create 'spaces' in the midst of the fighting where humanity can prevail and no fighting should take place. Clearly, then, the 'bearers' of that message of humanity should not themselves carry weapons or allow weapons in their 'space'.

But consider the limitations of IHL, which essentially applies to organised warfare between states and, by extension, to organised non-state armed groups. Its authority derives simply from an agreement among states, and possibly non-state groups, to abide by it. Humanitarian action can be allowed by armed groups, if they consent to it. The problem is: what happens if armed groups do not consent to and respect (from a security point of view) the presence and activities of humanitarian actors, and cannot be persuaded to do so, while endangered populations are in pressing need of protection and assistance? There is also another possibility: that there is no organised armed group but only criminals or, for example, demobilised soldiers who are no longer under a command structure and who turn to banditry. The question of obtaining consent from them does not even apply.

Consent

The notion of 'official consent', like the concept of 'sovereignty', has come under debate in recent years. Like the question of in whom sovereignty is ultimately vested, in the government or in the people of a nation, so too the question can be asked: whose consent counts most, that of the power brokers or of ordinary civilians? Is consent the key criterion, or compliance with international standards and norms? It is useful here to look briefly at 'neutrality' in terms of military peace-support operations. In such operations UN troops are required to be neutral. Neutrality implies avoiding taking sides and using excessive force. It does not, however, mean passivity. Neutrality can be principled. Principled neutrality requires responding to what a violent group is doing – not because of which faction or side they belong to but because their acts are a violation of basic human rights and/or the standards of international law. It does not mean abstaining from the use of force under all circumstances, but using the minimum force necessary to obtain compliance with agreed norms, rules and laws.

Compliance

Those accepting that force can be used, under certain conditions, for humanitarian purposes, might point out that this may not meet with the consent of the party to which it is applied, but, importantly, may well have the consent and acceptance of the population at large. Endangered and abused populations have sometimes lost confidence in the international community, because it refrained from using force where it mattered. Somalis came to wonder what the purpose of 'Operation Restore Hope' was if it was not going to disarm the predatory militias. There is still deep resentment in Rwanda because UNAMIR troops withdrew when the genocide started. And in Sarajevo and elsewhere in Bosnia, people have been exasperated that UNPROFOR at times did very little to protect them effectively from shelling, mass expulsion and massacre. The principled, targeted, measured and accountable use of force to obtain compliance with basic international standards and norms which exist for the public good, may enhance acceptance among the population at large.

Public security

Note that in this reflection we have moved from the consideration of armed protection for the private security of aid agencies and peacekeepers, to that of armed protection for the public security of endangered people. A major consideration would be who benefits from the armed protection: is it only the aid agency and its staff, or can the protection provide wider public benefit and enhance public security? Are you contributing to the 'privatisation' of security, whereby those who are able to pay can buy security while others have to live in fear, or are you contributing to increased wider, public security?

Armed Protection 6

6.2.3 Armed Protection and the Local/Global Arms Race

From a radical, anti-arms point of view, you will refuse armed protection because its use, as a matter of principle, contributes to the ongoing production and distribution of arms. Using armed protection, practically and morally, sends 'the wrong message'.

A more conditional perspective might focus not so much on the production of arms per se but on their uncontrolled proliferation – ie, the loss of a monopoly of violence by the authorities responsible for security and law and order. Armed protection which is not provided by the authorities would stimulate that trend.

Ultimately you may have to weight the two together. You can do this from a principled or contextual point of view: what matters most takes priority: controlling arms proliferation or securing urgently needed humanitarian assistance (and protection for civilians)?

6.2.4 Paying for Armed Protection

Following experience with the protection rackets of some Somali militia guards, some aid workers have argued that aid agencies should never pay for armed protection. There are ethical and practical arguments that may be invoked when making this decision.

Weighing the value of life

On the moral level one could argue that the value of the resources lost or stolen cannot be weighed against the value of a life lost in an armed confrontation, be it the life of a guard, an assailant or a bystander. Yet the situation may be one in which not assets but people themselves are targeted. The investment in armed protection is therefore meant to save lives. One could also argue that in situations of acute need the cost of a life cannot be weighed against the cost, in terms of suffering and possible death among endangered populations, of not getting urgently needed relief goods through.

The use of charitable donations

Another moral, and perhaps legal, question is whether paying for armed protection is a legitimate use of donations for charitable purposes. Is it, as a matter of principle, an abuse of such donations, or is it warranted as an inevitable cost to present the theft of the resources bought with the donations? From the latter point of view you could weigh the cost of armed protection against the value of the assets that might be looted, and against that of the insurance cover for assets and people in high-risk areas.

The economic arguments

From a pragmatic and economic perspective one could argue that some law and order service is (still) a necessary part of the functioning even of democratic and peaceful societies; in functioning democracies part of one's tax contributions finance the police, the national guard and the armed forces. Paying directly for armed protection only makes more transparent a reality that is otherwise less visible.

Whose responsibility

In some countries the government security force, police or armed forces are ineffective for lack of resources. As a result there have been instances in which aid agencies have supported the state materially, for example, with vehicles, to enable it to perform with some effectiveness. While this is ultimately the responsibility of the national government, a large proportion of international relief and rehabilitation assistance already provides services that government would normally be expected to provide. If aid pays part of the bill for health and education, for example, can it also pay part of the bill for security?

Case Study: One Possible Policy

Under the policy of one agency, armed protection can be considered when:

- large numbers of lives are at risk;
- the threat is banditry, not political;
- the provider is acceptable;
- the deterrent can be effective.

6.3 Questions of Context

You have decided that you have not yet passed the threshold of acceptable risk and you want to continue operations. You have also decided that armed protection is not excluded as a matter of principle. Now you need to consider other questions:

- What are the threats and where do they come from?
- Is armed protection the only possible and the best answer?
- Does armed protection reduce or increase the risk?
- Who benefits from the armed protection?
- Who provides the armed protection?

6.3.1 The Nature and Origin of the Threats

What/who is armed protection supposed to protect you from? Where do the threats come from and why? The question of armed protection often arises when there is a risk of targeted assassination of aid personnel, of kidnapping, of armed robbery, and/or of ambush and robbery or destruction of aid convoys. Your deeper analysis (Chapters 3 and 4) will have given you some idea about the 'who' and perhaps even the 'why'.

6.3.2 Is Armed Protection the Only Possible and Best Answer?

Threats or incidents may occur for 'political reasons', for example, because the agency is not perceived as neutral in its operations. Armed protection may increase that perception. An approach might be to aim for a more balanced 'neutral' political positioning, increased dissemination about who you are and how you operate, and more active consent-seeking and acceptance-building.

You may not find this desirable: If you are driven by a solidarity agenda you will not wish to establish relationships with an oppressive government, for example (just as it is conceivable that on moral/political grounds you do not want to have relationships with a violent rebel group).

Or you may find it impossible: Attacks on aid workers may be part of a broader strategy of intimidation, terror and oppression, and those pursuing such a strategy may be deaf to your arguments. Similarly, threats can come from criminals, bandits and militias with whom it is difficult to cultivate 'acceptance'.

There may be alternative strategies. If new 4-wheel drive vehicles are the attraction, use second-hand 2-wheel drive ones – as long as they are in excellent operating condition. If international agency convoys and warehouses are a target because they are outside the 'social system', you could use, for example, local traders and merchants who are more protected because they are 'within the system'. If internationals are the only target of kidnapping, national staff could run the programme.

6.3.3 Does Armed Protection Reduce or Increase the Risk?

Even where armed protection seems justified, the question is: will it provide a reasonable deterrent or will it increase the risk? For example, if burglars suspect that a resident has a firearm, they may turn violent if surprised in the act. If road bandits see a lightly armed convoy they may shoot before they loot. If armed protection is provided by government forces, you may turn yourself into a legitimate target in the eyes of the armed opposition.

Men and women may have different perceptions about this. Female staff may feel an added risk from armed men around them, who might become a threat.

Another important point is that reduced risk for you may mean increased risk for other people. For example, if some agencies use armed protection and others do not, this may increase the risk for the latter who, by comparison, become the more vulnerable target.

Finally, while armed protection may be the decision of the individual agency, it has implications for all agencies. Indeed, a sound operating premise is that people do not differentiate between different aid agencies not even between NGOs and the UN. One agency with armed protection will influence the image and perception of all humanitarian agencies, and therefore potentially affect everybody's acceptance and relationships.

6.3.4 Who Benefits from Armed Protection?

Typically in dangerous environments we tend to think about measures that will enhance our own security. It seems worthwhile, however, to consider whether and how security could be improved more generally. It might be possible to deploy armed protection in ways that enhance the general security instead of only that of the aid agency. For example, if you deploy armed guards in a refugee camp, can you do it in a way that protects not only your staff but also the refugee women who are at risk of sexual assault when they collect water and firewood? Can you develop a system whereby armed guards of several individual agencies patrol the neighbourhood and therefore increase the security of all? Your guards will themselves prefer clear and limited responsibilities and may not immediately warm to this type of approach, but there will be benefits to be had from it.

6.3.5 Who Provides the Armed Protection?

The decision to use armed protection must not be taken until you have considered a number of critical issues. You can draw up a list of potential providers and write a commentary for each, with their advantages and disadvantages in the light of your criteria. Different sources of armed protection include the national army, the national police, an armed resistance group, UN military peacekeepers and UN police, local militia men, private security companies and armed guards on the agency's payroll. Questions to consider are:

- What is the 'political' position of a provider of armed protection in a given conflict – in other words, will you be seen as 'taking sides' if you associate yourself with a certain provider of armed protection?
- What is the public image and reputation of a provider of armed protection? If, for example, the national army or police is broadly perceived as an instrument of repression and exploitation, or if an armed faction has a reputation for brutality against civilians, using their 'protection' may damage your public image.
- How important for the provider of the armed protection is the extension of that protection to an aid agency compared with its other objectives? The provider may have another agenda that in critical moments may override concern for your security.
- What is the 'integrity' of the potential provider? If the police force harbours known war criminals you may not want it to provide you with protection. If a private security company can provide you with protection but also provides or manages the armed guard of government officials and/or transnational business interests who profit from the instability and are involved in illicit resource extraction, again you may not want to associate with them (Annex 5).
- How professional is the provider? Are the guards well trained, provided with functioning equipment, well instructed, supervised and disciplined?
- How much management control do you need, and do you want, over the provider? National security forces, rebel groups and UN police and peacekeepers, for example, will have their own chain of command where decisions are made. Hired militia, private security companies or guards on the agency payroll could come more under your command. Having more direct authority over the providers of armed protection brings them more under your control but also makes you directly accountable for their behaviour and actions. The advantages and disadvantages will have to be weighed in context.

It is conceivable that you will find yourself not opposed in principle to the use of force and that you judge armed protection to be an inevitable measure in your particular situation. Yet because none of the potential providers is acceptable and effective you may decide not to use armed protection. You must then run the risk, or withdraw.

6.4 Managing Armed Protection

As suggested above, when you hire armed protection you have more management control than when you request the assistance of external security forces. Nevertheless, even in the latter case a number of management questions have to be considered. It is advisable to discuss and negotiate them as clearly as possible with 'external' security forces, and to spell them out on paper in case of later disputes.

Overall the key questions to consider are:

- Do you have the in-house policies, procedures and management competence necessary for handling this relationship?
- Do you know the necessary contractual stipulations?
- Who maintains command and control, and who has authority and responsibility for what?

Internal management questions might then include:

- Who in the aid agency makes the decision/approves the use of armed protection?
- What knowledge and experience will the managers need to deal with it?
- How do you draw up tenders and assess the bids from local private security companies, if that is your choice?
- How can you make inquiries about the professionalism and integrity of a potential service provider?
- How do you check on the criteria for a selection of guards in terms of training, experience with handling weapons, etc?
- Who in the country office has the daily responsibility for the management of the guards, and does that person have the necessary competence and confidence?

6.4.1 Contractual Stipulations

There are a variety of stipulations that you will need to elaborate in an agreement or contract. These include:

- Guard selection criteria such as age, health, literacy, no use of alcohol or drugs, no other employment (at least to the extent that sleep is adequate).
- Essential requirements of supervisors and minimum standards in supervision.

- Minimum standards for recruitment and further in-service training: You may wish to stress certain basic training items such as local law and the power of arrest, fire and explosives, log-keeping, office evacuation, vehicle and body search procedures, package and mail search, first aid, etc.
- Ending of an agreement or contract: The need for armed protection is a dynamic variable and you may wish to end a contract quite suddenly for a variety of reasons. Make sure to spell out clear criteria and procedures for the early ending of the contract or agreement. Shorter-term, renewable contracts give you more flexibility but may also expose you to inflating price demands.
- Liability in case of an exchange of fire leading to injury or death: There are legal 'rules' governing liability and compensation, though in some situations it will be customary law that applies. Who is responsible for the injury or death of a guard, assailant, or bystander in an exchange of fire? Can your liability be restricted to actions that fall strictly within the agreed terms, or only when carried out following orders?
- Remuneration: In terms of salary scales or the payment of incentives you may have to find a balance between your wish to avoid stimulating a lucrative market in privatised security with the need to maintain motivation and commitment and, perhaps, loyalty to your agency. Guards often work long and unsociable hours and do a potentially dangerous job. Too low a salary may lead to low standards of performance.

6.4.2 Command and Control

A crucial question is who is in charge of what? To whom are the guards answerable; who has the authority of command; who is in charge of their discipline? Where external security forces provide armed protection, what is the relative authority of their commander versus that of the agency manager? Who, for example, determines the rules of engagement and who ensures that the guards have fully understood them? Rules of engagement concern the circumstances under which the guards can use force, in particular, their weapons and the proportionality of the force used.

Another important point is to agree procedures and approaches. It is advisable to determine or to discuss and agree on procedures for a number of possible scenarios, for example, what to do when a visitor refuses to be body-searched or insists on bringing in his own armed guards, or how far to go in the pursuit of fleeing robbers or attackers. Also, what disciplinary procedures apply for what sort of offence or non-performance of duty, and how you deal with the situation where you feel that a guard under external command needs to be subjected to disciplinary procedure.

Take note that in a multinational peacekeeping force, for example, different national armies tend to come with different traditions and cultures, including with regard to command and control, rules of engagement, and what is considered 'appropriate' or 'excessive' use of force. Detailed in-depth consultation with field-level commanders may be required to ensure a common understanding between you and the provider of your armed protection. Similarly, the national army may be deploying changing contingents of troops to provide you with protection. Different commanders will have different understandings and interpretations. This is why you need a detailed written agreement with a senior commander. Monitor to make sure replacements are fully briefed.

6.4.3 Weaponry and Other Equipment

Agreement will also have to be reached about:

- The type of weaponry the guards will use (eg, pistols, single shotguns, or machine guns). Who is responsible for providing the ammunition and for checking that the weapons are well maintained?
- Who is responsible for the provision of additional equipment such as rainproof clothing, flashlights, good boots, etc?
- Armed guards do not normally come with vehicles. Decisions will have to be made about if and when they can use agency vehicles. For example, can a local army contingent guarding the refugee camp use your agency's vehicle to pursue robbers of another agency's vehicle in the camp? In some instances agencies, after removing their logos, have made vehicles available to the army to escort aid convoys through bandit-infested areas. Alternatively, vehicles may be rented for the armed guards but the risk that the vehicles are damaged in crossfire needs to be anticipated. Who will be responsible for the damage?

It is conceivable that you will find that armed protection is necessary, and that the potential provider is acceptable, but that no satisfactory agreement can be reached about aspects of command and control. You may then decide to do without armed protection, and run the risk or suspend your operations.

Case Study: An Offer of Armed Protection

An agency was operating in a republic in the northern Caucasus at a time of increasing risk of kidnapping. The local authorities had been urging it for some time to take armed guards, which the agency did not want to do. One day, five government guards simply showed up. The implicit message was that the agency had to accept them or leave. The authorities wanted the agency to provide the guards with uniforms and pay them, to which the agency could not agree. It felt uncomfortable as it had no reference for the guards. A relative of their landlord who had good contacts with the local authorities arranged for the guards deployed to be men whom he knew. The government guards stayed outside the compound, while the agency had its own unarmed guards inside the compound. However, it never felt happy with the arrangement and eventually left.

PART IV
THREAT MANAGEMENT

7 Battlefield Survival

Battlefield Survival

This chapter considers the threats of bombing and shelling, crossfire and sniping, and landmines. There are other battle-related threats not considered here, such as relief planes being shot down or sea-mines. Two particularly useful pocket-sized publications for wider staff use which deal with these and other issues are D Gowdey (1997) *Landmine Safety Handbook*, published by CARE, and D L Roberts (1999) *Staying Alive: Safety and Security Guidelines for Humanitarian Volunteers in Conflict Areas*, published by the ICRC.

7.1 Core Questions and Core Advice

Key issues to consider and questions to ask in the face of active battlefield dangers concern:

- **The threshold of acceptable risk:** Should your agency be or remain there at all? Is the risk of shelling and bombing, crossfire and sniper fire still within your threshold of acceptable risk? Are there significant non-combatant assistance and protection needs that warrant the agency's presence?
- **The risk-benefit equation:** Are the conditions such that you can still effectively do something for the non-combatants or are you just staying as 'witnesses' and 'out of solidarity'? Is yours the best organisation to play that role: is something being done with the testimony that it provides; how many of your staff have to remain to fulfil this function?
- **Medical assistance:** Medical personnel in particular tend to stay or even move in closer to help the casualties of battlefield actions. The same key questions should be considered: Is it your organisation that has to go in, or can you get others such as soldiers to evacuate the casualties to your more withdrawn and therefore safer health post? How effective an operation can you maintain in the midst of battle? Do you have supplies or are you only providing moral support to local health staff and psychological comfort to wounded combatants? How many of your staff have to stay exposed under these circumstances?

Core advice for staff when coming under fire:

- Don't be macho or a hero. Don't stand around trying to find out where the fire is coming from, who is firing, or what sort of weapon is being fired. This is not the moment to test and develop your knowledge of weaponry. You will not avoid bombs and shells by being a weapons expert.

- Your immediate survival decision whether to stay or to leave, followed by the logical steps resulting from that decision.
- Use the best natural defences you have: your own fear and common sense.
- Seek cover, get out of sight, get out of fire.

7.2   Shelling and Bombing

7.2.1 Types and Tactics

Shelling and rockets may come from howitzers and heavy artillery, from tanks and rocket launchers, or from smaller portable mortars. The most common mortars have a range of about 6km, whereas other types of artillery can have a range of up to 50km. Being behind a hill will be no protection as shells can be lobbed over the hill. Simpler 'Scud' or more sophisticated cruise missiles can cover much greater distances than artillery. Fighter planes can drop bombs, shoot rockets or pepper you from machine guns. Helicopters can fire rockets or use machine guns. Bombs can be dropped from fighter or bomber planes. Bombs or rockets can be launched a long distance to their targets and you will not hear the planes first.

In terms of tactics basic distinctions can be made between 'random or saturation fire', 'predicted fire' and 'observed fire'.

Random or saturation fire

This is highly inaccurate and you are at equal risk wherever you are in the target area. It can be a result of the type of weapon used, such as multiple rocket launchers which 'saturate' an area with shells (used by the Russians against Grozny in the second Chechen war), or 'cluster bombs' which scatter hundreds of smaller 'bomblets' (used by NATO over Kosovo). Or it can be the result of a deliberate tactic, such as an 'artillery barrage' or so-called 'carpet bombing'.

'Predicted' fire

This means that the artillery crew is aiming on the basis of calculations from a map, with no capacity to adjust to a specific target, or that pilots are shooting rockets or dropping bombs at a target more often than not in a single overflight – ie, without a prior trial run or a second return run with a better adjusted aim. The behaviour of pilots and therefore the accuracy of fire from a plane or helicopter depends very much on whether the enemy can detect them early on by radar, and whether they expect to be attacked by anti-aircraft fire or enemy fighter planes. Radar installations, enemy airfields and anti-aircraft installations are primary targets, either through high-altitude attack, missile attack or low-flying surprise attack. While the enemy may not have the technical means just described it may still dispose of shoulder-fired surface-to-air missiles such as were provided to the 'mujahedin' in Afghanistan in the mid-1980s and were suspected to be in the possession of the LTTE at the start of Eelam War 3 in Sri Lanka in 1995. Planes and helicopter gunships then tend to reduce their vulnerability by dropping bombs from high altitude, staying further away from the target, or coming in low in an attempt to surprise. This does not help the accuracy of fire which may very well hit the aid agency compound, however well identified. Consider yourselves to be at high risk.

'Observed' artillery fire/air attack

'Observed' fire means that there are one or more observers who watch where shells/rockets/bombs land, and relay directions for more accurate targeting to the firing crew. There are two commonly used techniques to adjust artillery fire on to the target: 'walking towards you' and 'bracketing'. In both cases the observer first directs the artillery crew to a 'firing line' – an imaginary line between the observer and the target – and then closes in on the target. In 'walking towards you' the shells get successively closer to the target. In 'bracketing', the shells are fired alternately before and beyond the target with the 'bracket' getting smaller and smaller. If you are the target, or very close to it, and alert, you will realise it as the shells start coming closer to you. You may not be the target but in the firing line, in which case the shelling may shift its focus elsewhere. But while the crew is adjusting you may still be hit. With 'observed fire' there is a shorter or longer time interval in which you may be able to get yourself out of the firing line.

7.2.2 Risk Reduction

Reduce risk

In order to reduce risk put yourself in a 'safe' location:

- Do not locate your offices and warehouses close to obvious or likely military targets such as the airfield, military barracks, fuel depots, official buildings, or strategic crossroads, railheads, power stations, radio and TV buildings, etc. If you put staff up in a hotel choose one that is away from potential targets.
- If your agency is in a town of strategic military value that is likely to come under fire move as far to the outskirts or the nearby countryside as you can without losing operational capacity.
- In hilly or mountainous areas avoid siting on high ground where you will be very exposed. Find relative safety from shelling and bombing at the foot of a steep hill or mountain.

Identify your location

The agency flag will not be visible from a distance or on a windless day. Paint the logo in bright colours on the roof and the side walls of the compound to make it visible – though this will not offer protection against random or hasty firing!

On the other hand this may increase the risk because pilots may use, for example, your visibly identified rub halls near the airstrip for better aim.

Reduce potential impact

This may not help much against a direct hit but it can reduce the damage of 'close calls' and the effects from blast and shrapnel.

Glass

A major risk to life and limb are the thousands of small glass fragments blown in by blast. You can reduce this blast effect with wooden planks, shutters, special blast curtains and strong self-adhesive role (transparent polythene sticky roll called '3M's Scotchshield') on the windows and glass door panels. This will not stop shrapnel or bullets, however.

Blast walls

These stop shrapnel and bullets only if correctly built. Use sandbags (alternate between 'stretchers' and 'headers' and build solid corners to strengthen the construction), oil drums or boxes filled with earth and/or rubble or strips of grass pods reinforced by vertical timber stakes. Build blast walls higher than a standing person, except perhaps for the one protecting the route to the shelter behind which you can run crouching. Blast walls themselves should not block passages, certainly not the ones to the shelter! Areas to protect with blast walls are the guard house, the doors and windows of the building, the radio room and fuel depot, and the entrance route to a shelter. You may also want to create a blast wall 'bay' in the house, ideally on the ground floor and in an inner room, ie, with at least two walls between the shell and you. Building a good blast wall requires some expertise (Roberts, 1999, pp75–86). Poorly built blast walls can collapse onto occupants in the house, and therefore themselves can become a danger.

Shelter

The best place is underground, often a cellar. The second best place is the reinforced room on the ground floor, as mentioned above. The ceiling can be reinforced with wooden logs or tree trunks. The larger the shelter, the weaker the construction is likely to be. It would be better to have two smaller ones, although they need to be large enough to accommodate all staff, vital equipment, possibly food and water, and a toilet facility, while also leaving some extra space. Ideally they should have two exits, so that you can get out if one is blocked by rubble. Shovels, pick-axes, etc, will help if you need to dig yourselves out.

A shelter will not be very helpful if your staff have to run 800 metres to get to it. Set a time-limit, for example, one or two minutes. Any staff in the vicinity who cannot make it from where they normally work within that timeframe need their own shelter/bay nearer at hand. If you are in a town under siege and the authorities have identified or constructed public shelters, no one should set out without clearly knowing where the shelters are along their route.

Refuge trenches and foxholes
If there is a risk of suddenly incoming mortar shells or strafing by low-flying planes or helicopters, you may want to add some emergency trenches/foxholes in which to take immediate cover. Make them deep (2 metres) but narrow, and large enough for two to four people. A good construction is an L-shaped small trench, with two entry/exit points. The top can be protected with tree logs and two layers of sandbags. Remember that these too need maintenance: rain can cause the entrances to crumble and flood them inside. Snakes may also make a fine nest in them.

Thicknesses
You need 20cm of concrete, 40cm of brick, 75cm of sand, 90cm of wood or 1 metre of soil to adequately protect you from small arms fire and blast. A car and a normal house wall alone will not do!

Be prepared and remain alert
When there is an identified risk of shelling or bombing, your protective measures should be in place at all times. When the firing has started it is too late to build a blast wall or stick on the adhesive tape.

If you keep the shutters closed and are routinely concentrated in the central rooms you may not immediately hear shells or planes coming in or the air raid siren. Keep a permanent 'look out' at the entrance who can immediately sound the alarm. If you have to drive around in a danger zone keep the radio off, the window down, and your ears open. You will not always hear a plane: modern bombs, rockets and missiles can be launched from a great distance from the target.

Inform people of your location/movements

- Do you have contacts with the combatants? Are they inclined to want to protect aid agencies? Would such contact compromise your perceived 'neutrality'?

- Can you provide detailed coordinates of the location of your buildings, and/or advance information about the routes and timings of your movements? Does this constitute a communication for 'information' with a request to avoid hitting you, or does it turn into a situation of 'seeking clearance' via prior permission?
- Do the army and air force command communicate with each other? Does the Ministry of Defence pass on information to the operational commands? Can you directly get in direct touch with the operational commands?

Guidelines: What To Do Under Fire (shelling and bombing)

What you do when under fire is partly a matter of situational judgement. It will depend on where you are when the shelling or bombing starts, where it is directed (if at all), and where the nearest effective cover is. In general:

- **Seek immediate cover:** Seek immediate cover in the nearest shelter or emergency trench. Standing around 'studying' the situation, or adopting a fatalistic attitude that a bullet or shell might have 'your name on it', is not appropriate. As aid workers you have a job to do which you can't do if you get injured or killed.

- **Seek solid cover:** If you can't reach the bomb shelter seek cover that protects you not only from glass but also from blast and shrapnel. A tree, a wooden fence, or a car will not do. Something much more solid is needed, for example, several walls, concrete, or rock. If you are very or totally exposed, lie down flat. Exposure to blast can damage your eardrums: remember to cover your ears with your hands and keep your mouth slightly open.'

- **While driving:** When caught while driving it will be your judgement whether to accelerate and try to get out of the firing zone, or abandon the vehicle and seek cover. If the shelling is close by or you are stuck in a convoy you should get out and seek cover away from the vehicle. (In the vehicle you are at risk of flying glass, shrapnel piercing the car or the fuel tank exploding if you are hit by a shell.) If the artillery fire is not too close (yet) and you can drive off, vary your speed or the artillery gunners (on sight or from the dust cloud you throw up) will be able to calculate your movements and aim better. If you drive off under machinegun fire, go for speed. A trained machine gunner will not be much hindered by you alternating your speed.

  Under air attack one must always assume that one's vehicle will be targeted. Get out and seek cover.

Preparation for Shelling and Bombing

- Material resources: sandbags and strings to close them, shovels, pick-axes, wood, nails, a saw, etc., to construct shelters and blast walls, and for emergency rescue.
- Skill to build good shelters, blast walls and foxholes.
- Competence in identifying buildings and compounds that can be protected, and where shelter is available.
- Alertness to potential military targets in an area from which one should physically distance oneself.
- Alertness to warning signals, a spotter plane, sounds of planes, anti-aircraft guns opening up in the distance, air raid sirens, civilians running for shelter.
- Psychological preparedness for the nerve-racking effect of the sounds of battle, ie, of incoming shells and bombs and deafening explosions, and preparedness to spend perhaps many hours if not days cramped in a shelter living with uncertainty.
- The mental habit of 'terrain awareness': physically familiarising yourself with the public shelters in town; constantly asking 'where would I take cover here'? when moving around.

7 Battlefield Survival

7.3 Crossfire and Sniper Fire

7.3.1 The Difference

Crossfire refers to any small arms fire to which you may be vulnerable as it is exchanged between combatants or used indiscriminately against anything that moves. This includes grenades and rocket-propelled grenades (RPG).

Sniper fire is targeted. Snipers are very good shots, who can pick out an individual target from a long range, also while no active battle is ongoing. Snipers may have special rifles with telescopic and night sight. Snipers may be trained experts; they may also be individual 'good shots', a skill perhaps acquired during hunting.

Snipers are deployed to harass the enemy force and cause disruptions to its movement, or to terrorise a larger 'enemy population'. They do this by taking up advanced positions or by infiltrating enemy territory, for example, to target officers or delay a convoy by killing the driver of the first truck, or simply to cause terror by suddenly and unexpectedly killing a civilian. They operate by stealth and surprise. If their position is distant and not threatened they may maintain it for a long time. In other circumstances they may shoot and kill and then shift position to strike from somewhere else.

7.3.2 Risk Reduction

The best prevention is to stay away from places where small arms fire is exchanged or where snipers operate. In much contemporary warfare, however, you may get caught in sudden crossfire. Also, it is only possible to avoid snipers if they are fairly static or are only 'covering' an identified area. But the presence and reach of a sniper often become known only through his/her casualties.

Guidelines: What To Do Under Fire (crossfire and sniper fire)

Passive measures: 'hardening the target'
Blast walls
When well made and sufficiently thick, blast walls also offer protection from small arms fire (though not from a direct hit by an RPG). Snipers can use armour-piercing bullets which pierce normal blast walls. Their protection then is that they keep you out of sight, rather than out of fire. Stay away from windows and doors; try and get at least two walls between you and the bullets. This will also increase protection from 'ricochets' – bullets bouncing off another object they hit first.

Flakjackets
These are designed to protect parts of the body from blast, flying glass and splinters, and shrapnel. They will not stop a bullet. Ballistic or bullet-proof jackets give more protection. The basic jacket needs to be worn with the ballistic plates and a helmet. They are heavy (up to 12kg) and expensive.

Armoured vehicles
These vehicles with armoured cabins will provide protection from rifle fire and from the blast effects of shells and smaller mines. They are very expensive and so difficult to drive that they often get involved in collisions. The thicker the armour, the heavier the vehicle. Special driving training is needed to handle them. They do not provide adequate protection from a direct hit by artillery, a bomb or an RPG, nor from specialist sniper fire which may use armour-piercing bullets. Unless specifically designed as a mine-proof vehicle (V-shaped underbody) they will not provide adequate

protection from the blast and shrapnel of an anti-tank mine. When driving in an armoured vehicle a helmet and flakjacket or ballistic jacket should also be worn. Armoured vehicles should also move around in pairs.

Evasive action: reducing exposure
Situational judgement
When suddenly under close fire, your staff and yourself will need judgement as to whether to try evasive action, whether to stop the vehicle and jump out, whether to run for cover or drop down and lie flat where you are and wait for a lull in the firing, or crawl on elbows and stomach or roll swiftly towards cover.

Your judgement will be influenced by where you are and how far it is to cover, how close the firing is, and whether or not you are being targeted.

While driving
When under close frontal fire you probably need to stop the vehicle, jump out and seek cover; stopping and reversing or turning and exposing the flank of the vehicle will take too long and leave you an easy target. When trying to take evasive action from small arms fire in a vehicle, go for speed. When there is no choice but to cross a 'killing-zone', again go for speed and/or from cover to cover along the shortest possible route. Avoid 'swerving' or 'zigzagging'; it does not make you harder to hit. In fact it lengthens the route and thereby the time that one is exposed to fire. There is also the risk of a serious car accident.

Solid cover
When seeking cover remember that 'solid' cover is what is needed. Crouching behind an ordinary car may keep you out of sight but not out of fire. 'Solid cover' means rock, a crest of soil, concrete, several layers of bricks etc. Bushes, trees, wooden fences and ordinary cars are not solid cover (there is a lot of misconception about the latter point from TV police shows). When under cover, think. If you have reasonable cover take time to consider your position and options:

- Is it general small arms fire and from which direction, or is it targeted towards you?
- If aimed at you, is it meant as a warning shot to make you retreat, or is it intended to hit you? Is it general small arms fire, or precise sniper fire?

Continued...

7 Battlefield Survival

The military say that if you wonder whether or not you are being targeted, you are not! In other words, you will know when you are. Experience will teach you the difference in the sound of a very close bullet (a whiplike cracking sound) and bullets at some distance (a hissing or whining sound).

If you want to take a look do not stick your head up from where you went into cover: a rifleman may be waiting precisely for you to do so. Try and move carefully to another observation point without being seen. Beware reflections, for example, from spectacles, binoculars or a camera lens, as this may give your position away.

When and how to shift position

If you have good cover can you retreat from the danger zone safely or not? If not, do you need to move or is time on your side? If the exchange between armed men or from a sniper in a static position, the safest option may be to sit it out. If moving brings you back into sight and therefore into the range of fire, then your moves should not become predictable, for example, running from tree to tree in a straight line and at regular intervals. By the fourth run, a rifleman may be in position to get you. Similarly, if there are more than one move all together in a group. If you go one by one a rifleman will be in position to get the third or fourth member of your party.

Still, it is important to keep things in perspective: you should not assume that in an exchange of fire people aim properly before they shoot. Bullets will be flying everywhere, and not getting hit will be as much a matter of luck as of what you do and don't do.

Preparation for Crossfire and Sniper Fire

- 'Terrain awareness' for small arms and sniper fire.
- Inquire about known sniper areas and 'killing zones'.
- Ability to recognise the sound of a shot, sounds of small arms fire.
- Understanding of the difference between 'out of sight' and 'out of fire'; of what is 'solid' cover and what not.
- Drill to go flat and/or get under cover, then to study the situation and think.
- Basic knowledge about types of injuries caused by types of small arms ammunition and essential do's and don'ts of first aid

7.4 ■ Landmines and Unexploded Ordnance (UXO)

Never touch. Never Approach. Mark and report!

7.4.1 Types and Tactics

Types

Mines can generally be categorised into anti-tank and anti-personnel:

- **Anti-tank mines** are larger and have greater explosive power. They typically require a heavier weight or movement to activate, but this may not be the case when they are old and unstable. They will break a tank track and damage part of its suspension, but will cause almost total destruction to a non-armoured vehicle.
- **Anti-personnel mines** are smaller. Some are designed to injure a person by blowing off a hand or foot. Others, however, can do much more serious and lethal damage.
- **Unexploded ordnance** is any type of ammunition ranging from missiles to hand grenades to simple bullets that have been fired but not gone off, as well as fused ordnance that has not been fired. A threat that has gained more attention recently is that of armour-piercing bullets made of depleted uranium. These have been used in the Gulf War and more recently by NATO over Kosovo. They carry the risk of radioactive contamination. A much greater threat, however, is posed by cluster bombs that behave like anti-personnel mines but have a bigger explosive charge and lethal effect.
- **'Booby traps'** can be ordinary-looking objects. The most common ones are not specially designed and manufactured (for example, a pen), but consist of a firing mechanism and explosives linked to items in daily use or attractive (a window shutter, a toy, a lamp, a musical instrument, the winch of a well, a tree branch, etc). The term booby trap is also used to describe the process of linking an anti-personnel mine to an anti-tank mine, or putting a mine on top of a buried drum of petrol.

Impact

Anti-personnel mines injure or kill through blast or fragmentation. Fragmentation mines are mines whose casing breaks into small fragments or which contain fragments that are dispersed upon explosion. Most anti-personnel mines are buried in the ground. Some have a first explosive charge underneath which, when activated, makes the mine 'bound' about 1 metre above the ground where it then explodes causing havoc in all directions.

7 Battlefield Survival

Directional mines are positioned above ground and attached to trees or fixed objects. They are normally remote-activated but can also be linked to trip wire or booby trap systems. Several anti-personnel mines can kill within a range of 35-50 metres, and cause severe injury up to 100 metres. If you find yourself in a (suspected) minefield, careful extraction is the only option (Section 7.4.4). Just 'walking' in single file does not significantly reduce the risk.

Anti-tank mines do not normally explode when a person walks on them as they need a heavier pressure to be activated. Sometimes an anti-personnel mine is put on top of an anti-tank mine, the smaller explosion causing the detonation of the larger mine. A number of anti-personnel and anti-tank mines have protective mechanisms to prevent their being recovered or disarmed. They will explode if you try to do so. That is why you should also not approach.

Some mines are detonated by trip wires which are generally hard to see and are very dangerous. Some mines have fusing systems that are pull-activated: they detonate when pressure is put on the trip wire. Others are triggered by pressure release: they detonate when the trip wire is cut. Never try to cut a trip wire! Don't approach and don't touch. If you come across a trip wire, leave the area in the direction you came from checking systematically for trip wires along your extraction route, and avoiding them. Note that trip wires are not put only at ankle height, but can be higher, for example, at breast level.

Some anti-personnel mine systems are interconnected and have sensors. If someone approaches one mine will explode. The others will explode when a second person approaches – for example, a rescue team – to help the victim of the first mine.

Most mines have a metallic content which is why metal detectors are used. In some situations, notably with some mine types that have no or minimal metal content or in metal-saturated ground, metal detectors will be of limited use. Some mines have a magnetic-influenced, anti-handling device – ie, the magnetic field of the metal detector will trigger detonation. Fortunately these are rare.

Tactics

Mines are generally laid for three purposes:

1. **As part of a battle strategy:** Armed groups lay mines to defend their military positions, to disrupt enemy movements, to try and deny the enemy access to a certain route, and/or to channel the enemy on to a certain route. Minefields can therefore be expected around bunkers and trenches, static tank positions, on and/or alongside bridges and roads, etc. Where towns and cities are

besieged both sides may be laying mines: the defenders to disrupt an attack, the attackers to prevent the defenders from getting supplies and from breaking out. Mines are often laid in non-systematic ways: they can be 'scattered' into enemy territory from planes and helicopters, or delivered by artillery. In guerrilla or (counter-) insurgency warfare, many groups plant mines indiscriminately without ever keeping or passing on records. It is not surprising therefore that forces of the same group wander into minefields laid by their colleagues. Knowledge of where major sieges and battles have taken place and of where major defensive positions were, as well as more daily 'terrain awareness', will make you more alert to obvious risk areas.

2. **Around socioeconomic targets:** Targets such as power pylons, water and electricity plants, a railroad junction, etc., can also be surrounded by mines to protect them from sabotage and attack.

3. **To cause general terror and dislocation:** Mines are also used in more 'generalised' warfare where civilians and their assets are targeted: grazing and agricultural land, irrigation canals, wells, forest areas where firewood is collected, temples and even village paths can be mined. The purpose is to dislocate the local population who may be providing infrastructural support to the enemy, and to create discontent among them that could be directed at the enemy forces.

The purpose of booby traps can be to prevent the removal of other explosives. More commonly they are planted to complicate and render more 'costly' the re-occupation by enemy forces and/or civilians, usually of a built-up area that is being abandoned by the force installing the booby traps.

People planting mines may well be smart: they will anticipate the reactions of an enemy force, or of civilians. Hence a bridge over a shallow river may be mined, but so too will the slopes next to it for those who cross through the water instead. A major access road may be mined – with alternative access roads perhaps mined as well.

Case Study: 'Anticipatory' Mining

In 1995 an NGO vehicle hit an anti-tank mine on a road in Central Africa. The force of the explosion hurled the double-cabin, pick-up vehicle 12 metres and turned it round completely. Two passengers were killed and three injured. During the night anti-personnel mines were planted around the wreck. The next day a local woman who had come to look stepped on one and lost her leg.

Mines also 'migrate': they are moved by rain, flooding, mudslides, tidal action on the beach, etc. Eight years after the war in Mozambique the heavy flooding in early 2000 swept mines potentially anywhere and destroyed the existing markings of identified mined areas.

7.4.2 Seeking Out and Sharing Information

The golden rule: actively inquire (also when the war is over)

Nobody is likely to come to you and volunteer information or ask what your movement plans are in order to give you warning. Your predecessor may even forget to brief you properly in the course of a handover! You must inquire yourself, and collate information from various sources. When the war is over mines do not disappear because the fighting has stopped. Mines (and UXOs) can remain active for decades.

Specialist information sources

Prior to departure obtain general information about the mines in a country (eg, from the *Landmines Monitor Report* compiled by the Geneva International Centre for Humanitarian De-mining and published by Human Rights Watch et al, 1999).

Specialist humanitarian de-mining agencies (such as the Mines Advisory Group and Halo Trust in the UK, Handicap International in France and Belgium, and Norwegian People's Aid) may be able to offer information or referral to sources (see RRN Network Paper 32 on humanitarian de-mining for contacts and other information on the mines sector)

In-country, your main sources of general and locality-specific information will be:

- a national mine action agency and/or the local authorities and security forces;
- de-mining organisations working in-country, and a central UN mine action centre, if there is one;
- UN military observers/peacekeepers;
- hospitals and health posts where mine casualties may be seen;
- your own staff;
- local people.

Local knowledge

When venturing into a new area where there is active fighting or there has been in the past, always stop regularly and inquire actively from local people.

Making time to inquire

While this takes time, it may save lives. In addition, you can learn something about the area you are going through and can explain who you are. Build this extra time into your journey plan (Chapter 8).

The quality of inquiry

The more precise your questions the more likely you are to get a precise answer. Rather than asking in general whether there are mines and/or whether a road is used, inquire about:

- how long the respondent(s) have been (back) in the area;
- the local history of fighting;
- the local history of accidents: have there been cases of vehicles; and also people and especially animals being hit by mines, and when and where?
- where local people do/don't go;
- whether the respondent him/herself has been using the road, and if so, when, and how far?
- how the respondent/village people use the road: only walking and/or on bicycles? In which case anti-tank mines may not have been detonated and will remain a danger. Be careful about definitions: in Mozambique, for example, people classify a bicycle as a vehicle!

The quality of local knowledge

Do not overestimate the reliability of local knowledge. For example, if people were refugees and have only recently returned they will not know where the mined areas are. Even if they have been around for a long time they may not know.

Case Study: Limitations to Local Knowledge

Two years after the end of the civil war in Ethiopia in 1991, an aid agency vehicle drove down a dirt road in the north. Several local people accompanied the agency staff, and other vehicles had occasionally used the road. Nevertheless, they were all killed by an anti-tank mine that had been buried in the middle of the road. Upon inquiry, former guerrilla fighters confirmed that they had put two anti-tank mines on that road in the past, and that only one had been recovered. The local people did not know this.

7 Battlefield Survival

The fact that most of the mine casualties every year are local people indicates that they are not necessarily an accurate source of information. Moreover, even if they are knowledgeable, they often take risks: they simply have to venture into uncleared areas for economic reasons and/or to recycle mines for scrap metal, explosives for fishing, or even doorstops or weights.

Local people may also (re) plant mines to protect their assets such as a well, a granary, a contested piece of land, etc. Ask about this, and only move around with local people on their own terrain.

Case Study: Civilians Recycle Mines

Virtually all Albanian Kosovars returned to Kosovo in the summer of 1999. Most inhabitants of a village on the border, however, had remained in Albania. UN peacekeepers who were de-mining the heavily mined border area found that some local villagers had recycled mines and put them on the forest tracks crossing the border from Albania to prevent Albanian citizens coming to loot the houses in their village.

Local people may become over-confident and act foolishly. Do not trust untrained people to handle mines and UXOs. You may very well be invited by villagers to take a look at their cupboard full of such 'curiosa' or recycled pieces, or at a 'work party' digging up mines. Any of these items may be unstable and explode even if it has been handled before. Stay away or leave immediately.

Most mined areas are not clearly marked by the military or de-mining organisations. Local people often create their own 'warning signals', but these are hard for outsiders to identify. They may be no more than a small heap of pebbles or two crossed branches lying at the start of a path. Actively inquire from local people what signals they use, and whether a common system is used: if everybody does it his/her own way, there is no 'signal'.

Report the information
It is not common practice for aid workers to circulate the information they obtain about mines. Yet wherever possible mines or mined areas should be marked and reported, ideally with a sketch map if you have nothing else. Aid agencies involved in curative medical work should actively report on the profile of cases they see due to accidents, violence and mines.

7.4.3 Risk Reduction

Guidelines: Basic Do's and Don'ts for Risk Reduction

Don't touch, don't approach, but mark and report.

- **UXOs:** Generally visible, although they can be partly or even wholly buried. Presume they are unstable and can explode simply when touched. Never touch them. Mark their position and inform the authorities. In certain countries there is an active scrap metal/recycling industry and UXOs are touched and handled. Even when handled several times, they may still contain explosive and can detonate at any time.

- **Booby traps:** The object that is booby-trapped is generally visible, but not the explosive linked to it. Presume that virtually anything in an uncleared and not yet re-inhabited, or only recently and partially re-inhabited area, can be booby trapped. Don't touch anything, don't pick anything up, do not push shutters or doors, etc. Don't 'explore' empty buildings or ruins, even for the 'call of nature'.

- **Mines:** Generally not visible. Never touch; don't try to remove; don't try to make them explode by throwing rocks at them, etc. If you know that mines have been used in the conflict, and you are not absolutely certain that the road is clear, don't venture on it. If you notice a mine, mark the location very clearly and inform the authorities.

Possibly the most common situation in which aid workers expose themselves to high-risk areas is on assessment missions. Ask how essential the trip is – not for agency profile and fundraising for new project work, but effectively to meet need? If you go into a high-risk or unknown area, should you be (among) the first to go? If a route between certain locations is known to be occasionally mined (eg, by guerrillas) do you have to drive. Could you fly? Could several agencies pool resources to charter a plane?

Impact reduction

A non-armoured vehicle cannot be protected from an anti-tank mine. However, some people believe the risk of serious injury can be reduced by putting sandbags about 10cm thick on the cabin floor under each passenger, as well as a layer or two of sandbags in the back of a truck. Unfortunately this may make all the difference in terms of downward pressure which makes an anti-tank mine explode. You also risk being blinded by sandblast if you run over a mine. A marginally better trick might be to fill the wheels with water, although this works best with larger truck wheels because of the volume needed to make a difference.

Remain alert and cautious

- When driving, avoid your vehicle being the first on the road. If commercial traffic uses the road don't set out at 5am but rather go later on after other vehicles have passed. If in a convoy protected by the military allow military vehicles to go first.
- When driving, try and use tarmac roads only. Avoid driving into potholes as these may be mined. When the tarmac suddenly ends and becomes a dirt track and you have no status report beyond, it may be wiser to turn back.
- Instruct your driver and insist on his/her discipline in:
  - sticking to well-travelled routes and not going cross-country;
  - always driving in existing tracks;
  - not driving over obstacles on the road (a big branch or some debris that may conceal a mine) nor driving round them without first checking whether the road surface has been disturbed (the obstacle might be placed there precisely to 'channel' you on to a mine on the other side of the road);
  - not driving on to the sides of the road to avoid an obstacle, to turn round, to overtake another vehicle or to give way to an oncoming vehicle: the sides of the road may (still) be mined.
- Watch for 'obvious' signs: a crater from an explosion, a torn shoe, the carcass of an animal, a wrecked vehicle, a road that appears not to be used, a field that is overgrown and not cultivated in an otherwise (re-) populated area, a building with the roof, shutters and doors intact while other buildings have had these looted/ removed, etc.
- Stay on the beaten track. Never walk off the road or path into the bushes or an abandoned building to go and relieve yourself.
- Look out for marked areas. Professional de-mining teams will put up very visible markings of known or suspected mined areas. Local people may use their own signals. Note, however, that markings could have collapsed or become less visible or covered by rain, snow, mud, etc. Note also that you may sometimes see a mark, without being clear as to which side of the mines it is.
- If in doubt, turn back! This is probably one of the most difficult recommendations for an aid worker to absorb or to instil into her/his colleagues, as by nature aid workers tend to be enterprising and adventurous and committed to alleviating the needs of others, and not properly concerned about their own safety. Nobody is helped by your losing life or limb.

- Leisure can kill. Expatriates, often more than local people, tend to go for walks in the countryside for leisure. It is relaxing and helps release the stress. In such a situation your alertness to danger may be lower, particularly if there is no fighting in your area. The area may still be mined!

Guidelines: What to Do in a (suspected) Mined Area

Mines are seldom planted alone. Your basic assumption must be:

Where there is one mine, there are more.

When a mine explodes or you suspect that you are in a mined area:

Never act impulsively.

- Do not jump out of your vehicle if it has exploded a smaller mine but is not on fire.
- Do not drive impulsively up to another vehicle that has hit a mine.
- Do never rush in to help another person who has just been injured by a mine.

Control yourself and your colleagues and act carefully and cautiously to avoid more casualties.

Extraction
The basic principle of extraction is to retrace your steps or return along the tracks that you followed to get to where you became stuck. This is easier in theory than in practice.

Evacuating a vehicle
When your vehicle has hit a mine but is not on fire or at risk of further explosion, evacuate it in a controlled manner. You should not step on the ground around it except in the tracks where you have driven, behind the vehicle. So climb out through the rear door, or from the back by first getting on the roof, and step in your own tracks. When you are on solid tarmac or the vehicle tracks are sufficiently visible, you can walk back – in single file and spaced out – to the last known safe point, or to a point where you think there is no more risk of mines. When the tracks are not clearly visible you must prepare yourselves for an extraction process with prodding that will

Continued...

7 Battlefield Survival

probably take several hours. If night falls you must prepare for a probably uncomfortable night until dawn allows you to get back to work.

Prodding

Prodding means that you search cautiously every inch of ground before you step on to it. You should first ascertain that there are no trip wires before you start prodding. Mines can be triggered by trip wires. Trip wires look like fishing lines or thick spider threads; they are barely visible and can be covered by leaves and branches. The trip wire feeler helps you identify them. Place it horizontally in front of you holding it between thumb and forefinger. Then gently raise it, keeping it horizontal. As soon as you encounter any resistance immediately release the pressure and check whether it is a trip wire. Try and find another path avoiding the trip wire. Never touch or try to cut a trip wire: some trip wires will cause a mine to detonate when pressure is put on them but some work through tension release. If you cut a tight trip wire the mine will also explode.

Next delineate a space shoulder-length wide and systematically prod it. The best way is to lie prone (first clear an area before you stretch out), otherwise do it kneeling or crouching. Prodding means sticking the prodder carefully into the soil at an angle of 30 degrees, gently feeling for any hard object. If you come upon a hard object – and in stony ground there may be hundreds – very carefully clear the side of it until you can see what it is. If it is a mine never touch it or try to remove it, but mark it and move your prodding path around it. You will have to control your anxiety and impatience and that of your colleagues to get out.

Rescue

Few situations are as difficult to confront as someone stepping on a mine in your vicinity. Staff should be carefully instructed:

• Never to rush in to help, even if the victim is screaming for help and risks bleeding to death. They should always bear in mind that where there is one mine there are likely to be others, and no one is helped by increasing the number of victims.

• Only to attempt a planned and controlled rescue operation when the victim is still alive, when no specialist teams can be called to the site within a reasonable time, and when there is a reasonable chance that they themselves will not become further victims.

In essence a rescue operation will consist of:

- Talking to the victim and getting the message across that s/he should not move as there may be more mines in his/her vicinity.
- From the closest safe spot checking an access area of about 1.5 metres wide by prodding. Also clearing an area around the victim to allow first aid to be administered. Checking carefully under the limbs and body of the victim for other mines.
- First aid will consist of trying to stop the bleeding by putting bandages on serious wounds. If there is no pressure bandage available or it doesn't work, a tourniquet should be applied a little above the wound. The risk of gangrene is often greater than that of haemorrhage: a tourniquet has to be released for at least 30 seconds every 10 minutes to control the risk of gangrene. If there are broken bones likely to swing during transport, you should try to bandage them to a limb or a splint.
- Don't give the victim any food or drink if you are not absolutely certain that the digestive track is not pierced (and you are unlikely to be able to determine this for sure).
- Extract the victim only along the path you have cleared. Wrap the patient in a blanket and continue talking to help stave off shock while transporting him/her to the nearest medical facility.

Recovering a damaged vehicle

Care is equally required in the operation to recover a vehicle damaged by a mine. The risk of other mines is real.

Case Study: All Staff Need to be Knowledgeable!

In 1994 an aid agency truck was slightly damaged in the rear by a home-made mine planted, as it turned out, by a small rebel group. Its crew and food cargo were rescued and loaded on to a commercial vehicle that had been following the truck. Shortly afterwards, the agency's area manager had to intervene to prevent the team of nationally recruited mechanics from going out with another truck to recover the damaged one, without any preparation or caution. He established radio communication and medical back-up and went along. Close to the site of the incident, an escort of army soldiers was picked up as guard against further rebel activity. As it turned out, the soldiers, experienced former guerrilla fighters, proved extremely careless. The project manager again had to intervene very firmly to ensure that the damaged truck was approached and pulled out with the greatest possible caution.

7.5 Preparation and Training

Appropriate training

As a manager you need to consider the following:

1. What do you want to train people for?
2. Who needs to be trained in what?
3. What do the staff need? What can be mere awareness; what must be knowledge; and what must be 'skill through drill'?
4. Who can provide the right training for you?

Training aid workers about mines (but not UXOs) has become more frequent. Some of this training, however, has very little impact because it is poorly conceived. It is about mine awareness rather than about operating in a potentially mined area. Typically, the technical names and characteristics of various mines are presented with the help of slides and posters. The key advice given is: stay away from mined areas. The training is further animated by the display of mines on a table, perhaps with a series of slides of parts of mined landscapes or wreckage from mines and a short exercise in which course participants are made to tread on a buried dummy mine or against a trip wire. This may be necessary but is far from sufficient.

Awareness: Staff need to be aware that mines and UXOs constitute a major danger at all times; also in post-conflict situations; potentially almost everywhere. But preparation for operating in a potentially mined area demands good knowledge and an emphasis on personal movement and behavioural discipline.

Basic knowledge: Some of the core knowledge about mines, UXOs and booby traps includes: where one might expect them and therefore how to avoid them; locally used warning signs; misconceptions about mines; mine clearance and local knowledge, and what to do if it is uncertain whether or not an area is mined; the do's and don'ts when one is confronted with mines; how to get out of a (suspected) minefield; and reporting on identified or suspected mined areas.

Skill and drill: Above all, mine training should emphasise behavioural discipline. Aid agency staff will generally not heed the advice to turn back when in doubt, unless that message has been instilled in them through simulation exercises and reinforced in daily operations by programme managers. In high-risk areas, the drill should include inquiring from local people, discipline while moving, extraction from a vehicle and then from an area by feeling for trip wires and prodding.

First aid training: If you are operating in an area where specialist rescue is more or less everywhere at hand, such as in Kosovo in late 1999/early 2000, your staff may not need training in first aid. But that will be the exception. Staff operating in more remote areas away from specialist support will need basic medical training

Note: Such training is more staff- and time-intensive, and likely to be costly.

Quality briefing

New staff arriving in an operational area where there are known to be minefields and mine risks should be briefed in detail. Ideally you will actively familiarise them with the vicinity and point out known mine areas and the signals that help to identify them. Real life exposure and visual memory will stick more thoroughly than verbal and/or written information. A proper briefing should also instil the necessity of marking any (suspected) mined areas that the staff member may come across, and reporting in detail on this.

Supervision and reminding

Managers and supervisors should regularly remind their staff of the importance of remaining alert to the dangers of mines. On a field trip do not hesitate to challenge a staff member over undisciplined or careless movement decisions.

Essential equipment

What to take with you in risk areas:

- a radio in the car;
- if possible hand-held radios for those moving away from the car while one person stays with the car;
- a good first aid kit – take it along when you go on foot;
- prodding/feeling equipment (a prodder can be a long screwdriver or a strong knife with a blade 12–15cm long. A trip wire feeler is a light, flexible rod 100–130cm long, a thin piece of strong wire or a flexible stalk or branch).

8 ▶ Vehicle Safety and Travel Security

8 ▸ Vehicle Safety and Travel Security

Road accidents remain a major cause of injury and death for aid workers. At least half of all security incidents occur during travel.

8.1 Risk Reduction

8.1.1 Vehicle Choice and Safety

Vehicle choice

Choice of vehicle can impact on safety and security. Consider, from a safety but also from a security point of view, the choice of 2-wheel or 4-wheel drive vehicles, passenger vehicles or pick-ups, diesel or gasoline engines, new or secondhand vehicles, engine and fuel tank size, short or long wheel base. New 4-wheel drive passenger vehicles are very popular among aid agencies – and among warlords and car-jackers!

Vehicle safety

Condition of the vehicle

Vehicle safety partly depends on the vehicle being in good working order: water, oil and fuel levels checked, tyres in good condition, seat belts installed and used, essential equipment (jack, spare tyres, first aid kit, etc) present. Make sure that drivers check their vehicles daily, that vehicles are cross-checked before serious journeys, that you identify a quality garage, and that a logistics manager keeps a servicing and maintenance schedule. You do not want the vehicle to break down at a critical moment. Car users need to be taught basic emergency repair techniques.

Safe driving

Safety on the road further depends on safe driving. This tends to be a major problem area for expatriates and local drivers alike. Usually the driving conditions carry a heightened risk: less disciplined driving behaviour under an 'emergency' mentality; animals, cyclists and push carts on the main roads; sections of a road under repair not marked or illuminated at night; muddy rural tracks, dangerous mountain roads, crossing rivers after heavy rains, etc.

Safe driving requires mastery of the:

- **Vehicle:** Mastering your vehicle means, eg, knowing how to operate a 4-wheel drive vehicle properly, knowing the capacities of the engine under various circumstances (acceleration, steep uphill, etc) and appreciating the stability of the vehicle on different types of surfaces.
- **Terrain:** Mastering the terrain means being able to drive safely and competently on, for instance, sandy or icy tracks, on mountain roads, or being able to cross a river bed.
- **Traffic:** Mastering the traffic means understanding that many other road users do not obey traffic rules or drive in disciplined ways. It will be crucial to adopt an anticipatory or 'defensive' driving style.

All drivers need to be trained for this.

Speed
Speeding always increases the risk of road accidents. In practice both expatriates and local drivers often need to be tightly disciplined or speeding will occur. Only in exceptional circumstances, for example, in a zone with potential sniper fire, can high speed be justified.

Seat belts
The procedure should be that seat belts should always be worn. Only very exceptionally when there is a high security risk of aerial attack (Chapter 7) or armed robbery/car-jacking on the road, can a situational judgement be made not to wear seatbelts; under such circumstances you would want to be able to get out of the car as quickly as possible.

Windows
At moments of higher security risk it is advisable to drive with the windows down and the music off in order to hear planes approaching or small arms fire. Under shelling or bombing this will also prevent glass splinters being blown inwards by blast. In winter conditions or in very dusty environments this will be difficult; at least maintain silence in the car in these environments.

The radio aerial
The radio aerial on the car should not be put on or taken off or even touched unless the radio is switched off to avoid getting radio frequency burn (Chapter 17).

8.1.2 Drivers and Safety and Security

Recruitment

The recruitment of drivers is a critical management issue for at least three reasons:

i. they need to be technically competent and safe drivers;
ii. travelling a lot, and being able to influence decisions at critical moments, means that drivers have an important role to play in security management;
iii.as they come into contact with a lot of people, drivers informally represent your organisation and therefore affect the image that people form of you.

When recruiting, therefore, there are various criteria you must consider:

- valid driving licence;
- language skills (essential or desirable);
- good eyesight (test);
- driving experience and driving record;
- technical competence in maintenance and repair (test);
- driving style in difficult terrain and undisciplined traffic (test);
- reliability (don't recruit people with links to criminal gangs intent on stealing your cars; get a social reference; Chapter 20).

Moreover, in insecure environments you may also want to consider other aspects:

- ethnic identity;
- local language skills;
- age and temperament (is s/he likely to be observant of rules and regulations; how will s/he behave in a threatening situation) ;
- analytical and observational skills (can the driver communicate a useful report on an incident?).

Driver training

When you have a number of drivers it is worthwhile training two or three of them as driver-trainers. They in turn can then train other drivers in driving safely. You could hire a driver-trainer on an interagency basis or find a competent person locally.

Induction, briefing and training

Drivers not only need training and supervision, they also benefit from briefings and training.

- As they informally represent your organisation they need to be able to give a succinct but accurate picture of what your organisation is, what it does in the country, and what its status is in the conflict.
- As drivers are vulnerable to security incidents and need to observe the overall situation from a security point of view, they need essential security training.
- Regular driver meetings, with the logistics manager and/or security manager present, can reinforce their ability and effectiveness from a logistics and security point of view.

Driving policy

Establish a driving policy for staff who are not drivers: can other national and international staff drive vehicles? If so, under what conditions? This can involve introducing driving tests and training for others. As for the drivers, this policy should clarify liabilities in case of an accident caused by an agency staff member.

8.1.3 Approaches to Passengers and Accidents

Drivers and senior programme staff travelling in vehicles should have a clear understanding of your 'approach' to picking up passengers who are not employees of your organisation, and to accidents involving other people. The term 'approach' has been chosen deliberately because, unlike rules and regulations, it will be partly influenced by your security strategy (Chapter 5). In practice you will probably combine strict rules with guidelines and situational judgement.

Rules could be such that:

- no weapons can be carried in your agency vehicles;
- no cargo other than that of the agency can be transported;
- your vehicle cannot be driven by anybody who is not an (authorised) employee of the organisation;
- a vehicle on-mission should not be left unattended (ie, perhaps guarded by a local person).

Passengers

You may choose to provide guidelines regarding passenger policy. These can be printed onto a laminated card in the local language(s) for drivers to show that they are acting under orders. It is of course possible to insist that nobody other than identified aid agency employees can be taken as passengers in your vehicle. However, this may be untenable and self-defeating: in many situations you may have to take a local person as guide to find the route, or you may give local people in your project area or who have provided you with hospitality a lift as a measure of reciprocal hospitality and building up good relationships. You could have a 'waiver of liability' document in the car which you make any passenger who is not an employee of the organisation sign when they travel with you. But if the social custom holds that in cases of injury or death of a passenger compensation is paid by the 'socially recognised host', you must acknowledge that your 'signed paper' will have little local value. If you are concerned about liability and payment of compensation you would do better to discuss this in advance with community leaders and the close relatives of your passenger.

Soldiers

'Lifts' to soldiers are another difficult issue. You may be strict about not giving lifts if they carry arms; but what if they are not armed but in uniform, or sick or wounded? Again, an element of situational judgement may come into play:

- Is your agency operating in a zone where several opposing parties move about and where its image of 'neutrality' can easily be compromised?
- Is it operating in a zone of criminal activity where it may need temporary (armed) protection?

Causing an accident

It will be important to have guidelines on how to react in case of an accident, especially if it causes injury or death of local people. In certain countries the advice might be to stop and help the victim; in others not to stop but to continue onto the nearest police post or agency office as bystanders are likely to attack the driver and his vehicle whether or not the accident was his fault. If this is the case your agency, perhaps with the local police, needs to come back and sort out the matter. Do not leave disputes unresolved (Chapter 4): local people may attack the property of your agency or others in revenge later on! While guidelines may differ between areas in the same country this should not prevent you from using your situational judgement. Note also that a situation can turn 'understanding' or 'hostile' depending on how you behave at a critical moment (Chapter 18).

8.1.4 Protective Devices

Protection against theft

There are a number of devices that help protect vehicles from theft: lockable fuel filler cap, lockable wheel nuts and a strong steering lock are all easy to install. An electronic immobiliser may need some specialist input. A hidden fuel cut-off switch can prevent car robbers from getting very far. Avoid, however, instant fuel cut-off devices as you may become the target of the anger/frustration of the attackers if they can't get the vehicle running. A simpler measure, for overnight protection and when facing the risk of looting, is to remove the distributor rotors from petrol engines, to release the air from all tyres, or even to remove the tyres for the night. Removing injectors from diesel engines is not so simple: when reinstalling them all the air will have to be bled from the fuel system before it will work and although many modern engines are largely self-bleeding, it still thrashes the battery to turn over the engine to bleed it. It may also lead to dirt getting into the fuel lines and injector failure just when you don't need it. On the other hand, removing some of the fuel pipework can be just as effective in disabling a diesel engine vehicle, and is less trouble to restore. Of course all these measures can increase the frustration and aggressiveness of would-be robbers, and also hamper your escape when you need to move away fast.

Radios

Radios are generally very helpful devices as they allow others to monitor vehicle movements and drivers to report on problems and call for assistance when/if stuck. But they also defeat any attempted strategy of keeping a 'low profile': driving around with huge antennae marks you as very visible 'outsiders' and perhaps as worthwhile targets for militias or criminals.

Vehicle tracking system

The decision to install a tracking system will depend on cost considerations but also on what you want to do with it. A tracking system follows a vehicle and can indicate its location on maps stored in the control station computer – on a regular basis or in response to a distress signal. It can also be programmed to send a warning signal when the vehicle is approaching an exclusion zone that you yourself have defined. It can therefore have a preventive function, ie, to signal to the vehicle's occupants that they are entering a high-risk area or crossing a border that is not physically marked. A precondition, however, is that you input good maps with precise geographical coordinates and geographically demarcate the exclusion zones. Locating the vehicle following a distress call is useful but it does not tell you what the problem is, nor does it on its own put you in a better position to respond. Finally, in principle this system will enable you to track and locate a stolen vehicle. This is useful provided that someone is willing and has the capacity to chase and retrieve the vehicle.

Flashing lights

In areas with a risk of aerial attack agencies have installed blue or orange flashing lights on the roofs of their vehicles to increase their visibility and identification. However, do monitor that armed forces do not copy your practice or it will lose its protective value.

Essential documents

Keep a list of engine and chassis numbers of all your vehicles. One day it may be proof that the vehicle once belonged to you before it was stolen (Chapter 15).

8.1.5 Journey Planning

When going on a journey that carries a certain risk, two key principles apply: think through your journey in advance; and establish a journey monitoring system. Journey planning takes time. This is no reason not to do it. The additional complications that arise when a problem occurs and that result from not having prepared in advance will take even more time. If you travel regularly in the same area you will not have to start from scratch each time; you can simply revive and perhaps adapt an earlier journey plan. Plan your journey with a map.

Guidelines: Planning Your Journey

- Keep your journey plan confidential if there is a risk of targeted attack.
- Study the route and all possible problem points from a natural perspective (eg, flooding, snowed up passes, etc) or that of man-made conditions (known checkpoints, good areas for ambush, etc) and from lack of information (where might you get lost?).
- Estimate travel times rather than distances, and plan your journey so that you arrive well before nightfall or curfew hours. Build in time for local inquiries, eg, about the risk of mines (Chapter 7). Anticipate possible delays and build these into your timing. You can then indicate estimated departure time, arrival time and return time.
- Emergency options: are there alternative routes, fall-back places where you might get help, or find security?
- Establish a monitoring system: radio call times, from where and at what intervals; who decides about deviations from the journey as planned – the 'leader' on the journey or a senior person at base? Define code words or coded phrases if necessary (Chapter 15).
- Inspect and prepare the vehicles in advance: have they been serviced and are they ready? Do you have all the necessary equipment depending on the context and possible scenarios? Do you have all the necessary documentation for vehicles and passengers to show any authorities you may encounter? Are copies of all key documents available at base?

Team briefing and debriefing

Prior to departure it is useful to have a team briefing in which the journey plan is reviewed and discussed so that everyone is well informed. Equally good practice would be to suggest that a returning team is debriefed on any changes encountered in the travel on the route taken.

Exploratory missions

It will be quite common to venture into unknown territory on an exploratory/ assessment mission. Take the time to inquire about the 'landscape' ahead of you, ask questions of local people, and stop regularly to ask more of people you meet on the road. If a local guide is accompanying you, elicit details before you set out. You will probably have experienced the tendency of local people to seriously underestimate travel times if asked for a straightforward answer to 'how long will it take'? A more useful approach is perhaps to ask for details of the route ahead, useful reference points, road conditions, etc, and to work these through on a sketch map. When venturing into 'unmapped territory' notes should be taken on the route and sketch maps drawn for the benefit of those following after. Keep track of distances using the mileage counter.

8.1.6 Checkpoints

Aid agencies tend to focus on the checkpoint as a critical moment in a journey. This is generally correct: armed men manning a checkpoint can harass, intimidate and even threaten you. The situation can spin out of control because they are already tense or drunk when you arrive, or because they find offence in what you represent, carry, say or do. Staff interaction with those at the checkpoint will influence how your agency is perceived and how other aid personnel trying to pass it after you will be dealt with.

Rapid assessment

Not all checkpoints are equally critical. A key skill to develop – which also requires constant alertness and quickness of mind – is the 'assessment at a glance' at what type of checkpoint you are dealing with: where it is located, who is manning it, and what appears to be their mood. Checkpoints at crossroads, bridges, mountain passes, town entrances and exits, etc, are to be expected and are likely to have been set up for the general monitoring of all passers-by. Checkpoints in the middle of a forest or on a mountain road away from habitation may exist for a more ominous purpose. Checkposts manned by regular army and police forces may be less problematic than those manned by irregulars. Checkposts manned by drunken, frightened or recently defeated and revengeful soldiers can be more problematic than those manned by bored troops on duty. If a checkpoint looks or 'feels' suspicious, stop some distance away and study the situation. This in turn may arouse suspicion among those manning the checkpoint: if you proceed have an acceptable and defusing answer ready about why you stopped.

When approaching a checkpost, signal clearly that you have no harmful intentions:

- put the car radio on very low volume or turn it off (it is generally not advisable to start talking over the radio while at a checkpost. Inform base before approaching it and resume contact when you have passed it. Turn it off if you feel that it might attract unwelcome attention);
- put the window down;
- after dark turn on the light inside the car cabin so that all passengers are clearly visible;
- slow down;
- stop the car a few yards from a barrier, but always keep the engine running unless ordered otherwise. If there is more than one vehicle, the next one keeps a certain distance;
- take off sunglasses so that people can see your face and eyes;
- avoid any brusque movements in the car, and keep your hands clearly up and visible.

The spokesperson should be identified beforehand. Drivers often play a lead role either because they talk the team through the checkpoint or because they also act as translator. They should have a clear understanding when to switch role from spokesperson to translator.

Any team member could potentially be interrogated. It is therefore necessary for all to know what cargo the vehicle carries and to have the same story about what their organisation does and what the purpose of the journey is.

It is useful to carry small 'presents': cigarettes, sweets and pens are common, but in certain situations a tape with local music or local newspapers or magazines may be highly appreciated. However, try not to use them if you can avoid it. There are ample examples of 'inflationary' demands for 'presents' by people manning checkpoints.

All passengers should have identification in the local language(s) on them other than their passports, and passports should not be handed over if it can be avoided. If asked to go inside a guardroom, try to avoid leaving the vehicle unattended. If one of the vehicle occupants is considered 'vulnerable' or 'at risk', accompany that person if s/he is called away from the vehicle for interrogation or document inspection.

8.1.7 Convoys

Convoys and security

There are some general guidelines for convoys but you also need to consider what sort of convoy: two or three passenger vehicles of NGOs driving together to reduce the risk of road banditry; a food convoy as often run by the WFP; a convoy of returnees as run by UNHCR; or a convoy evacuating people at risk, as sick and elderly, perhaps run by the International Red Cross.

How does the type of convoy relate to security? A big convoy may reduce risk through strength in numbers, but it also moves more slowly. It can also portray an image of power and wealth, which can stir up resentment. And it may be mistaken from afar for an army column on the move. Smaller convoys may be more vulnerable to ambush but are perhaps easier to negotiate through checkpoints and less likely to come under aerial attack. Consider your context.

The type of convoy will depend on:

- **Vehicle composition:** the numbers and types of vehicles, and the type of cargo. This will determine the length and speed.
- **The 'human population':** busloads of passengers have special requirements in terms of water, food, comfort, medical care, etc.
- **The organisational composition:** convoys need to be managed, but convoys composed of vehicles and/or passengers from different organisations need additional coordination. One component of this will be the 'image' projected by its constituent elements, which will reflect on the collective image. If one vehicle is full of rowdy aid workers who turn up the radio volume and dress in culturally inappropriate ways, by association this will reflect on the others.

The convoy leader

A 'convoy' must have a leader. When different agencies participate in a convoy, or when they join a convoy under armed protection from national army troops or international peacekeepers, there is often reluctance to accept leadership. This can affect discipline. It is incorrect, however, to join a convoy for one's own security and then try and 'change the rules' or break the convoy discipline. This stimulates lack of discipline in risk environments and creates bad feelings among different actors. This in turn undermines the solidarity and collectivity when confronted with a threat.

Guidelines: How to Prepare For and Manage a Convoy

Planning the journey
- Draw up a journey plan and establish an assembly point and assembly time well before departure.
- Obtain precise details of all vehicles to be expected, the passengers and cargo.
- Inform yourself about all documentation that will be required.

Constituting the convoy
Think about how to order the line of vehicles. This will depend on the number and types of vehicles there are and what cargo and resources they are carrying, as well as on the types of threats/problems you anticipate. A simple way to plan this, and to discuss the rationale for your sequencing, is to draw each vehicle and each 'asset' and on a piece of paper and then assemble a 'paper convoy'.

- Assets are both organic and inorganic: the convoy leader; the deputy leader; a local guide; the commander of the military troops; a long distance radio; short distance handheld radios; medical personnel; mechanics; the water tanker; the recovery truck, etc.
- What type and numbers of vehicles do you have: trucks; buses; 4-wheel drive passenger vehicles; pick-ups; a recovery truck; a water tanker; an ambulance; an armoured personnel carrier, etc?
- What 'assets' do you have and where will you put them: the convoy leader; the deputy leader; a local guide; the commander of the military troops; long distance radio; short distance handheld radios; medical personnel; mechanics; the water tanker; the recovery truck, etc?
- What are the problems you anticipate: a vehicle getting stuck in the mud during a river crossing without a bridge; heavy trucks not able to climb a snowy road to a mountain pass; a road block by irregulars; mines; physical aggression by local people against the returnees from an ethnic minority you are escorting back home, etc?
- In the light of the possible scenarios how will you line up your 'assets'? If you expect manmade problems you may want to have a 'scouting vehicle' ahead of the convoy. This needs to be able to maintain radio contact; it probably should not carry the convoy leader but perhaps the deputy? Will the local guide go with it or stay with the main convoy? The convoy leader will be in front, but the rear of the convoy should

Continued...

also be made up of someone with experience and decision making authority. Can you maintain radio contact between the front and the end of the convoy? If not, is it possible to establish a signal code (with car horns and headlights)?

• Armed escorts should be in separate vehicles. If the armed escorts do not have their own transport, aid agencies may provide a vehicle but all agency identification marks should be removed. Ideally an armed escort should be split over more than one point in the convoy.

• Buses or other vehicles full of passengers should be in the middle, with the medical resources and food, water and blankets among them. You need to add spare vehicles for passengers in case one of the buses breaks down.

Check before departure

Prior to departure the convoy leader must check all vehicles: are they adapted to the expected journey (for example, are trucks of a height and weight so that they can pass all bridges and tunnels); do they all have enough fuel, and spare tyres; are all 4-wheel drive vehicles if these are indispensable to pass difficult terrain; do all have the necessary documentation required to pass official checkpoints, etc? It is very important for the convoy leader to know the details of the cargoes carried, and s/he must have the right to inspect the cargoes of constituent vehicles prior to departure.

Articulate and communicate the convoy rules

• **General movement rules:** these include such things as the speed of the convoy (it will travel at the speed of the slowest vehicle); minimum and maximum distances between the vehicles as a function of safety and security; lights on for easier visual contact; regulations on radio use; agreed stopping and resting points.

• **General scenario rules:** how does the convoy act when approaching a checkpoint; what will the convoy do when one vehicle experiences problems at a checkpoint while the others get clearance; what will the convoy do when a vehicle breaks down but cannot immediately be repaired? (There have been instances of truck-drivers being killed when their vehicle broke down and they stayed behind.)

• **Allocation of authority:** a clear identification of the convoy leader and his/her deputies. Drivers need to be clearly instructed about the convoy rules.

Distance keeping

Distance between convoy vehicles is a difficult issue in practice. Vehicles should never be so far apart that visual contact is lost; at the same time they should not be so close together that they get caught in the same incident (ambush, slipping into each other on an icy road, damage from a mine explosion). What is appropriate varies according to the terrain and the weather and security conditions, and may have to be adjusted several times during the course of one journey.

8.2   Car-jacking and Armed Robbery on the Road

8.2.1 Threat Analysis and Preparedness

Car-jackers will want to steal your vehicle. Armed robbers may only want your valuables, although they could use your car to make good their escape.

Vulnerability and pattern analysis

A good incident pattern analysis (Chapter 4) can identify high-risk zones. It can also suggest high-risk times, for example, that car-jackers seize vehicles when their owners get into them to leave in the morning, or when they return home in the evening. Under such circumstances you should closely watch your surroundings before getting into your car, and perhaps even walk around the block first in the morning, or drive around the block when returning home in the evening, looking for anybody suspicious.

Alternatively car-jackings may occur at a stopping point. In some African cities cars are stolen at a red traffic light. This is complicated, and you could try to reduce the risk by trying never to be the front car waiting at the red light. It is more common for car-jackers and sometimes armed robbers to follow you for a while in another car and then suddenly overtake you and force you to stop.

Another possibility is that your regular route is known and the attack has been planned, in which case the attackers may be waiting for you and suddenly block your route by parking their vehicle in front of yours. Another technique is for the robbers to deliberately fake an accident by bumping into your vehicle to make you stop and get out of your car. If you know this has happened before then do not stop immediately but signal to the other car to follow you and try to reach a well-lit area with more people around. Constantly monitor whether another vehicle is following you, and test this by changing speed and turning into side streets.

Door locks and seatbelts

Whether drivers lock the car doors when driving or not is again a contextual decision. When thieves operate generally without weapons (eg, snatching a bag from the passenger seat while you are waiting at a traffic light) or with knives, this offers protection and gains you seconds in which to accelerate out of danger. However, when an incident pattern analysis reveals that armed robbers are likely to shoot when they encounter any obstacle that frustrates their attempt it may be safer not to lock the doors and perhaps not even to wear your seatbelt.

8.2.2 When an Incident Happens

Trying to escape

Specialised security training teaches drivers how to throw their vehicle into rapid reverse, to hit a vehicle trying to push them off the road or to 'crash' through the roadblock of another vehicle. You may want to try this if you consider yourself an expert, but this is not advisable. You are likely to provoke gunfire or even kill yourself in a car crash.

Whether you should try and reverse or accelerate to escape an imminent ambush is a judgement call. Always assume, however, that the attackers are armed and that shots will follow if you try to escape. Of course, if your threat analysis has indicated that people are often shot and killed in the course of a car-jacking you may decide to try evasive action.

Types of attackers

Bear in mind that the armed robbers may be of two types: inexperienced opportunistic robbers, often adolescents, or experienced robbers.

- The experienced robber is likely to practise techniques of intimidation and submission: he/she may force you to face the car, or go down on your knees, hands behind your neck, pistol against your head. You may be hit hard on the head or neck to signal that you should not try to resist; what you do not know is how likely they are to pull the trigger if you perceive you are resisting.
- Experienced robbers may also practice ambush techniques: they will block you in front and behind to prevent you escaping. Your attempt to reverse or accelerate out of an ambush can have been anticipated and will be met with gunshots.
- The inexperienced robber is even more dangerous: he/she may be far more nervous, pepped up with drugs or alcohol, not in control of his/her own weapon or of themselves; a weapon can go off very easily and almost unintentionally.

In general any robber will be watchful for anything that signals resistance on your part, and nervous about delays. Remember:

- no vehicle or amount of money is worth your life;
- never put your life at risk by resisting an armed robbery;
- keep your hands visible, make no sudden moves;
- avoid displays of anger, rudeness or aggressiveness;
- give up the vehicle and/or valuables as instructed.

This latter point is to be taken fairly literally: comply swiftly with the attackers' orders but do not initiate any action such as getting out of the car or handing over wallet or car keys, unless 'instructed' (verbally or with hand signals).

Danger moments

Getting out of a car is a dangerous moment. The attackers may suspect that you too carry a weapon or will try some manoeuvre; their finger will be on the trigger. Never spontaneously grab for the door handle, release the seat belt or touch the hand brake without alerting the attackers to what you are doing: they may think you are grabbing a weapon. Keep your hands visible, and say or signal what you must do/intend to do before making any movement. Leave the car door open when you are out of it. Surrender personal items on demand. Don't show fear or anger.

Negotiating

There may be circumstances when you could try to negotiate – for instance, so that you can keep your passport and/or the radio, so that you are allowed to first make a distress call, or so that you keep a supply of water and food (when ambushed in a remote area and a long walk from a help point). This again is a situational judgement: in general, avoid negotiating when the attackers are very nervous, visibly anxious to get away as quickly as possible and/or highly aggressive.

Vehicle Safety & Travel Security

8.3 Preparation and Training

For drivers and field staff
• map reading and use of compass;
• testing and training for mastering the vehicle, terrain and traffic;
• a 'get yourself home' basic car repair;
• instructions on driving discipline and convoy discipline;
• key messages about the agency and its mission in your context;
• simulation: under aerial attack; in a mined area; armed robbery on the road; checkpoint passage; journey planning; venturing into unknown territory.

For logistics managers
• knowledge of advanced vehicle repair;
• driver training skill or clear criteria to identify a good driver-trainer;
• competence in installation and use of protective devices;
• management of vehicle pool and maintenance and repair scheduling;
• simulations on journey planning;
• simulations on convoy constitution;
• security management.

For field managers
• policy on driver recruitment criteria;
• driver policy and disciplinary policy (who is allowed to drive what and when);
• passenger and accident policy (procedures/guidelines);
• simulations on convoy constitution.

9 Site Protection

9 Site Protection

The purpose of site protection is to deter or stop intrusion, and to delay attack.

The focus of this chapter is on office and residential protection. It is also necessary to consider site security for staff in programme settings, for example, staff residing in refugee camps or in a hospital or school building/compound where your agency provides assistance. If the site is not formally under the control of the agency (the hospital or school is run, for instance, by the local administration), you will need to think about how to manage this (the requirements for a site to serve as an assembly point in times of crisis are addressed in Chapter 14 on evacuation).

Most principles can also be transposed to the protection of warehouses. This chapter does not deal with theft and pilferage from stocks which should be monitored via the normal checks and balances.

9.1 Site Selection

Site protection starts with site selection. The most common criteria are location (access/logistics), floor space and price. From a security point of view, however, you will need to take into account other criteria, such as:

• What are the known or potential natural and man-made threats?
• What are the physical strengths/deficiencies of the site from a security point of view? Which deficiencies can you live with/improve? Will physical improvements be allowed by the owner; which improvements will cost most, and are they affordable?
• What is your security strategy? If you believe an acceptance strategy will be fairly effective then you may want to reside in an area where local people live with a low profile and close contact with neighbours. If you pursue a deterrence strategy you will choose a different location – one difficult to approach and easy to defend.

In practice you will have to balance various considerations. The perfect choice will seldom exist. But consciously consider the pros and cons of every site from a security point of view, in the light of how you will be perceived, of your security strategy and your contingency planning. Identify the weaknesses in the choice you make and do something about them.

9.1.1 Environmental and Social Criteria

The neighbourhood

If you are considering a particular district check an area of at least 1.5km radius thoroughly to get a closer feel for it. Questions to explore with local residents and authorities include:

- What sort of neighbourhood are you in? Are most people local residents or does the area have quite a fluid population with workers coming in daily from elsewhere or travellers passing through on their way to other places? The more local the population in the vicinity, the more difficult it will be for outsiders to watch you and/or carry out an attack on you or your property.
- What local authority and rescue services are there in the area? Where is the nearest fire station? Where are the police posts? Where do the influential local leaders live? Find out if there is a police patrol and which are the more regularly patrolled areas.

Consider the potential vulnerabilities of the neighbourhood:

- **To military activity:** Are there military installations and government buildings and/or important socioeconomic targets?
- **To political unrest:** Demonstrations are likely to turn against government buildings. However, if foreign intervention is resented demonstrations may target diplomatic buildings; a university area may be susceptible to student unrest; a market place can be a target for a terrorist attack. In addition, a neighbourhood where a minority group lives could also be vulnerable to mob attacks.
- **To crime:** Note that the highest incidence of crime can be in the wealthier areas but could also be in poor areas. If you choose to reside in a less wealthy area you must not appear – outwardly and in lifestyle – to be attractively wealthy.
- **To flooding:** Close to the river, landslides, or avalanches, etc.

The landlord

Try to find out more about the landlord, his/her occupation, social background, possible role in the local community, political affiliation, etc. You do not want to rent a warehouse or an office from a person involved in suspicious dealings, someone who is politically prominent, or who is a leader (or close family member) of a group that is involved in the conflict. In places with a more tribal background the clan affiliation of the landlord will be important to consider. The tribal tradition that a host is duty-bound to protect his guests may come into play if your landlord sees you as guests. In other places the fact that your landlord belongs to a minority group could constitute a risk factor.

9 Site Protection

REMEMBER: Before signing a lease negotiate in detail permission to make alterations to the building to increase its security.

> **Case Study: A Secure Site in Ossetia**
>
> For reasons of security an aid agency decides to relocate from Ingushetia to North Ossetia. When looking for a secure site it notices that the international staff of another agency are housed in flats (it is the agency's policy for staff to find their own accommodation). It does not like the dark entrances and alleyways to the blocks of flats and it decides to search for a compound where office and residence for the international and some local staff can be combined, vehicles can be parked, and telecoms set up. First the male logistician finds what looks like the ideal place in terms of access and space. Female staff, however, notice that the neighbourhood does not look too good. Upon inquiry the agency learns that there is indeed criminal activity about. In the end a local person who had already been acting as an adviser to another agency, finds a compound on the outskirts of the city. This building has the necessary physical security requirements and is in an area where the 'newly rich' live with many guard dogs and high security awareness.

9.1.2 Physical Criteria

The perimeters

The physical strengths and weaknesses of the outer and inner perimeters are discussed below.

Concealed approaches

Avoid areas that offer many possibilities for concealed approaches and escapes, for example, areas with dense bush or a dry river bed, with narrow, dark alleyways, with factory grounds, storage spaces and warehouses that are largely abandoned at night, or with damaged and destroyed buildings.

Single or multi-tenant occupation

Consider whether to go for single or multiple tenant occupation:

- The advantage of multiple tenants is that the presence of other people around you offers additional surveillance and protection. Rent office space or a flat between the third and the fifth floors: the ground floor is more vulnerable to intruders (but also more accessible to disabled people) and the higher floors unreachable with emergency equipment (eg, in case of fire). The disadvantage may be that it is more difficult for you to know/observe who belongs to the building and who does not, and to make overall security changes to the general access. You may also not be able to put your vehicles inside a compound. If the roof is accessible, perhaps from a neighbouring building, then do not choose the flat just under the roof.

- Whether a block of flats increases or decreases risk depends very much on the stability and social cohesion of its resident population. If this is high, you probably have a good implicit 'neighbourhood watch' scheme. If low, then there may be general lack of interest in the security of one's neighbours and strangers may have easy access to the building.
- Single-tenant sites may be more fully under your control. You could get some of the advantages of 'strength in numbers' if several agencies occupy sites close together. This will also make it easier for guards to help each other.

In general it is advisable to get to know your neighbours.

9.1.3 In a Hotel

When you have to check into a hotel in an area where you don't know the threats, do not simply accept the room that you are given. Check its location and the access points (doors/windows) from a security point of view. Factors that are likely to increase vulnerability to burglary, robbery or sexual assault are:

- a room at ground floor level, especially with a covered approach (eg, from vegetation);
- a room at upper floor level close to a fire escape or service stairs that are accessible to an intruder;
- a room at the end of a long corridor away from the main movements of hotel personnel and guests, where suspicious noises from inside are less likely to attract attention;
- a room with a door that can easily be forced and no security lock/security chain; a room with a window that is easily forced, especially when at ground floor level;
- a room without good curtains that can conceal who is inside, and without a functioning telephone to hotel security;
- a hotel without guards or poorly guarded and a hotel without night-service at the reception desk to respond to an emergency call;
- admitting into your room someone you don't know well, for example, somebody you met during the day and who drove you to the hotel, the taxi driver bringing up your luggage, or someone whom you haven't called, for

example, a 'service staff' member bringing food or drinks that you did not order;
- single occupancy: balance your need for privacy with the need for security, perhaps sharing a room with a colleague or at least getting adjacent rooms and returning to the hotel at the same time.

If you are unhappy with the room that has been booked for you ask for another one. If you can't get another one; consider changing hotel. If you don't know the surrounding area, consider whether it is wise to go out after nightfall.

9.2 Perimeter Protection

The actual building or flat constitutes the 'inner perimeter' the compound walls or larger grounds in which it is set the 'outer perimeter'. Do some scenario-thinking and even roleplay: put yourself in the shoes of a potential attacker and study the site for its weak points.

9.2.1 The Outer Perimeter

- If the approach to the site is full of vegetation have it trimmed or removed where it offers hiding places for an assailant, or replace it with thornbushes.
- A wall at least 2.5 metres high increases the protection of the compound. You can top this with barbed wire, but that can create quite a provocative image. A more 'modest' version could be broken glass on top. If there are trees on the outside, by which the wall can be scaled, you will need to do something about the trees or the wall at these points.
- Consider the gates: high walls are little use, if the gate is a weak point because it is easy to scale or is only closed with a padlock and chain, either of which can be broken open quickly.
- If there is a risk of armed robbery in the building, or of mob violence, a second exit point is needed, apart from the main gate. The second exit point should not be a weak point for those trying to enter with malicious intent.
- Improved lighting is likely to reduce certain risks. But it may have the opposite effect and make the premises stand out in the street, and draw attention to the fact that there is something to protect. This is the constant dilemma of security measures that raise profile. Sensor lights that light up for a limited time and only when someone approaches, can solve this dilemma. The problem is that they, like any regular lighting, are dependent on the reliable availability of electricity. If lighting is installed or improved, it should be installed within the perimeter. In the absence of electricity or if there are regular power cuts, you

could consider the strategic placement of some hurricane lanterns, if there is a guard to monitor them.

- It is a contextual decision whether to put the agency logo on the outer perimeter, depending on whether in your assessment it will reduce or increase the risk.
- Dogs can be an excellent early warning help and often a deterrent. Get a proper guard dog, not a pet that sleeps all the time.

Guards

Unarmed guards are commonly used at residences, warehouses and for agency offices. In many cases, however, they are ineffective because they are untrained, poorly instructed, poorly equipped and poorly managed. It is not uncommon to find a bed in the guardhouse of aid agency compounds. This could lead to the guard falling asleep on duty. In recruiting and managing guards, the following are useful points to remember:

Guidelines: Recruiting and Managing Guards

- Select a physically fit person.
- Get reliable social references.
- Hire and deploy enough guards to challenge at least two intruders working together.
- Include contractual stipulations against the use of harmful substances (eg, alcohol) while on duty, and against additional jobs, for example, during the day, that are likely to affect guard performance.
- Provide essential equipment: rain clothes, torches, a whistle or other sound-alarm, possibly a strong stick, and a handheld radio or separate telephone in the guard house.
- Provide a logbook with instructions on keeping the log and on reporting, as well as a list of key contact numbers.
- Provide clear instructions and training on what to do/say and not to do/say with regard to visitors and their cars, 'service personnel' presenting themselves for meter readings or repairs; people asking for information regarding the whereabouts of residents; and when they discover an intruder, etc.
- Provide clear instructions about monitoring the surroundings, patrolling the compound, the rules regarding gates, doors, windows, keys, etc.

Continued...

9 Site Protection

- In areas of high risk of armed robbery, you may want to instruct guards on deployment procedures: for example, a routine inspection schedule alternated with variable timings of rounds, and especially the separation of guards. There have been instances of guards being easily overpowered, in which case they can become a liability; they may be forced to produce the keys of doors and vehicles, and may even be used to blackmail the residents into opening up, under threat that otherwise the guard will be killed. To reduce this risk, spread out the guards, with at least one in a position where he cannot be easily observed and overpowered, for example, on a roof terrace – to immediately sound the alarm.
- It is good practice to supervise the guards, including surprise spot checks. But don't get yourself shot by accident if they are armed!

Parking vehicles

Where there is the threat of vandalism, car theft, mob violence, or bombing, vehicles must be parked in the compound at all times. Make sure there is enough parking space when you select your site. Depending on the type of threat, you may have different guidelines for parking and fuel levels:

- If the threat is from car thieves breaking into compounds to steal vehicles, make sure to park the vehicles with their rear facing the exit, perhaps immobilise the vehicles at night by removing the distributor rotors from petrol engines, deflate the tyres or remove the wheels, and keep fuel levels low.
- If you need to escape quickly or carry out a rescue, then park with the front of the vehicle facing the exit, and keep fuel levels high.

9.2.2 The Inner Perimeter

Walk around the building with the eye of an intruder and look for weak spots.

- All entrance doors need to be strong. The strength of a door, however, also depends on its frame and hinges. Avoid or replace doors which have any glass, but do install an optical viewer (peephole) and a primary and auxiliary lock on outer doors. On the inside install a safety chain and a sliding dead bolt or strong bar across the door. Heavy duty padlocks on the inside, at the top and bottom of the door, are an additional means of creating a 'safe house', especially if the padlock rings are welded on.

- Windows can be protected with bars, grills or shutters, especially at ground level. Check how easy it is to reach an upper floor window, for example, by climbing on the kitchen or garage roof or a fire escape, and respond accordingly. Thick thornbushes as under ground floor windows can further impede access.
- Check whether it is possible to enter the house through garage doors or a cellar or small bathroom window.
- In case of fire, intrusion or rioting an alternative exit may be needed from the house. The escape exit should be easy to open from the inside. Rehearse an escape, thinking carefully about where you will end up when you leave the compound through this alternative exit. You don't want to be lost in a labyrinth of alleyways.
- Use of burglar alarms and closed circuit television (CCTV) cameras is not common. Both typically depend on electricity supply, although some burglar alarms work on batteries. If you're going to be robbed at gunpoint, a CCTV is little deterrent if the intruders don't know what it is and does, or if there is little chance that they will ever be apprehended.
- Don't place a panic button and the telephone close to the entrance door where an intruder could block your access to them.
- Smoke alarms are cheap and battery operated. You also need fire extinguishers: at least one in the kitchen and one on every floor. (For electric fires, you'll need a CO_2 or powder-filled extinguisher, and a foam or water-filled one for other fires). Check and have the extinguishers serviced at least once a year. Identify fire escape routes and ensure that, when locked from the inside, they can be opened instantly. In larger buildings, organise fire escape drills regularly, especially if you have a high turnover of staff.
- At night, routinely close curtains to make it difficult to observe who and how many are inside. When going out, leave a light on to give the impression that someone is in.
- Regularly check that all locks and bolts, etc, are in good working order and routinely lock everything as night falls or before going to bed. Limit the number of keys available and closely control who has access to them.

9 Site Protection

> ### A Safe Room
>
> The Afghan conflict has multiple layers. In the 1980s it had Cold War A 'safe room' is a place where quick refuge can be found from intruders. It will be strong enough to withstand any normal attempts to break into it. It should have a reinforced door and protected windows. Ideally it will have a telephone and a list of key contact numbers, plus torchlights or candles/matches. It may not continue to offer effective protection if you rather than your assets are the target of the attackers, and no rescue party can come to your help.
>
> The purpose of a safe room is to protect people, not assets. Although some valuables will probably be kept in it, it is not a good idea to put the office safe in it, or all your portable assets. This would frustrate most armed robbers who don't want to leave with empty hands and who therefore may take more drastic measures, such as blowing up the door with a hand grenade. As with all situations with a risk of armed robbery, let the robbers get something, if not everything.
>
> A safe room is not the same as the bomb shelter (Chapter 7). The bomb shelter is likely to be in a cellar, which would take too long to reach in case of an intrusion by armed robbers. A safe room is also not necessarily bomb and shell proof.

9.3 Site Security Management

9.3.1 Managing Access

An appropriate security strategy

You will need to manage visitors to the office, residence or warehouse from a security point of view. This is delicate and related to your overall security strategy, and strongly influences how your agency will be perceived. If an acceptance strategy is adopted, you will not want a completely 'open door' but probably a 'low threshold' for visitors. With a deterrence strategy you will discourage visitors or direct them to a separate building away from the main one. With a protection strategy you will allow access, but only if it is closely controlled.

There are degrees of security control. For example, having visitors sign in and out is hardly a security measure in itself, as anyone can still get in. Stricter standard procedures would be to have:

- all employees wear a visible photo ID when on the premises. These are collected upon termination of contract/employment;
- all visitors show/leave an identification and possibly be given a visitor's ID or visitor's pass that is collected when they leave;
- no visitors allowed in unless there is explicit authorisation from the person they want to see or who agrees to see them;
- no visitors allowed in unless accompanied by a staff member.

Still stricter procedures would be:

- routine checking of visitors' bags;
- routine manual or electronic body checking of visitors.
(Female guards and special training for all needed here.)

A visitor waiting space
This needs to be easily visible to security personnel and/or the receptionist. No uncontrolled access to the building should be possible from a toilet used by waiting visitors.

Clear policy and practical instructions for access

- **Visitors' vehicles:** Are they allowed into the compound or not; where are they to park? For example, if there is a bomb threat you will want to make sure that there are no non-agency vehicles in the compound. You should even prevent them from parking around the compound. You may instruct your guards that all vehicles need to be searched. Searching vehicles is a skilled job and guards need to be trained to do it effectively.
- **Body guards:** Should visitors who come with their own bodyguards be allowed to bring them in, and if so, with or without their weapons? Are you liable (socially/politically) in the case of an attempt on the life of the visitor whose bodyguards you did not allow in? Maybe the meeting could be in an annex of the building/on a verandah where bodyguards could be permitted.
- **Services access:** These include maintenance, repair and utilities personnel in delivery vehicles with cargo that has been ordered. Are they allowed into the premises in your absence? Can their arrival be planned and scheduled so that it is expected? Is it clear what they are supposed to do? What sort of ID do they need to provide and what is to be done if they arrive unannounced or cannot provide a proper ID? In the case of street vendors with fresh fruit and vegetables, who may be undercover 'scouts', give clear instructions to the guard and house staff to buy outside the gate.

In times of high risk, the policy should be that anyone unknown, unauthorised or unable to provide convincing identification should not be let in. If this occurs

9 Site Protection

at the office or warehouse, a supervisor can be called. If at a residence the person can be asked to come back at another time.

Keys

Locks and keys are only useful when tightly managed. The number of keys, and access to them, must be tightly controlled. If in doubt, locks should be changed! Keys should be identified, generally in code. All personnel with keys, including house staff, should be clearly instructed that:

• keys should be carried on the person and not left on desks, in cars, or in unattended coats or bags;
• keys should never be allowed to be duplicated, except under specific instruction from the agency management;
• loss of keys has to be reported immediately.

On the other hand, avoid situations where your practice of tightly managing keys gets you trapped, for example, in a building on fire because you don't have the key to the emergency exit door; in a residence where intruders have entered; or unable to respond to an emergency call from a colleague because the keys of the vehicles are locked away and the logistician lives the other side of town.

9.3.2 Suspicious or Threatening Phone Calls

Problematic phone calls can range from fairly innocent 'crank calls', to sexual harassment calls or bomb threats. Staff should be instructed that the general rule with phonecalls from people they don't know is to:

• insist that the caller identify him/herself and the precise purpose of his/her call;
• give as little information as possible about themselves and try to get as much as possible about the caller;
• give no information about their movements, when they will be in or out, and whether they are alone or not;
• request a number that they can call back;
• report all such calls to the security supervisor.

Sexual harassment calls can sometimes be stopped by having a male co-resident answer the phone. If the caller persists, change the telephone number. Female staff, in particular, (perhaps all staff), should not put their residence phone number on their visiting cards.

When a phone call contains a threat it is important to remain cool and practical, polite and courteous. Encourage staff to do the following:

- If the threat is vague and general try to elicit more detail about the reason, the precise target and whether the problem can be solved in another way.
- If there is a bomb threat ask when and where the bomb will explode and state that there are many people in and around the building who will be hurt if it does. State what the organisation is or what residence it is, and make the caller confirm that it is indeed the intended target. Ask what the reason for the threat is, and listen sympathetically.
- Try to write down exactly what is being said, or try to commit it to memory.
- Listen for any clues about the identity of the caller: male or female, tone of voice, agitated or calm, language and accent, smoking while talking or not, background noises, etc.
- Unless absolutely confident that the threat is not real, immediately evacuate the building.

9.3.3 Frontline Site Security Staff

Guards are an important part of your human security cordon. But in order to play an effective role, guards need to be fit and alert, well trained and clearly instructed, and supervised.

Even when there are guards, site security is everybody's responsibility. Everyone should remain attentive to anything unusual or suspicious and to neglect in security procedures (doors or windows left open, keys left lying around, etc). They should then take the responsibility to act directly or inform the designated supervisor.

Three other groups of people play a direct and important role in site security:

- **Receptionist/telephone operators:** These staff must monitor visitors and telephone calls with security awareness, and report on anything and anybody that could be a security threat.
- **Non-employee family members:** It is no good you being aware of residential security if your spouse and children are not, as they are likely to be at home when you are not.
- **House staff and office cleaners, including gardeners:** These too may be in the residence or at the office when no one else is. They should not let unknown people in, give information to unknown phone callers, give details about the office layout, or allow their keys to be duplicated etc. They need careful instructions about how to respond in different scenarios, and how to report anything unusual immediately.

10 Crowds, Mobs and Looting

10 Crowds, Mobs and Looting

In tense and conflictual settings, crowds can turn menacing or violent. This can lead to the looting of assets and aggression against staff. Common scenarios involve civil unrest, ethnic or communal violence, disorder around relief distribution, and soldiers or armed fighters, who go on looting sprees – irrespective of whether they have won or lost. Such violence can erupt spontaneously; it can also be planned and instigated.

10.1 Risk Reduction

10.1.1 Situational Monitoring and Analysis

Noticing tension

Anticipating crowd and mob violence is not an exact science. However, the possibility of it occurring needs to be considered as part of your ongoing situational monitoring and analysis – at the general national level (with often a higher risk in the cities), or at the local operational level (especially in camps of displaced people or in shanty towns). Growing tension and frustration can often be picked up in advance by the astute observer. Local people, tuned into the local media and informal circuits of information, are often aware that something is brewing, although they are not necessarily better placed to predict exactly what will happen, when and where.

Vulnerability

You need to consider whether you are, or might become, a target and where you are potentially exposed. What is the cause of the tensions, and at whom is the resentment directed? Are foreigners, or aid agencies, the object? Can local authorities deflect resentment directed at them onto foreigners or aid agencies? Are some of your local staff more at risk because of their ethnic or social identity? Has there been public anarchy in the past; where did it start; how did it evolve? Is there a pattern that could repeat itself? Are you indirectly exposed, for example, because your office or warehouse is close to an area where demonstrations tend to take place, or located in a minority neighbourhood, or because you have to travel through areas that can be a flash point?

Trigger events

Tension that has been building up for a long time can suddenly escalate because of a trigger event. Potential triggers can be identified, for example, the decision by foreign powers to intervene militarily, a fairly sudden economic crisis because of international trade conditions or a government decision to cut the subsidies of essentials such as food or fuel, or to close a refugee camp before people are willing to return, etc. Others cannot be predicted but can be recognised as likely triggers, for example, the arrest or assassination of a prominent figure, the defeat of troops that held a strategic position defending the town, or an unpopular measure by an international peacekeeping force or authority.

Case Study: A Mob Against Aid Agencies

In the autumn of 1995 the war in Sri Lanka once again turned into a dramatic confrontation. Despite this the NGO Forum on Sri Lanka, a group of international and national NGOs, chose to hold its annual meeting in the country. In earlier years it had concentrated on human rights, fair elections, and issues of equity and poverty. Now for the first time humanitarian action was on the agenda. A few days before the meeting an article, triggered by an expatriate Sri Lankan organisation in London, appeared in a national newspaper. It accused the Forum of supporting the rebels and alleged that the meeting was in reality a rally against the Sri Lankan government and its war effort. The details of the meeting, and this message, were picked up by a local radio station. An angry mob of up to 3000 people came to the venue and threatened the participants. The Forum moved to another venue, but again the details were broadcast over the local radio, and violent protesters came to disrupt the meeting; they even raided the hotel in which some of the foreign participants were staying. The situation did not calm down until members of parliament and government ministers intervened. But for weeks following the incident a climate of suspicion and hostility towards NGOs was noticeable in the whole island.

10.1.2 Preventive Action

Proactive information

The more misinformation which exists, or is spread, about your agency, the greater the risk that collective frustration and anger will be directed against it.

As suggested in an earlier chapter a general acceptance-promoting approach is useful. More specifically, expectations should be managed proactively. For example, discuss with people what they can realistically expect, and inform them immediately if there is a delay or a change of plan. Sitting together to listen to criticism and search for alternatives can help to prevent frustration turning into anger. Do not just talk with a few representatives, try and make the information publicly known.

Proactive crowd control

Never encourage a crowd to gather unless you can meet their expectations. Organise in advance events (meetings/distributions) where crowds will gather. Work out procedures with local representatives. Try to avoid or minimise uncontrolled crowd movements, long queues and waiting times: multiply distribution points; schedule distributions throughout the day for different sections of the population; create waiting areas with shade and water and make those waiting sit down; provide precise information about the nature and quantity of hand-outs; designate crowd control staff who will turn back whoever does not belong there and further assist the crowd with information and movement procedures; physically channel people into a manageable queue/through small avenues; arrange for an exit route away from the entry points.

10.1.3 Protection

Reduce exposure

Consider tactics such as cutting down on movements through risk areas, relocating sites away from risk areas, withdrawing staff considered to be at risk, limiting or reducing stocks in warehouses, temporarily moving valuables such as office equipment to the residences of local staff, etc.

Reduce visibility

You could do this by removing agency logos and flags from buildings and cars, perhaps limiting the movements of international staff who will stand out among local people, and renting local cars or using taxis rather than the high-profile 4-wheel drive agency vehicles.

Reduce surprise

In a period of rising civil unrest and regular demonstrations, closely monitor the nature of the demonstrations and the direction they take.

Crowds, Mobs & Looting

10

Case Study: Monitoring Civil Unrest

Operation Desert Storm against Iraq in 1990 led to widespread daily street protests all over Pakistan as the population rallied in support of Iraq. Aid agencies, most of whom had offices and residences in the same neighbourhood, were concerned that the demonstrations might turn against them. One agency therefore deployed local staff to monitor the demonstrations constantly: their size, behaviour, the slogans they adopted and whom they were addressed to, and the attitude of the police. The monitors had hand-held radios, to give an early warning in case the demonstrations got out of hand and turned towards that specific neighbourhood. Meanwhile, the international staff did not go out unless dressed in local clothes and accompanied by local staff. Posters of Saddam Hussein had been put up everywhere in town and one agency put some on its car windows too.

10.1.4 In a Time of Crisis

If you are pursuing a deterrence strategy you will probably post more guards around your compound and/or ask for special protection from the authorities. This can be a very effective strategy if the authorities are willing and have the ability to exercise effective control over the crowds. However, this may not always be the case: police from local stations may be part of the local community and unwilling to antagonise an angry local crowd. In addition, the government may be unwilling to expend its 'political capital' by intervening too quickly or too forcefully to control a crowd that is made up of future 'voters'. On the other hand, the authorities may be willing to 'impose order' with more force than you are comfortable with. While you don't want your sites looted, you also don't want the police or army to use excessive force or even to shoot at a crowd and possibly injure or kill people on your behalf. When asking for armed protection from the authorities, make sure to discuss the rules of engagement that will be used to protect you (Chapter 6).

10.2 Crisis Management

10.2.1 Negotiation

When confronted with an angry crowd at your office you will want to try to defuse the anger. At the same time you must be prepared to protect yourself from a rapid degeneration into mob violence. Key tactics are the following:

- Seek advice from local staff who can understand what is being shouted, and who may gain an impression of who the demonstrators are as well as who appears to be controlling/driving them.
- Gain time; negotiate with the demonstrators on the basis that talks should take place with a small number of their representatives.
- Hold these talks in the compound, not in the heart of the building. Do not go out to negotiate as you may be attacked or taken 'hostage'.
- Adopt an anger-defusing negotiation strategy (Chapter 18). Listen attentively and respectfully; avoid making quick promises about the issue in contention, rather signal that you are taking note of the grievances and are willing to pursue the discussion further but not under threat or duress. In other words, try to negotiate an agreement to have talks but in a setting where the angry mob is not at the door.
- Inform the authorities of the situation, but also indicate your position with regard to the use of (excessive) force.
- Meanwhile, all employees should prepare for evacuation from the building. You will need to consider whether to take essential items with you such as vital diskettes, portable computers, satellite telephones, radio equipment and essential files. This will not be possible when you are forced to 'escape' (see below) or when, once outside, you want to blend into the local scene. Lock the doors of all rooms that are vacated; exit the compound at a place where the crowd has not yet gathered and where you are not visible to it. If safe evacuation is not possible gather all the staff in one place where there is no easy access once all doors are locked.
- If local staff believe that the crowds are being stirred up by troublemakers who are not the normal community leaders, they may contact the latter and make them come to the scene of confrontation to calm the crowd.
- Designate one person to contact immediately other agencies who might be at similar risk.

Following such an event make sure to:

- maintain heightened security alert for some days until the situation has clearly calmed down and there is no perceived risk of perhaps individual retaliation;
- consider very carefully your public relations position and messages, from contacts or not with the media, to what messages local staff may informally pass out;
- stick to your word: hold talks, even if you have now increased police protection. Don't only have talks with the formal authorities but communicate with a wider environment of ordinary people; you will need to re-establish relationships and perhaps repair your 'acceptance' in your environment.

10.2.2 Escape

A well-chosen site should have a separate emergency exit which is not visible from the main entry/exit point. You should familiarise yourself with alternative back routes in advance. It is a situational judgement whether you run and thus draw attention to yourself, or walk, pretending everything is normal.

10.2.3 Surviving Looting

Looting, not only of warehouses but also of convoys, offices and residences, is a not infrequent occurrence. Your response will depend on your situational judgement. Key principles to bear in mind are: to protect your life; to protect vulnerable staff; and to try to maintain communications.

The first two principles are the same as for surviving armed robbery. Don't resist, and try to prevent aggression against staff members by allowing the looters to take what they want. Don't show fear: signs of high vulnerability may give some looters the confidence to turn on you. Remain calm, retain your dignity, and try to defuse the anger (Chapter 18).

In general, it is advisable to leave the place being looted in case the situation escalates. This may not always be possible; it could be even more dangerous outside. This may occur in a situation of forced 'hibernation' (Chapter 14).

If this is the case, you will probably have to prepare for several hours, even days, of ongoing anarchy and widespread looting. The looters may come in waves, eventually stripping the office/residence/warehouse of its last valuable piece.

Anticipate that the risk may increase. Over time there will be fewer material possessions to satisfy the looters, and alcohol, drugs, and blood already spilled may release greater aggression.

Try to hide, and retain a means of communication. It may be possible to hide a hand-held radio, mobile phone, or satellite phone, or negotiate for one telephone to be left (if the lines are not cut). You will need to retain or re-establish contact with your colleagues as soon as possible.

Case Study: Surviving Waves of Looting

In the face of an advancing rebel force an aid agency had evacuated all non-essential staff. However, some international staff chose to stay in the office in a 'popular' neighbourhood out of solidarity. The agency's analysis was that it was unlikely that the government army, although being pushed back, would start looting, as the army patrols were composed of soldiers from the four major sections of the army, who effectively restrained each other. But a change was triggered by the assassination of the general in charge of the city's security. As a result the soldiers started looting and shooting. On the first day, it was possible to pay off those soldiers wanting to commandeer the agency car. A second group, however, were more aggressive; they fired shots into the house and stole the satellite phone and other electronics and valuables. Then civilians arrived to loot everything portable. The following day, the agency was attempting to tidy the ransacked house when a third group of soldiers entered. They mistook the cleaning up for an attempt to hide something, and became very aggressive and intimidating. It took great persuasive skill to convince them that there was in fact nothing left. Luckily staff had managed to hide a mobile phone and a hand-held radio. When staff eventually established contact with colleagues elsewhere in the city they learned that the rebels were entering the town, and also that their agency had issued an international press statement condemning the rebels for a massacre elsewhere. Having had all their clothes stolen they were left with only their agency T-shirts, which had suddenly become a liability.

10 Crowds, Mobs & Looting

11 Cash Security

11 Cash Security

This chapter is only concerned with theft and armed robbery by persons external to the agency. Obviously external actors may have been 'tipped off' by someone among the staff. Contextual factors again play a role. The following are therefore only tips for local adaptation.

11.1 Reducing the Use of Cash

In order to reduce the use of cash, your agency could use other formal financial mechanisms:

- **Credit cards:** statements should be checked regularly as not everyone will always be discreet about your personal code.
- **Traveller's cheques:** follow the security instructions issued with them.
- **Payments by cheque and/or bank transfer:** where possible ask all staff to open a bank account as this minimises your risk. The agency could even agree to pay any costs involved.

If there is a sizeable cashflow you should inquire into the cost and conditions of insurance against loss and theft.

The agency might also use informal credit and transaction systems. In a number of places there is no functioning banking system, for example, in Somalia. Under such circumstances, traders and money suppliers have constituted a network to minimise cash transfers and the associated risks. Some of these networks may only operate locally; others may have 'nodes' with international connections. This would allow you to deposit a sum as credit in a foreign account to cover payments made locally on your behalf by a third party. The system works on trust, and increasingly by satellite telephone. Make enquiries about this with local staff, local traders, contractors, service providers.

11.2 Discretion

If you have to ask for, move and/or keep cash, communications about it should be discreet: The less people know, the less they can, intentionally or not, give away. Communications over the telephone or radio should be 'encoded' and you need to code the 'money' – the amounts and type of currency. As with all coding systems use one that is clear and unconfusing – but not one that allows a 10-year old to understand after five minutes that you are talking about money!

If you withdraw money from the bank make sure to organise this with the bank in advance and be discreet about the transaction. If you make large payments, for example, to a supplier or contractor, do the same.

A common and sometimes unexpected problem is the actual 'bulk' of the money. A somewhat extreme but good example was the monetisation of many tonnes of food aid in Somalia; the resulting payment in Somali shillings took up no less than 17 cubic metres of space. More common perhaps is the volume of local currency that the bank gives you (for what is still a fairly modest amount of international currency) and which still may fill a suit case. See if you can ensure in advance that you will get higher denomination notes and hence less 'bulk'. If there is a subsequent problem with payments in high denomination notes you will need to think of a solution for that. If there is no alternative option, you will need to reduce the visibility of the money transfer, and to protect and/or spread the 'bulk' size of the pile of money.

11.3 Limiting the Exposure

Reducing the amounts

It is common practice to put a ceiling on the amount that can be withdrawn, transferred and/or kept in the safe. Ceilings can differ between different transactions, in respect of the cash requirements and the potential risks. The consequence is that you may have to make more transfers. The size of your 'vulnerability' will become smaller but the 'frequency' higher.

Reducing the number of transfers

If the highest risk is during the cash transfer, rather than when the cash is in the office safe, you may want to reduce the risk by moving larger amounts of money but less frequently. This may be your choice if there are the occasional opportunities to move cash more securely, for example, by a helicopter flight or large convoy every two months.

Just-in-time payments

If the highest risk is when money is in the office then you should organise the timing of your transfers in such a way that the period the money is in the office is kept to the absolute minimum.

Transferring the risk

You could reduce your own movements of cash by making those whom you need to pay, for example, contractors, suppliers and service providers, come to collect it rather than you taking it to them. Staff in field-locations could even collect their own salaries, for example, on the occasion of a staff meeting.

To help you think through these different scenarios you could draw a flow-chart, identifying the money and cash transfers and 'storage points' within the organisation from your headquarters to the final payment to someone outside the organisation. Consider the respective risks and risk-reduction measures at the different nodes and transfers within the chain.

11.4 Spreading the Risk

If burglary, hold-up and robbery are risk factors then it is advisable to spread the risk: do not keep all your money in one place, though you should keep a certain amount in an obvious place so that robbers in a hurry are quickly satisfied and will not harm you in order to find out where the money is. This means having some money easily accessible on your person, in the car and at residencies, and other money better hidden.

In times of high tension when you might need to withdraw, relocate or evacuate, it is advisable to distribute cash among those leaving not only to spread the risk, but also to give them financial means in case they get isolated (Chapter 14).

11.5 Considering Predictability

Routine increases risk. Some of the more common predictable 'money concentrations' are:

- the monthly payroll for which cash is accumulated;
- special payments to national staff prior to evacuation;
- international staff arriving at the airport and transferring to a hotel or the office in the city (professional robbers may monitor the arrival times of international flights, and prey on official taxis and vehicles of foreigners on the main route into town);
- the accountant or finance manager going from the office to the bank and back along the same route, often around the same time.

11 Cash Security

These are high-risk moments and movements for which you want to take extra security precautions or reduce the predictability. For example:

- use an unmarked rented or local staff vehicle and/or a back route to bring staff from the airport to the office/hotel;
- change salary periods and payment times in order to reduce the predictability of the payroll;
- authorise additional staff members to go to the bank, or have the accountant/finance manager follow different routes.

11.6 Reducing Vulnerability

Ideally the safe will be anchored to the floor so that it cannot be removed. Good practice suggests that you should have two keys to open it, which are held by different people. However, if there is a risk that armed robbers will use violence against staff if the safe is not opened alternative options may have to be considered. One might be to keep money in a locked and portable box to which only the accountant has the key. In this scenario the key(s) to the safe itself are accessible somewhere in the office (or residence if staff reside in the same building where the office is). For example, an emergency key could be kept behind a glass window that has to be broken (like an emergency brake or emergency door lock). In this approach there are the normal checks and balances to opening the safe, albeit somewhat reduced (hence the second locked box). However, in a worst case scenario the safe can be opened and the violent robbers can get away with the smaller box.

When it comes to transporting cash the most common method is by car. At least two people, and possibly more than one car, should be involved. A more extreme method would be to use an armed escort and/or an armoured vehicle. The latter is clearly a 'high visibility' approach, which will attract unwanted attention; it requires a very effective deterrent capability. On the one hand, in a fairly established situation where the office has been running for some months, the meaning of two easily identifiable aid agency vehicles outside a bank is also fairly clear. An alternative option may be for trusted local staff to withdraw cash in an ordinary vehicle. It is the eternal question of what is most likely to reduce risk: high profile or low profile?

12 Sexual Aggression

12 Sexual Aggression

12.1 Definitions and Scope

Rape is understood here as sexual intercourse without consent and against the will of the victim. The classic understanding of rape is vaginal penetration by a penis. However, men are also vulnerable to rape. Sexual assault is an act of aggression that may be differently understood in different legal traditions, but also by different individuals in your organisation. Stripping someone naked is a form of sexual assault that falls short of rape. However, oral and anal coitus or the insertion of objects into the vagina or rectum are very likely to be experienced as rape, although they may not always be understood as such. Sexual assault and rape are usually carried out with the threat or actual use of violence. The victim is forced to submit out of fear or because s/he is physically intimidated or overwhelmed. The relationship between the victim and the assailant(s), any present or past intimate relationships, past sexual acts or behaviour, etc, do not indicate consent for current unwanted sexual involvement.

Intimidation and sexual harassment of women constitute forms of gender-based violence which have psychological effects that can turn into physical symptoms. Your organisation should have a policy on sexual harassment and make sure to apply it. This chapter, however, focuses specifically on direct assaults on the physical integrity of a person. Because the overwhelming majority of rape victims are women it is written from this perspective.

There are various reasons for sexual aggression. Those common to the environments in which aid agencies often operate include the fact that:

- certain categories of women ('Western', 'low caste', or a particular ethnic group) are seen labelled as morally loose and 'available';
- rape can be politically motivated and designed to intimidate your agency and/or international intervenors in general;
- rape and the domination of women enhance the feeling of power in the rapist. This could constitute an individually savoured feeling of power extended to the social/ethnic group to which the rapist/s belong;
- rape as a weapon of war is intended to destroy the social bonds in the 'enemy society' and undermine the determination of the men in the opposing group;
- gang rape is a 'bonding' ritual. It strengthens the sense of social cohesion and group identification among those participating in it.

Rape is about power more than it is about sex:

- power rather than sexual lust and its fulfilment is the driving motive;
- the intention of the rapist(s) is to humiliate his victim and/or the people associated with her.

Hurting and demoralising the 'enemy' by violating 'his' women is a common tactic of violence. Rape may therefore become part of a major 'protection' (security of civilian populations) concern. This is outside the scope of this manual. The extortion of sexual favours for material and physical protection often occurs when men control resources (eg, food rations, access to a safe place, or vital documents) or otherwise have power over women. Although there is not a direct threat of violence, this remains a form of 'enforced consent'. Women on the move – IDPs, returnees, those in refugee camps – may be particularly vulnerable; so too are economic migrants who are often in weak social and legal positions. Some of these may be employed by your agency. They therefore fall under your responsibility and within the scope of this manual.

12.2 Risk Reduction

12.2.1 Awareness and General Risk Appreciation

Risk reduction starts with the organisational and individual acknowledgement that rape constitutes a real risk. This is currently not the case: sexual assault and rape of aid workers are still taboo subjects and absent from most security guidelines. It is important to recognise that women of all ages can be at risk. It is also important to recognise that working in violent environments can increase the risk of particularly traumatic forms of sexual assault and rape. There may be a greater risk of gang rape or of repeated rape, for example, during a period of captivity. It is even possible for women – though perhaps more often local women than foreigners – to be abducted and forced into sexual slavery and/or enforced 'marriage' with a fighter. This could happen to a staff member.

Rape is a risk in any society at all times. However, in theory aid agencies should have a fair idea of the countries where rape constitutes a higher risk for aid workers than others: Sierra Leone and Afghanistan as compared with Sri Lanka, for example. Too often the lack of risk analysis and poor incident reporting mean that impressionistic assessments are more common than informed ones. There are, however, general contributing factors which heighten risk, even without focused inquiry: the presence of many young men with access to arms; war or

Sexual Aggression **12**

conflict in which rape has often been used as a weapon of war; in a conservative society which restricts contact between unmarried men and women, etc. Where it is common practice to extort sexual favours, the risk of rape may be reduced as certain men have other means of dominating women sexually; on the other hand, it signals a habit of abusing power to physically abuse a woman.

12.2.2 Risk Mapping and Patterns

Focused risk analysis will identify places, times, situations and categories of people that constitute a higher risk. You will also assess if there are certain groups or individuals that are more likely to commit sexual assault and rape than others. Areas of higher risk may include districts in which militia operate; the area surrounding a refugee camp or the periphery of the camp; certain neighbourhoods in the town or city; prisons (men and women detained in police stations or in prison are often the victim of rape); certain types of hotels; or private residences. There may be certain times when risk is heightened: after dark; during great festivities and celebrations; at the time of aid distributions; at the time when women go to the bush to collect water or firewood or to go to the toilet; when armed groups are fleeing in defeat; or when victorious but revengeful troops enter the town they have just captured, etc. There may also be certain categories of people at higher risk: your local staff or a certain ethnic group; local female staff who have been relocated and are living in an environment where they have few or no social ties; Western women; widows or female heads of household; teenage girls because they are believed to be less likely to be HIV-infected, and so on. Certain groups may also constitute a higher risk: the paramilitary compared to the regular police, for example; government soldiers compared to rebel movements; demobilised and unemployed soldiers; armed robbers whose primary intent is to steal but who will often rape if they find a woman in the residence.

12.2.3 Sources of Information

Rape is generally a taboo subject among local people, expatriate aid staff and rape victims alike. It is therefore not always easy to obtain reliable information. Possible sources include local female staff; local women's activist groups; human rights organisations and human rights lawyers; women's groups in refugee camps; expatriates with good contacts in the community such as religious workers or long-term aid workers; security focal points at embassies. It may not always be advisable to ask straightforward questions; rather, be sensitive and move the conversation to the subject discreetly. An informative approach would be to ask local authorities and local health centres for statistics:

their reactions will give you an indication of the sensitivity surrounding the subject; they could also lead to a discussion about legal requirements and local responses to sexual violence and set you on the road to finding out about legal and medical resources.

12.2.4 Reducing Vulnerability

Measures by the individual

The general recommendations about personal competence with regard to security (Chapter 18), ie, low profile and 'determined' appearance, are also relevant here.

Female staff should generally dress inconspicuously and adopt a low profile approach as and when necessary. However, it is also important to display clear determination, familiarity with their environment and self-confidence. This will give the impression to anyone watching the staff member that she cannot be easily surprised or overwhelmed.

Personal appearance is a sensitive issue as it is regarded as within the private realm. At the same time women's hairstyles, dress and behaviour can be misinterpreted by others in terms of being seen as overtly sexual. This happens in all societies. Both male and female staff members need to adopt a culturally sensitive approach to appearance which could be viewed as being more 'modest'. In certain cultural contexts this will make male and female staff more socially acceptable. This will facilitate their work and perhaps contribute to reduced vulnerability to assault.

In addition, a whistle or other form of personal alarm may help to deter the 'opportunistic' rapist (eg, the solitary and unarmed burglar). So too pepper spray or tear gas. But remember that these could also be used against the intended victim. Where rapists are armed and operate in numbers, such devices are unlikely to be of much help.

Measures by the organisation

Be careful about which hotels female staff stay in, insist on a room that offers maximum protection from intruders, or simply adopt a policy of lodging female staff with colleagues or in host families. Normal residence security should be observed (Chapter 9). Gender identifications (Miss, Mrs, Ms, or a recognisable female first name) should not be put outside the residence or in the telephone directory. Perhaps employ a male housekeeper to answer the door during the day. If using an answerphone, a male voice should record the outgoing message.

12 Sexual Aggression

Women receiving anonymous calls should report this to the office. It might be a good idea to adopt an incremental strategy depending on whether or not the calls persist: have a male pick up the phone for a while; report the incidents to the telephone company; change the telephone number; change the residence.

Possible incremental policy measures could include:

- **Agency transport:** Female staff considered at risk (international and/or national) could be picked up at home and returned from work in an agency vehicle. Where a female staff member lives alone or stays in a hotel, instruct the driver or other person accompanying her to take the her to the door of the residence and perhaps even to check the house or flat to make sure no intruder is waiting.
- **Constant accompaniment:** You may institute a policy whereby female staff do not move around on their own, but are either in groups or accompanied by a male staff member – both during work but also when going to or coming from the airport, when on a morning jog, or at the weekend when going shopping or going out. The accompanist could be another woman or a man. Clearly the accompanying male should be trustworthy and of known loyalty.
- **Policies to prevent isolation:** Make sure that your policies and practice are such that, in a hostile environment, everything is done to prevent a female staff member from being isolated, even for a short period of time.

Case Study: Being Aware of the Threat of Rape

During the war in Bosnia an international aid organisation helped evacuate local people from Srebernica. As usual, all buses were checked by Serb forces. During one such inspection a young local Muslim female staff member was ordered out of the bus to 'have her papers inspected'. She returned half an hour later but had been raped. It is not known whether the international staff members on the bus tried to insist that she should not go by herself, but this would have been the recommended good practice.

- **Differential security procedures** can be adopted for male and female staff in high-risk areas. For example, no female staff should stay overnight in a project area even if the male staff do. Such measures tend to be contested as 'discriminatory'. Their intent, however, is to reduce an identified risk, not to discriminate. One perspective would hold that individuals, when fully informed of the risk, should be able to make their own decisions. Another perspective is that the repercussions of an incident go beyond the individual and would affect the operations of the agency as a whole, which justifies the agency taking the final decision.

- Female staff could be **relocated** away from high-risk neighbourhoods or camp areas.

- There can also be **withdrawal or preventive evacuation** of female staff at times of higher risk – for example, when opposing armed groups are fighting for the control of a town where your agency has a project and where the defeated and/or the victors may engage in rape.

- In high-risk countries or areas a policy of last resort may be **not to deploy female staff members**. However, this is obviously drastic and will have serious repercussions in terms of accessing women through your programmes.

These policies can be selectively applied depending on your assessment of your vulnerability. For example, you might decide to adopt such measures for national female staff only rather than international ones, for the younger women, or for women of a certain ethnic identity, etc.

12.3 Surviving Sexual Assault and Rape

The available guidelines on this are very much based on Western psychological models. These may or may not have relevance for non-Western people. It is recommended that you discuss this with your national (non-Western) staff in a sensitive way.

12.3.1 Experiencing Sexual Aggression

Preserving life

There is no general rule on how to behave when faced with the imminent threat of sexual assault and rape. The most common reactions are:

- **Active resistance:**
  - screaming; blowing the car horn; shouting for help;
  - running away;
  - fighting back.

- **Passive resistance:**
  - talking to the assailant to try and make him change his mind (knowing a few sentences in the local language would help greatly in this regard).

What happens and what the staff member does will depend on the circumstances (if there is a gradual build-up of the threat; how many assailants there are; if they are armed; where the attack happens; if there is help nearby, etc) and on her personality and preparedness.

The key message to staff should be: Protect and preserve your life.

If there is no way out survival should be the priority, followed by minimising the physical and psychological harm that is done during the sexual assault or rape. This may mean 'accepting' that submission is forced, and not resisting.

Psychosomatic responses and survival mechanisms
The following can be discussed proactively with staff at risk:

- **Do not face the attacker:** There are two reasons for this. First, the attacker may fear later recognition and decide to kill his victim. Second, the victim may 'see' in her mind the face of her attacker for many years to come, which can make it harder to survive the event.

- **Psychological defence mechanisms:** As in other acute security situations it is likely that psychological defence mechanisms will be active. These differ between people, and frequently include:

  - dissociation: it is as if the victim is watching a film and experiences it as an observer;
  - denial: a 'this is not happening to me' message goes through the victim's head;
  - suppression: an 'it will be over in a few minutes; this is not the end of the world' message goes through the victim's head;
  - rationalisation: a 'poor characters; what a cheap way of satisfying your need to feel power to fight your little war, but you can't really hurt me' message goes through the victim's head.

  While these are healthy survival mechanisms to adopt during the attack they should not mislead the victim into believing that she has not been deeply hurt.

- **Physical reactions:** There can also be physiological or psychosomatic responses during or immediately after a rape such as vomiting, hyperventilating, urinating, choking, losing consciousness, etc. These are normal reactions to the psychological and physical experience of being 'invaded' and having one's most intimate boundaries violated.

It is not recommended to discuss the fact that prolonged rape, such as a gang rape that lasts a whole night, may defeat the initial psychological defence mechanisms and stimulate a profound 'mental numbness' which is more a direct expression of deep psychological trauma. Such a message will not enhance 'preparedness' and may actually undermine the victim's ability to cope with the threat or with the occurrence. Those likely to provide immediate support, however, should be aware of it.

Report the attack

It is a common response to not want to mention to anybody that one has been sexually assaulted or raped. The survivor may feel shame and guilt and also fear the reactions of family, friends and colleagues. This is a normal reaction, and an understandable one. At the same time s/he runs medical risks and will have been deeply hurt. Not mentioning anything to anybody deprives the survivor of the possibility of getting medical assistance and psychological support, which will help recovery and start the long process of healing. If there is a persistent risk but no alert then not reporting what happened may also contribute to other women/men getting raped.

12.3.2 Witnessing a Sexual Assault

Attention also needs to be paid to the people, often men, who are forced by the assailants to 'witness' rape. This applies to civilians as well as to agency staff. Male civilians and aid workers can be forcibly prevented from stopping the rape of their mother, wife or daughter taking place in another room or in their vicinity, and can even be forced to watch it. This risk is real, and awareness and preparedness need to be created. Those who witness such an event will also require competent support.

The key message is the same: Protect and preserve life.

Staff should be advised:

- To try and make those threatening rape change their mind by talking to them, and by insisting that they cannot leave the woman alone.
- If their active or passive resistance becomes life-threatening they should not persist. No-one is helped if the witnesses are badly injured or killed; if violence is used first against male colleagues or relatives there is a greater chance that it will subsequently be used against the woman during or after the rape. Colleagues in such situations should be advised to avoid provoking the assailants into unnecessary violence, but rather focus on preparing themselves mentally to help and support the rape victim(s) when the attack is over.

- Being unable to prevent a rape is in itself a deeply shocking experience, apart from the mortal fear for the witness's own life that the situation may evoke. The witness will have to deal with his/her own emotions afterwards. As mentioned above, concentrating on how best to support the rape survivor immediately after the attack can be a strong coping mechanism during the ordeal.

12.4 Crisis Management

There are four major areas that need careful and competent management following sexual assault and rape: psychological support, medical support, legal issues, and communications. All of these need to be initiated immediately and simultaneously, which is easier when you have a prepared team of two or three.

12.4.1 Psychological Support

The key messages for those providing immediate support are: create a sense of safety, empathy and positive support. It will also be important to provide support to possible 'witnesses' and the rest of the team. The key person providing the support should be someone with maturity and sensitivity, who the victim trusts. This is not per definition the manager.

Restoring a sense of safety

A rape victim is a person who has been aggressed. It will be important to find a place where she can rest and recover with a sense of total safety and security. This sense will be influenced by physical location, which must feel secure, and by those surrounding the victim. An expatriate can be relocated in-country or to a neighbouring country. A national staff member may want, or have, to stay because of social and/or economic reasons. The person affected is best placed to indicate where she feels safest and most secure, so consult with her.

Also consult with her about companionship. She may want to isolate herself with her grief, shame and guilt. It will be important, however, to balance respect for privacy with a supportive presence in order to prevent the victim from going into a negative spiral of isolation at a time when she is highly vulnerable. Ask her whom she feels most comfortable with and trusts. This person can be in the vicinity and maintain close contact.

Try to limit the intake of caffeine and nicotine; ensure rest and good sleep, and that nutritious food is eaten and regular exercise taken. This will help restore a sense of physical balance which will aid psychological recovery. In the first few days a biological reaction, for example, to the adrenaline pumped up during the assault, may make it difficult for her to relax. Medicine or, if nothing else is available, the controlled use of alcohol may help the victim get through the day.

Empathy

Immediate emotional responses following rape can vary. The survivor might cry a lot and suffer from feelings of acute anxiety; she could be agitated and hysterical. On the other hand, she might be very calm and apparently composed, wanting to carry on as normal as if nothing had happened.

The most common feelings following a sexual assault or rape (for men as well as women) are:

- **Fear:** of being alone and/or of being in a crowd; of reminders of the event; of men in general; of going to sleep because s/he suffers nightmares, etc.
- **Guilt:** for having 'caused' the rape; by getting into that situation; by dressing the way she did; for not resisting more or for resisting too much; for 'engaging in sex' (with someone other than her partner).
- **Shame:** feeling 'dirty'; humiliated; fearing people can 'tell' that s/he has been raped;
- **Anger:** at the assailants; at the society they belong to; at colleagues and the organisation; at herself.
- **Lack of trust:** in others in general; in men in particular; in her own ability to make judgements.
- **Powerless and depression:** loss of control over her own body; over her emotional well-being; over her life.

Each person is unique so each victim should be helped to recognise and express their feelings as they experience them.

You will need to convey that all these reactions, which can also alternate, are normal. Being supportive will mean finding a balance between calming the person down when agitated (with the message that this is something one can survive and live through) and gently refusing to go along with an attitude of denial that pretends everything is 'normal' when clearly it is not.

Positive support

Your attitude in attempting to be supportive is very important:

- Empathise with the survivor and help her identify and recognise her own emotions. However, don't impose on her.

12 Sexual Aggression

- Avoid any statements or non-verbal communications that could imply blame or criticism. The survivor is already likely to blame herself. There is no discussion about who is to blame: the rapist(s). While the survivor may have increased her vulnerability by certain actions, she did not 'ask' to be attacked and did not consent to what happened.
- Allow the survivor to be in control as much as possible. Experiencing sexual assault and rape is disempowering, both in a physical and a psychological sense. Do not reinforce that experience and make it difficult for the survivor to regain control however much you want to protect her. Always ask, consult, and seek her consent rather than making decisions on her behalf. Do not be surprised if the survivor suddenly has an emotional outburst against you and says hurtful things that you do not deserve: you may have unknowingly put pressure on her by something you said or did. Enquire if that is the case. Alternatively it may simply be an expression of the emotions the victim feels towards others which suddenly get projected onto you. Don't take it personally.

Key Messages for the Survivors of Sexual Aggression

- The attack was not about sex but about power.
- You are not to blame, the assailant is to blame.
- You are not alone. There are people who support you and love you, and there are other people who have gone through the same experience.
- You can survive this and recover from it. This may take some time and needs attention, but this is not the end of your life or happiness.

Dealing with couples

If the survivor has a partner present in the field that person will also need to be supported whether or not s/he was present at the time of the assault. Three aspects will influence the situation and shape the support you give:

i.   the cultural backgrounds of the partner and the survivor;
ii. the personality of the partner;
iii. the length and strength of the relationship.

The fact that one's partner has been sexually aggressed is a very difficult experience. It can yield a variety of emotions, simultaneously or alternating: guilt for not having been able to prevent it; anger at the aggressors, but also anger at the victim for having put herself in a vulnerable position; denial and a refusal to accept that it has happened; rejection and a wish not to continue a relationship with someone who has been 'taken' by another and who – implicitly – may have humiliated the (male) partner. Rather than facing these impulsive emotions, which are not only strong but also difficult to accept, the reaction could be, or become, one of pushing away the source of the 'problem' and unease, that is, the victim.

The couple may be from different cultural backgrounds. Whereas under 'normal' circumstances the cultural differences may not matter much, sexual violence touches upon deeper and more intimate beliefs and attitudes which are also culturally and socially shaped. Both may discover that they have different perspectives on sexuality, sexuality in a relationship, sexual violence, and dealing with traumatic events, of which they were not previously aware. The result may be different reactions and expectations, and difficulties in communication and understanding. This only adds to the stress.

The event will also prove a test of the strength and depth of the relationship. If it is a mature one in terms of the depth of commitment, mutual understanding and experience, it is more likely that the partners will be able to support each other. When the relationship is newer, less clearly committed or with less profound mutual understanding this may be more difficult, and the survivor and/or the partner may actually be more hesitant and uncomfortable about being together. The event may therefore initiate the end of the relationship.

It is important to support and manage this aspect of rape survival and recovery constructively. For example:

- ask the survivor if and when she wants to see her partner;
- you should discuss with the partner what a rape survivor is likely to experience, and what attitudes and messages can be helpful;
- you should also provide support for and/or help the partner to see clearly in his/her impulsive emotional reactions.

If the couple are close and find support in each other, you can take a step back. If, however, the event and the subsequent situation create stresses and make communication difficult between them you may have to step in and constructively manage their interaction.

Support for the rest of the team

As mentioned before, those who were present and unable to prevent the aggression will also need support. If what has happened is known to a larger segment of the team you will have to attend to the sense of shock, disorientation, depression, anger and confusion that this may cause in the wider group. It is not inconceivable that other members of the team have been victims of rape in the past. Depending on their own healing process they may or may not be well placed to provide support for the new survivor. If the incident reawakens their own traumas they will then require support themselves.

Helping the helpers

Providing this support is stressful and demanding. Those doing so should also monitor their own emotions, which may become turbulent. They should find someone they can share their feelings with confidentially, and who has the maturity to talk the 'helper' through constructively.

12.4.2 Medical Care

A person may have suffered injury as a result of violence used by the assailant, and is further at risk from involuntary pregnancy and infectious disease. The following steps can be taken, but only after consultation with and agreement from the victim.

Post-coital contraception

Post-coital contraception (morning-after pill) can be administered within 72 hours of intercourse. The decision to take it or not rests with the person concerned but should not await the results of a pregnancy test which is generally not reliable within this short time span.

Sexually transmitted diseases (STDs)

Medication can be taken to prevent chlamydia, gonorrhea and trichomonas. If it is not known whether the assailant is HIV positive you must assume he was, and care needs to be taken during the medical treatment of the survivor. The risk of contracting HIV increases if penetration was violent and caused tissue damage. No preventive medication which is 100 per cent certain exists. Some agencies offer medication that consists of a combination of AZT/3TC, to be started within 72 hours and continued for four weeks on the basis that it may help. The medication can cause side-effects such as stomach aches, nausea, headaches, liver inflammation, etc, and must only be taken under medical supervision. Medical tests for STDs (sexually transmitted diseases) and HIV have to be repeated intermittently for up to a year after the incident.

Hepatitis B

If the rape victim is not immune due to prior Hepatitis B infection, and has not received a complete Hepatitis B vaccine series, then vaccination should be offered. This is effective when started within 14 days of exposure. Additional protection can be gained from Hepatitis B immunoglobuline.

12.4.3 Forensic Evidence and Legal Pursuit

Forensic evidence admissible in court

If legal proceedings are desired, prosecution would be in the country where the assault occurred. It is important to understand that prosecution in court requires medical evidence; and to be acceptable, such medical evidence needs to be collected and handled under certain prescribed conditions.

You will need to seek a reliable and experienced lawyer in advance. The embassy may help you find one. You need to find out from the lawyer:

i.   who has the legal authority to collect forensic evidence in the case of rape;
ii. what forensic evidence is admissible in the prosecution of a rape;
iii. what procedures of collection, examination and storage must be followed to ensure that the evidence will be admissible.

If a recognised medical professional is required you may want to identify one (preferably a female) before any such incident occurs.

This whole process is a delicate matter and requires sensitive handling. Two key principles are:

1. Forensic evidence should not be collected *without first informing the victim fully* of why it is being done and what, in practice it consists of, and *without her – written – consent.*
2. Collecting the evidence as required does not commit the victim to future legal action but preserves the possibility if, at a later time, she decides to do so.

Common evidence would consist of the victim's clothes (without washing), pubic hair, evidence of genital or other injury, and semen stains. Three common problems in collecting this evidence are:

1. The victim wants to wash and change her clothes as soon as possible because she feels dirty and stained. She may want to destroy everything that reminds her of the ordeal. This does not destroy all evidence, but will make it more difficult to collect.

12
Sexual
Aggression

2. Certain evidence, such as semen stains, vaginal secretions and evidence of genital injury, may require a medically trained person and the appropriate equipment to collect.

3. The evidence has to be sealed, handled and stored in a correct and appropriate manner, for example, in paper not plastic bags, sealed and marked; some of it needs to be refrigerated. There should be a minimum of transfers and people handling the evidence and a log kept of who handled it when (the chain of custody of specimens must be preserved). Often time limits are legally imposed within which the evidence must be collected and examined if it is to remain admissible in court.

Reporting to the police

The question of whether or not to inform the police is also sensitive. Ask your legal adviser in advance what the procedures and time limits are with regard to making a declaration to the police. Inquire if it is possible (ie, within the prescribed legal time limits) to collect the forensic evidence to 'keep the options open' without immediately going to the police, thereby giving the victim more time to reflect upon the course of action she will eventually follow.

Obtaining official documentation might seem bureaucratic, insensitive and less of a priority, yet it may turn out to be important at a later stage, for example:

- if the victim decides to press charges and initiate prosecution;
- to access legal abortion;
- to obtain HIV treatment at an affordable price.

If a child is born, a record of the birth may be required to access child support services at a later date. This may be particularly relevant for staff from countries with more 'conservative' legal and social welfare systems. All documentation should be kept in a safe, locked place.

Case Study: A Second Traumatic Experience

It is not uncommon for the victim to suffer a second trauma as a result of insensitive treatment by the police. In one case a female expatriate aid worker was sexually assaulted during aid work overseas. No one in the (well-established) organisation knew what to do immediately after the incident – not her female field manager or the human resource team at headquarters. The next day she was sent, alone, to her embassy to report the incident. The embassy sent her to the local police accompanied by the embassy security officer, a national. Once at the police station, four armed policemen interrogated her asking detailed questions about the incident. When she hesitated to answer the difficult questions they accused her of lying. During the interrogation other policemen kept coming in for a 'look' as they were curious. The police undertaking the interrogation insisted that she show them her injuries before she was allowed to leave the station. They then insisted on her taking them to the place of the incident for a 're-enactment', which they claimed was essential to the investigation. No real investigation ever took place. The assailant was never caught and the survivor learned later that is very rare for anyone in that country to be tried or convicted of sexual assault. Her experience at the police station was effectively a second assault and resulted in a second trauma.

A well-informed and trusted individual should always accompany the survivor to the police station, whether a lawyer, medical professional, or whoever. This then becomes part of the agency's 'protection' strategy to ensure that the survivor is not intimidated or further victimised at any stage, that interviews are conducted in a language that can be understood, and that the appropriate documentation and assistance are provided. It involves making interventions when the survivor's rights and dignity are not respected. The protection function is all the more important when someone in a position of authority is implicated as an assailant: a local official, an influential person, or even one of your own staff members who, for example, abused his authority over the distribution of relief supplies to extract sexual favours. It is essential that the protector assumes the identity of an organisational representative and is not perceived as acting in his/her individual capacity.

Prosecution

The decision to prosecute should be made by the survivor, who needs to be able to make an informed choice. To assist this decision making process the manager has to inquire about the practical details of an arrest and court proceedings: Will the victim have to identify a suspect before he can be charged? How does this take place in practice? Can a suspect be released on bail? Does the victim have to testify in court, possibly in front of the defendant? Can the prosecution proceed if the victim does not reside permanently in the country, or will it involve her having to return several times? What are the penalties if the assailant is convicted? Given the facts of the case, what are the chances of conviction?

As a manager you also need to consider the possible security implications for the survivor and for other staff members if a prosecution takes place – and if it

12 **Sexual Aggression**

does not take place. Bringing and pressing charges may expose the survivor, her relatives, and/or those supporting and accompanying her to further threat and aggression.

12.4.4 Confidentiality and Alerting Others to the Threat

From a management point of view sexual assault and rape should be treated as a medical emergency and as a security threat.

Medical confidentiality

As a medical emergency (medical in a broader sense than purely physical), the survivor can and must enjoy medical confidentiality. This is often additionally guaranteed by law (eg, by the Privacy Act in the US). The purpose of confidentiality is to make it possible for the person seeking medical help to discuss their medical and psychological concerns and problems openly and completely. Feelings of shame, guilt, humiliation and the fear of being judged by others will play a role in terms of the survivor wanting to keep her experience as private as possible. This is a legitimate concern.

Even if it is known that someone has been sexually assaulted, the survivor will not want the details to be widely known and discussed. It will therefore be the responsibility of the whole team, the manager and the organisation, to protect the individual identity of the victim and the confidentiality of the details of the ordeal. The manager must undertake immediate action to:

- ensure that other staff members do not mention the incident. It is advisable to give them a 'standard line' that they can use if questions are asked (eg, I cannot answer this question, please contact the resident representative);
- establish a direct line of communication with a designated focal point at headquarters. Communications between the field and headquarters should be managed and controlled and should not involve a series of intermediaries or a large number of 'alternates'. The situation should not be discussed where one can be overheard;
- take proactive action towards the press if it seems that the incident will get press coverage, impressing on editors and journalists not to use the full name of the victim, at most only the initials.

It is advisable to agree upon a code name, a code word or a case number as standard reference in the conversation instead of the victim's name.

Alert to a threat

There is a common, and dangerous, confusion between rape as a medical emergency and as a security threat. This has led to the current practice in which rape incidents are simply not mentioned among aid agencies in the field. The net result can be that other women, unaware, remain exposed to high-risk and may suffer what was, in many respects, an avoidable rape.

The Obligation to Sound the Alert

A number of organisations have field offices in a city that is outside the war zone of the country but where there are tensions between the local population and the de facto authorities, who are seen as an 'occupying force'. After nearly 20 years of war many male civilians have been brutalised and are armed. One night, three armed robbers break into a residence. While there they also rape an expatriate woman while her colleague is held at gunpoint. The woman is repatriated, but in order to protect her the agency decides not to mention the incident. Three weeks later armed robbers again break into the residence of expatriate aid workers of another agency. This agency subsequently reports that the expatriate woman was threatened with rape but that one of the robbers had stopped his fellow robbers with the argument that they 'had not come for that'. The staff are shaken and the agency decides to withdraw them from the city. Only now does the first actual rape become more widely known about among a number of agencies operating in the city, and only now are steps taken to control the vulnerability of staff.

It must be understood and explained to the rape victim that failing to make any mention of the incident could actually prevent others from being alerted, and thus be a contributory factor to other women getting raped. The strategy therefore should be one in which the confidentiality of the victim is protected, while the alert is sounded to prevent others from suffering the same ordeal.

Handover: It will be important to write a full report which can be handed over to an incoming manager. The new manager may have to continue to follow the legal pursuit of the attack, and will have to deal with the longer term emotional effects that the incident has had on remaining staff.

The embassy: It is advisable to inform the embassy even if you do not seek their assistance. The embassy can be a locus of 'institutional memory'. If you do not require diplomatic or direct legal assistance from them it will be possible to report without disclosing the identity of the victim.

12 Sexual Aggression

The family: The responsibility for dealing with the victim's family will lie with headquarters unless the victim's partner and possibly her children are also in the country of operations, as would certainly be the case for national staff. You must seek the advice and consent of the victim about this. She must be allowed to decide who will know how much, and when and who will tell what happened. In the case of a repatriation, however, a reason will have to be given to the family, and close consultation with the victim is required for this. If the press takes up the incident a more proactive approach towards the family will be required, with the organisation probably designating a contact person who relates regularly and closely with the family, as in the case of kidnapping (Chapter 13).

12.5 Recovering

12.5.1 Surviving

People recover from the experience of rape even if they never forget it. Most go through a difficult and sometimes traumatic period but eventually learn that these difficult emotions are part of their personal history and are not an obstacle to leading a fulfilling life. Recovery takes time, sometimes years, and requires personal effort and support from others. If a rape survivor continues in post, as would almost certainly be the case for national staff, it is important that the managers are aware that the experience may result in symptoms of prolonged concentration difficulties, for example.

12.5.2 Organisational Commitment

Aid organisations are often unable to provide long-term support, especially if the survivor leaves the organisation. It is the responsibility of headquarters, not of the field manager, to clarify what can realistically be expected from the organisation and what not. Sometimes former colleagues who lived through or were present at the time of the rape stay in contact and form an informal 'support group'. Otherwise there are rape survivor support groups and the organisation can help by providing information and guidance about these.

The recovery process evolves over time: the experience of the survivor will change which means that the management/support issues will also have to change. This is beyond the scope of this GPR but you should get specialist advice on it.

12.6 Cultural Differences

It is important to recognise the cultural differences in 'coping'. The Western approach is centred on the individual and on talk therapy whereby the survivor is helped to put the incident and her emotions and reactions in perspective. But people with different cultural backgrounds or worldviews may deal differently with the experience of sexual violence. For example, it may affect not only their psychological well-being but also their social future, for instance, their ability to marry or to continue life as a nun. They may seek to forget rather than 're-frame' the experience by means of acknowledging their emotions, or seek a ritual transformation perhaps with the help of a traditional healer. In addition, sexual violence, particularly in the context of wider persistent violence, may be dealt with much more from a political and social perspective rather than an individual psychological one.

What are considered as 'supportive' attitudes, therefore, may also differ culturally. In Western culture the survivor is encouraged to talk; in another culture she may be discouraged from recalling the experience by talking about it and people may actively seek to 'distract' her. You need to be open and sensitive to other ways of 'healing' when dealing with people who do not come from a Western individualistic background.

12.7 Preparation and Training

At organisational level
- An aid organisation that deploys staff in an environment where rape is a risk must be able to mobilise expert and effective support to field managers dealing with rape victims. If this expertise cannot be developed or retained in-house it must be readily accessible from external sources.
- As a matter of policy, all expatriate staff members (not only women) should be informed about the risk of rape prior to signing the contract rather than merely prior to deployment.
- Good organisational practice should include clear policy statements about what support a rape victim can expect from the organisation, and how the organisation intends to reconcile the need for the protection of confidentiality with the need to alert others to the threat. This should be specific in terms of how far the organisation is prepared

Continued...

to go: will it pay for an abortion; for a lawyer if the survivor decides to prosecute; for the travel and accommodation if a survivor returns from abroad to the country where the trial takes place etc?

• There should be detailed guidelines for field managers and, whether male or female, they should be prepared to deal with a rape situation through training and simulation.

At field level

• Managers are advised to consult and discuss with staff the threat of rape, and the basic guidelines for proper conduct as suggested in this chapter. At field level, if rape is no longer ignored or discussion of it seen as taboo, and if staff are sensitised to the risk and the requirements for proper support, it will become much easier to employ measures to handle the situation should it arise.

• It will be important to discuss with staff from other cultural backgrounds what protocol and support they find most appropriate. Local female staff may be less able to control outcomes and therefore more reticent about reporting sexual violence within the agency, and very concerned about confidentiality.

• In your senior management team discuss who can and might handle the various aspects of the immediate crisis management.

• In a high-risk area couples should be advised to discuss between themselves their understanding of sexual aggression and their mutual expectations in case it happens to one of them.

• As a rule, detailed knowledge should be sought about legal requirements and police and judicial practices and specialist medical support identified. This knowledge will then be in place if an incident occurs.

• If post-coital contraception and other specialised medication is not readily available from medical institutions in your operational area, you should ensure that these are somehow at hand.

At individual level

Individual aid workers, and especially women, need to examine their own preparedness. Women usually have a heightened awareness of the risk of sexual aggression wherever they are but it is important to note that in conflict-ridden environments there may be a higher risk of gang rape, of aggravated assault (ie, being threatened by weapons), and of HIV infection as a result of rape.

- It is important to recognise your own emotional strengths and limitations: can you cope with the risk? Would you be able to survive emotionally and recover from the experience?
- Will you be prepared to observe security measures intended to control the risk for you, even if they feel like an infringement of your personal liberty or equal rights?
- Consider, in advance, how you would deal with your partner, your family, perhaps your children, if you get raped? Could you discuss the risk and the subsequent scenario with your partner and find clarity about what you expect/can expect from each other, so that this does not become an additional worry and anxiety?
- Knowing some sentences in the local language may be critical in changing the intent of a potential assailant. Get some language training and discuss perhaps with local female staff what you could try and say or do when threatened.
- A more extreme form of preparation, as with other types of threat, would be to submit yourself to a simulated scenario (of the threat of sexual aggression) in order to gauge how you would respond and to hopefully reduce the shock of surprise and the sense of debilitating panic if you find yourself confronted with a real-life threat. Self-defence courses in Western countries are perhaps not really appropriate for the type of situation expatriates may find themselves in elsewhere. Simulations can be emotionally very powerful, and you must anticipate that you are likely to feel a sense of being over-powered and humiliated.

12 Sexual Aggression

13 Detention, Arrest, Abduction, Kidnapping and Hostage Taking

13 Detention, Arrest, Abduction, Kidnapping and Hostage Taking

13.1 What Sort of Disappearance?

When one or more staff members 'disappear', the first challenge for a field manager is to find out exactly what the situation is and what type of disappearance it is. It might take hours, and sometimes days and weeks, to become clear. Terms are used in different ways, but here we distinguish between detention, arrest, abduction, kidnapping and hostage-taking. All have in common the characteristic that people are deprived of their freedom of movement and could experience anything from polite pressure to a life threat, but the nature and/or motivation of the captors will not be the same. Therefore the crisis management strategies will not necessarily be the same.

13.1.1 Detention

Staff members are kept under the control of an individual or a group. While there is no serious threat to life, there is also no clear pre-condition for release.

Detention can occur quite frequently during aid work. Agency staff can be detained by a group of villagers, a local authority, or a group of soldiers/militia. Reasons that often trigger this situation are discontent with the project/ programme of the agency itself or another agency (people often do not differentiate between agencies), resentment that others are receiving project aid rather than those detaining the staff members, or a concern for the 'security' of the staff members. Although the people detained have lost their freedom of movement they are by and large treated reasonably.

13.1.2 Arrest

This term is used to describe detention by government authorities (normally the police, but also the army) or the 'presumptive authorities'. What distinguishes it from straight detention is that we are dealing with official authorities so that, in principle, the law can be invoked. The situation can be more difficult and dangerous when the government authorities arrest someone 'extra-legally', ie, secretly. They may then deny the arrest and/or refuse to reveal the whereabouts of the detainee. Alternatively the person may have been arrested by a secret police force, possibly operating in unconstitutional and/or illegal ways. This happened frequently during the civil conflicts in Latin America from the 1950s to the 1980s.

Case Study: Detention Because of Discontent

In west Cambodia in the early 1990s, the local driver and vehicle of an international aid agency were held by a local Khmer Rouge (KR) group. The group demanded to speak to a foreigner or they would kill the driver. The only foreign staff member in the area office was a relatively inexperienced woman. The agency had no policy for managing this sort of situation, except to follow the advice of local staff, and there was no radio link to the country office in the capital to ask for advice. The woman decided to proceed to the KR-held village. Her decision was informed by the fact that, up to that time, no foreigners had been targeted by the KR, and by the consideration that she could not risk the life of the driver (local staff had advised against contacting the government military for fear that it might lead to a confrontation and the immediate killing of the driver).

The woman set off with a VHF radio that enabled her to keep in contact with the local office of another agency. As it turned out the KR were upset about what they perceived to have been 'broken promises' about providing wells, a school and a clinic in the area under their control. These promises had been made by another agency which, in the meantime, had withdrawn without further word. The driver, the expatriate woman and two other local staff accompanying her were held for six weeks during which time they were treated reasonably. Negotiations took place between the agency and the KR, first through a monk whom both sides knew well, and subsequently over the radio. The KR opportunistically shifted their demands fairly quickly to a large amount of money. The agency remained firm that it would not pay a ransom. In the end the staff were released in return for a promise of community aid to the KR-held area on a par with what was provided to other areas.

13.1.3 Abduction

This refers to the forcible capture and removal of a person in an illegal way, but which does not lead to any demand. There can be various reasons for abduction: the Khmer Rouge and the Burmese army often abducted local people for the purposes of forced labour; young men can be 'abducted' into the army as 'forced conscripts';

young girls can be abducted and forced into 'marriage' or used as sexual slaves; or people are abducted for political reasons. In this last case they are often tortured and murdered – another frequent practice during the conflicts in Latin America.

13.1.4 Kidnapping

This refers to forced capture and detention with the explicit purpose of obtaining concessions from the captive or others associated with him/her. In this case the life and liberation of the kidnapped person is dependent upon the fulfilment of certain conditions. The concessions sought might be of a political nature (eg, the kidnap of a family member to force a politician not to stand for election, or of public figures to force a government to make legal concessions to the criminals), or they might be of an economic nature as part of an extortion tactic (eg, the kidnap of Basque business leaders who refuse to pay ETA) or simply for ransom. As the earlier example from Cambodia shows, a 'detention' can turn into a 'kidnapping'.

13.1.5 Hostage-taking

Kidnapping and hostage-taking are sometimes used interchangeably, but here the latter term is used to describe a situation of siege. In such a situation the criminals and their hostages have been located and surrounded by security forces; the criminals threaten the hostages as part of their strategy of escape. A kidnapping can turn into a hostage/siege situation when the security forces trace the kidnappers. However not every hostage situation is the result of a kidnapping. For example, criminals surprised during a robbery may decide on the spot to take some hostages to use in negotiating their escape.

13.2 Risk Reduction

In terms of reducing risk, a lot depends on the context and on where the threat comes from. Even then it is not always possible to anticipate and prevent such a situation occurring.

The type of detention referred to here can be prevented or at least quickly or fairly amicably resolved if you are aware of which areas and which groups benefit from aid and which do not and therefore might feel discriminated against, and consequently make sure that as many as possible in your areas of operations know who you are and what role you are playing. The way in which programmes are executed, and the interactional skills of programme staff, are important in this. Transparency, good communications, integrity and respectful attitudes help as well.

Abductions of social activists or perceived opposition figures, with the intention of torturing and/or murdering them, are not easy to prevent. Strategies used in Latin America often consisted of the person at risk going 'underground', staying with friends, regularly moving house, possibly changing appearance and, in extreme situations, being smuggled abroad. A less drastic form of protection consisted of constant accompaniment by foreign human rights/peace activists.

Humanitarian agency staff will not typically find themselves in this situation, though national staff may be potential targets. Abduction is a delicate issue, as the perception is that it is a political matter and aid agencies are wary of being seen to 'meddle' in local politics. This should not, however, be an argument for avoiding responsibility; a first step might be for the agency to clarify its ethical position and where it draws the line in terms of its responsibility in such a situation. The reverse can also happen: a person at risk could be recruited as a national staff member of an international aid agency as a strategy of protection. The effectiveness of this approach will depend on the perceived political importance of the person concerned and the influence or prestige of the agency's home government. In certain contexts this strategy can also be effective where categories of people rather than individuals are at risk, for example, young males at risk of being conscripted or abducted and murdered as supporters of, or sympathisers with, the 'enemy'.

The key question is whether membership of an (international) agency can override the social or political identity of the vulnerable person.

13.2.1 Strategies to Control Risk

In recent years attention has mainly focused on the kidnapping of aid workers (the situation in the northern Caucasus is a paradigmatic example). Strategies to control risk include the following:

Know the country you are going to
In the northern Caucasus, for example, kidnapping is a 'cultural tradition'. Past incidents have also revealed other countries to be higher risk, for example, Colombia, Somalia, Sierra Leone, Yemen, Tajikistan, Algeria.

Raise an immediate alert when a kidnapping is reported
Kidnapping, especially for ransom, is seen as a copycat crime; people realise that it is a quick way of making a lot of money and this leads to a rapid increase in kidnappings.

Put yourself under local protection

Foreigners may be a more desirable target for kidnapping (for ransom) because they are outside the local social system. Kidnapping a local person would mobilise large social groups into retaliation, particularly in countries/areas with strong clan or extended family dynamics and rules of collective responsibility. In environments where a host is responsible for the well-being of his guest and will mobilise his men to protect his guest as if he were one of his own, it might be a good idea to obtain local (traditional) protection. Likewise, taking respected 'elders' along when travelling may also offer a form of protection. Less drastic forms of this approach might include operating a policy of expatriate staff always having to be accompanied by a local person when they travel, and perhaps even co-residing with local staff. Only good knowledge of the context can say whether this tactic will reduce the risk rather than lead to a situation in which two or more staff members are kidnapped.

Reduce visibility

Expatriate aid workers have been kidnapped on their way to and from airports. Reducing visibility might mean staff travelling in a taxi rather than an easily identifiable agency vehicle. Of course, people have also been kidnapped by captors disguised as taxi drivers. You therefore need to make sure you have a bona fide taxi; otherwise use agency vehicles. If there is a suspicion that your radio communications can be overheard you could operate a policy of expatriate staff not identifying themselves when travelling. For example, only local staff might be allowed to talk over the radio (in their own language), as they would when travelling without an expatriate colleague. Information about movement plans, routes and travel times should be encoded (Chapter 16).

Reduce exposure

Reduction of visibility and exposure also extends to site protection measures, including avoiding a residence on the ground floor and strict rules for the identification of strangers (Chapter 9). A more drastic measure is to withdraw those staff members considered at risk. In the northern Caucacus, for example, as Chechnya became too dangerous, agencies moved their headquarters first to Nazran in Ingushetia and then even further to Vladikavkaz in north Ossetia.

Countersurveillance

In simple terms this means 'watch to see if someone is watching you'. A successful kidnapping normally needs planning, and the perpetrators will be watching the residence, office and movements of their identified target for some time before making their move. They may try to find out more about the residence by presenting themselves as a servicemen, or checking the locks of doors and windows while staff are away. They may follow you in a car to establish your routines and identify the ideal point at which to strike. Countersurveillance means being observant of your surroundings and watching for anything unusual. Doing this effectively requires skill, but also constant attention and knowledge about the local environment to the extent that you have a feeling about who belongs in your locality and who does not.

Avoid routines

People perceived to be at risk should try and avoid routine behaviour. This is not easy to maintain and often the options are limited. They are also still likely to fall into a pattern, but a more complex one. While this offers no absolute guarantee it does make them a more difficult target. The kidnappers may therefore decide to focus on someone else.

Armed protection

This is a more extreme form of hardening yourself as a target. If you are at risk armed protection probably needs to be full-time: at the residence, office and during all movements; also during the weekend and leisure time! Be aware, however, of certain caveats: your armed guards may not turn out to be as effective as you thought – either because they find themselves surprised and outnumbered and are not ready to risk their own lives, or because they are part of a social environment in which killings between 'locals' lead to group mobilisation and therefore escalation, which they are not prepared to carry out on behalf of a foreigner.

Public policy of no ransom

Aid agencies are urged to make it publicly known that they will not pay ransom. It is hoped that this will act as a discouragement. However, its preventive value should not be overestimated. If business people are being kidnapped in the same environment and if the business community pays ransom, criminal gangs or so-called rebel movements may still try their chances with aid workers. Also, maintaining the policy becomes very difficult if the kidnappers are prepared to start maiming and killing their captives.

13.2.2 The Limits of Risk Reduction

Nothing short of removing those at risk from the risk environment, or possibly enlisting the protection of a very powerful local authority/social group, will provide 'complete' security. In the northern Caucasus even people under armed guard have been kidnapped from cars and from their residences. A well-prepared, determined, well-armed, brutal gang is hard to stop.

13.3 ▌ Crisis Management: Detention, Arrest and Abduction

13.3.1 Detention

In case of detention the key issue for those detained will be to negotiate skilfully. As situations can differ widely, no precise guidelines can be offered, but certain principles seem generally valid.

Calling upon national authorities or adopting a heavy-handed approach to this type of situation can be counterproductive, and can increase rather than decrease antagonism towards you.

13.3.2 Arrest

Guidelines: Negotiating Release from Detention

Focus on negotiating – not a settlement, but a way out.

- The objective of your negotiation should be permission for you to return to base.
- A conciliatory method of communication should be developed rather than becoming antagonistic – ie, steer the situation towards defusion rather than escalation.
- To this effect, listen to those detaining you and try to find out what really motivates them and what they want or hope for.
- Do not make promises in order to obtain a quick release, but be sympathetic to the captors' requests and make it clear you are taking note of them and will follow them up. However, you should also indicate that you are not in a position to make final decisions or firm commitments. You can agree to meet again after you have returned to base and consulted with your colleagues.
- If the detention continues, or you cannot negotiate a way out, then make it clear that you have no decision making authority and must communicate with your headquarters. Negotiate to be able to be allowed to do this.

If a staff member is arrested and his/her whereabouts are unknown, the first priority is to establish where s/he is and under whose authority. For this you will need to be assertive and to visit all relevant local authorities. You will also need to inform the embassy in the case of an international staff member, and to be very persistent and insistent that you must know where the person is.

When it is clear who has arrested the staff member and where s/he is, the objective of your action should be to ensure that the person's rights are protected. Insist on his/her right to be visited and to medical and legal assistance; also insist on improvements in the conditions in which s/he is being kept if these are not acceptable. People are often arrested without formal charges being brought, in which case you should focus on a charge being articulated within a determined period of time. The charge may relate to the individual (for example, the accusation that s/he has been involved in some kind of crime) or the organisation (for example, the accusation of spying under cover of humanitarian work). In the latter case you will need to refute the allegation and clear the name of the organisation, and/or argue the defence. Insist on due process of law and seek legal advice accordingly.

In the case of an arrest you will need to liaise with, and manage, the family in the way as you would had there been a kidnapping (see below). Indicate the steps you are undertaking, maintain a direct regular line of communication, remain aware of what steps the family intends or is undertaking, and advise and talk with them if you believe some of these may be counterproductive.

13.3.3 Abduction

As defined in this GPR, abduction is an extremely difficult situation: you may not know where the person is or who has abducted him/her. Moreover, even if you suspect who the perpetrators are you may have no way of contacting them, and even if contact could be established you may have no bargaining power as the staff member has not been abducted to obtain something from you.

If someone has been abducted by a(n unofficial) 'death squad', the strategy of attracting immediate high-level publicity may be tried. This will signal to the authorities that there is widespread international awareness about the fate of the person concerned and that his/her continued 'disappearance' or murder would seriously damage the (inter)national image of the official authorities who fail to establish or maintain the rule of law. This may require rapid cooperation with human rights and other advocacy organisations which are better organised to create that type of publicity. In other cases you may have little option but to disseminate information and an identification picture of the person abducted, and try to find someone who can eventually provide a lead or a contact.

13.4 Crisis Management: Kidnapping

The management of a kidnapping takes place at three levels: at the level of the individual kidnapped, at the field office and at agency headquarters. More than any other incident kidnapping requires specialised expertise. This commonly involves actors other than the agency and management beyond the moment of release.

13.4.1 Surviving a Kidnapping/Hostage Situation

Guidelines: Basic Knowledge and Key Principles for Surviving a Kidnapping/Hostage Situation

• The most dangerous moments are: during the abduction, when the abductee/s is moved hastily because the captors fear that the authorities are near, during a siege situation, and during release. At these particular times the kidnappers will feel threatened and tense and will therefore be more given to violence. Stay calm and avoid adding to the kidnappers' tension through your behaviour.

• During an abduction you will be very probably be blindfolded and sometimes beaten. This is to break down your mental resistance and signal the dire consequences of any attempt to escape or otherwise trick the captors. In addition you may be drugged. Do not resist these tactics, the purpose of which is to keep you quiet. Quietness will actually help you regain composure, pick up information about where you are and who your captors are, and adjust to the shocking change in your situation.

• The place and conditions in which abductees are held can vary widely. You may be kept in the same place or moved several times; you may be alone or with other captives. In some situations captives have walked with their captors for weeks through the bush or the mountains. Some are held in reasonable conditions, others are kept chained to a bed or a radiator. The captors may simply treat you as pawns to obtain something from someone else, or they may show strong hostility towards you and accuse you, for example, of being a spy. It is common for abductees to develop some sort of relationship with their guards and find it difficult to adjust as the guards' change. You should also expect to meet other local people and may be confined in a house where the

Continued...

owners live and bring you food. While these people may be sympathetic to you, they will not take steps to inform the authorities or aid your escape.

- Be prepared to be held for a long period. Some abduction/kidnap situations end quickly, others last for weeks and even months. You should also prepare for ill-treatment, both physically and psychologically, and sometimes consisting of false promises of imminent release and even of fake executions. It will be important to maintain an outward dignity.

- If you are in a group you should try not to be separated. Being confined with someone else in probably difficult circumstances and for a prolonged period of time creates its own pressures, but by and large the ability to share experiences with at least one other person will be a source of support. If you are kept together as a larger group identify a spokesperson, on the basis of ability rather than formal rank to liaise with the captors.

- Securing release is not your problem but that of your organisation. Remain confident that your organisation is doing everything possible on your behalf and at the same time providing support to your friends and relatives – even if you don't hear anything or your captors tell them otherwise. Do not try to escape unless you fear that your captors are planning to kill you, or when you are in good condition, have a good notion of your environment, and are fairly certain of success. Otherwise you may put your life at risk, as well as the lives of others if you are held captive in a group. Play on the fact that you are of most value to your kidnappers alive.

- Never get directly involved in the negotiations for your release. This will only complicate matters. If asked to talk on the radio, telephone or on video say only what you are asked or allowed to say and refuse to 'negotiate' even if pushed forward by your captors.

An attitude of passive cooperation
The same principles apply as for surviving an armed robbery. In other words:

- obey the orders of your captors without appearing servile;

- do not talk tough or threaten your captors; do not threaten to testify against them;
- be careful about eye contact especially during tense moments: eyes can show fear, anger or contempt which can trigger violence. On the other hand, face your captors (it is more difficult to harm someone who is facing you) but avoid making eye contact;
- avoid surprising or alarming your captors: always say what you intend to do and get permission even for something as simple as opening the window;
- keep a low profile and avoid appearing to seek clues to the identities of your captors or to be actively witnessing criminal acts;
- offer persuasive reasons why your captors should not harm you;
- adopt a calm and dignified attitude even if you don't feel that way;
- be conscious of your body language.

Building 'rapport' when the situation appears 'stabilised'

- insist on your humanitarian role, and explain the mandate and operational motives of your agency;
- do not argue politics or ideology with your captors;
- you may develop some sympathy for your captors' cause and point of view. However, remember that this does not justify your abduction/ kidnapping;
- do not believe everything you are told by your captors, who will try to manipulate/destabilise you with good as well as bad news;
- try to build human rapport to generate sympathy as well as respect: do not beg, plead or cry, but do not hesitate to draw attention to human needs and ask for food, something to drink, the use of a toilet, washing facilities, a radio, things to read, etc;
- try to discuss family and children with your captors, ie, topics of mutual interest.

Maintaining physical and mental health
This is very important. You should:

- not give up your personal belongings such as clothes, wristwatch, spectacles, a ring, unless coerced to hand them over;

Continued...

- try to create 'structure' and 'order' in what will be a situation of disorientation, dependency and unpredictability: It is a good idea to organise 'living space', try to keep track of time, and try to establish a daily schedule;
- exercise daily, and stick to a daily fitness programme;
- try to maintain hygiene, stay well groomed and clean;
- maintain your strength by eating and drinking, and asking for palatable food;
- when necessary ask for medicines, books, writing paper, a radio, newspapers, etc;
- do not let your hopes soar when your captors indicate that your release might be imminent – it may simply be a lie or something may intervene;
- think positive, emphasise your values, focus on pleasant memories and scenes, recall plots of books and movies you enjoyed, etc;
- you may be deliberately subjected to humiliating or terrifying experiences such as mock executions. Try to come to terms with the fact that humiliation and fear of pain or death are very normal reactions, and that you should not lose hope.

Communicating

- be prepared to be ordered to speak into a cassette recorder, on the telephone or on the radio, and say only what you are told to say;
- ask whether you can write or send a message to your family in any other way, as well as whether you can receive messages from them;
- if you are 'shown' to one or more press people, bear in mind that the primary interest of the press is in a headline-making story and not in your release;
- avoid being drawn into the negotiation process.

The rescue operation

- try to avoid changing clothes, especially with your captors. This may put you at risk during a rescue operation;
- in the event of a rescue attempt, drop to the ground, seek cover, and keep your hands on your head;
- appropriate identify yourself and be prepared not to be immediately recognised by the rescuers who may handle you roughly until you are identified.

Case Study: Surviving a Kidnapping in Lebanon

In early 1988 an expatriate medical doctor was kidnapped from a refugee camp in Lebanon. He was released after 13 months. In the first few weeks he was treated reasonably: he was given fresh meat, a radio, and a French-language weekly. But the last six months were very difficult: he was moved to an underground cell of 2x3 meters and barely high enough to stand in; the radio and magazine were withdrawn; canned food replaced fresh food, and its quantity and quality deteriorated very much. Attempts were also made to disorient him: for two to three months he was kept in total darkness, then for a similar period in continuous light. The isolation and despair he experienced gave rise to feelings of wanting to commit suicide.

Throughout the ordeal it became personally important to him to keep track of time. This he succeeded in doing fairly well. Initially he had had the radio. Later the toilet-bucket became an aid: given his food intake it would take 10 to 11 days to fill up. Then there was the change in seasonal fruits, and the moment when a guard unexpectedly offered a few sweets with a 'Happy Christmas' in broken English. He realised this meant the end of Ramadan which in that year fell in mid-May. It also meant, depressingly, that he had already spent a year in captivity.

13.4.2 Organisational Management of a Kidnap Crisis

Managing a kidnap crisis is a dynamic process that can last from anywhere between a few hours and several years. It requires close collaboration between headquarters and the field office. Key issues are: the mobilisation of a competent crisis management team; dealing with the family, the authorities and the press; communications with the captors. This GPR highlights some major points for attention.

The critical incident report

A genuine kidnap or hostage situation cannot be managed at field level only. It requires extensive headquarters support. As soon as there is a suspicion or confirmation that a staff member has been kidnapped the field team should send a report with the information required by headquarters and others who will get involved.

> ### Example of a Critical Incident Report Form
>
> Information should be given on:
>
> - the problem (person missing, confirmed kidnapped, arrested, held hostage);
> - the victim (name, nationality, age, gender, position in the office, affiliation if staff of different organisations involved);
> - next of kin (notified or not);
> - what happened (what is known, what is speculation, what is not known);
> - where it occurred, as exactly as possible;
> - when it occurred, as exactly as possible;
> - who did it (known, suspected, speculation, unknown);
> - any contact with captors; what means of contact;
> - what demands, if any;
> - why it occurred (motive stated, speculation);
> - who has been notified/who knows outside the organisation/who you propose to notify outside the organisation;
> - what actions are under way or proposed;
> - whether the press is aware of the incident;
> - what the rest of the team know;
> - other relevant facts, eg, the captive has an injury that prevents him from walking long distances, or can hardly see without glasses that were left behind in the flat, speaks the local language a little or not at all, has just arrived and is totally unfamiliar with local context and culture, etc;
> - which channels for reliable and confidential communications are available with the field office, if any.

The crisis management teams

The field office will set up an incident management team, possibly with someone from headquarters coming down. Headquarters will also mobilise its crisis management team which has overriding authority – ie, the field team does not take decisions or initiatives without headquarters' approval. It is generally easier for headquarters to maintain a 'strategic perspective', and the withdrawal of authority from the field creates an obligatory time lag between requests from the captors and your response – a vital interval for reflection. A 'hot line' will be established between the field office and headquarters.

Kidnap crisis management is initially a full-time job. Staff involved need to be released from their other duties and shielded from unnecessary intrusions so that they can concentrate on the task. They will need their own working space and facilities. They will monitor the situation on a daily basis, and decide on and review policy towards the captors, the family, the authorities, the press, the other agencies. They will need regular rest and relaxation, and support during and after the crisis.

Note that maintaining a coordinated crisis management strategy is a major challenge – especially if people of several nationalities are kidnapped at the same time or are held by the same captors.

Chaos or Coordination in Interagency Crisis Management

Imagine a situation in which an interagency team travelling together is kidnapped. It comprises a Finnish national working for UNICEF, a Turkish national working for UNHCR, a Belgian working for MSF-Holland, an Australian working for CARE International, and a French national, seconded by the French Red Cross through the International Federation to the national Red Cross society.

Individual agency approaches clearly risk undermining each other or giving the captors room to play one off against the other. The different stakeholders must constitute one joint crisis management team (at field and HQ level). Obviously each of the relevant agencies will want to be involved. It is imperative, however, that members are chosen for their skill and competence in managing this type of incident rather than as representing their respective agencies. It is also strongly advised that outside experts not affiliated with any agency should be bought in to help the team maintain objectivity and focus.

Even if the captors make rapid contact you need to establish contact with the family and the authorities immediately, and develop a strategy towards the press. You will also need to manage the information with other agencies, and the impact of the event on the rest of the team in the organisation, in the country concerned, and elsewhere.

Managing relations with the family

Just as with other serious incidents, the family must be informed immediately. It is vital that they hear about the kidnapping from the organisation first, and not through the press or a third party, as this would immediately undermine their trust in the agency. The following is written with a focus on kidnapped international staff, but it can also apply to kidnapped national staff:

Establish and maintain trust
when the family do not trust the organisation, its competence in handling the situation, or its honesty in respecting their rights, they are likely to undertake their own initiatives and/or publicly criticise the organisation. This complicates matters for the agency.

Obtain information about the kidnapped person from the family
and perhaps from friends; general personality, mental state prior to the kidnapping; possible concerns on his/her mind; physical endurance, special needs, etc.

Develop a clear approach towards the family
you will need to balance the family's right to know and remain informed with the need to maintain the integrity of your crisis management strategy. Having an information strategy will help you to decide what to tell them/show them, and what not.

Point of contact
a senior agency staff member with good interpersonal skills should be designated as the focal point for the family. In principle, this person should be contactable directly and at all times. Maintain regular and sensible contact with the family: it is not helpful to inform them about every unconfirmed rumour, raising hopes that are dashed soon afterwards, nor is it helpful to maintain a prolonged silence for weeks on end because you have 'nothing to report'. This liaison person will also need support and occasional relief from what is a demanding responsibility.

The family will want time and attention from the agency
information; advice on what they can usefully do and perhaps should not do; and a feeling that the agency, with or without the authorities, is doing everything possible to obtain a safe release.

Expect fluctuating attitudes from the family
as the situation drags on. This is perfectly normal. They may come to voice doubts about your agency, the authorities, the strategy pursued, and so on.

Expect initiatives from the family
They will be tempted to undertake action themselves: to go to the press; to go to the country where their relative has been kidnapped; to seek to establish their own line of negotiation. The family will also be more prepared to pay the ransom and may start selling assets to collect the money. For them the life of their relative is worth more than any money; for the organisation and/or the

government, non-payment of the ransom is driven by the wish not to create a precedent and inspire more kidnappings. The family have their own right of initiative but you can advise them about the possible consequences of their actions and the risks to the ongoing negotiations.

This situation may be somewhat different when it concerns national staff. In such situations the family, because of its knowledge of the local culture and society and its own networks of contacts, may sometimes be better placed to take the lead. This may well be the case when the kidnapping is motivated by social or political rivalries between local social groups such as clans. But local people may be in no better position when a criminal gang or a politically motivated group is responsible for the kidnapping.

The family will need support
A third party close to the family, such as a friend or a priest or mullah, could play the role of close 'accompanier'. But it may be better to (also) bring in a professional counsellor, in which case it is in the interests of the agency and of the negotiations that a good relationship is developed between this person and the agency. In some cases a larger support group will materialise around the family. Become involved with them, give advice on what they can meaningfully do and what could be counterproductive.

Managing relations with the authorities
'Authorities' here refers to the host government and, in the case of an international staff member, the home government.

Invoking the authorities
In situations of detention an agency may try to solve the situation by itself. When it comes to kidnapping, however, it is generally advisable to inform the authorities at once as they will, in all likelihood, get to know at some point and will find it irritating if you failed to inform them. Even if a kidnapping occurs in an area of the country not under the control of the government, they should be informed. You will have to provide the facts about the kidnapping as well as details about the person kidnapped.

A policy towards the authorities
Headquarters and field staff will need to decide upon a policy towards the host and home governments. The national authorities may have access to information and networks that are not available to foreigners and even to individual nationals, and therefore be in the best position to secure the release of the kidnapped. At the same time their decisions may be guided by considerations other than simply the well-being of the kidnapped, for example:

13

Detention, Arrest,
Abduction,
Kidnapping &
Hostage Taking

- a concern to be seen to be assuming their responsibilities;
- a concern to appear, nationally and internationally, in control of law and order;
- distrust in the capacity of an aid organisation to manage a 'security' problem professionally;
- criticism of the aid agency for having failed to seek or heed guidance from the authorities regarding security;
- not wanting an aid agency to enter into negotiations with 'criminals', 'terrorists' or a rebel group (in some countries it is illegal to make and maintain contact with kidnappers);
- concern to bring the situation to a quick solution (often national authorities and national security personnel hold that this requires a combined strategy of negotiation and pressure on the captors, with the pressure coming from police search actions).

What you will want to negotiate and agree is:

- that the safety and well-being of the kidnapped should be the primary concern;
- that the authorities will refrain from a rescue attempt by force without the consent of the family and the agency;
- confidentiality vis-a-vis the media, unless a different strategy is agreed;
- involvement in the crisis management group set up by the authorities. If that is not acceptable then the involvement of an embassy official or at least an agreed framework of contact between the national authorities and the aid agency (the agency cannot abdicate its responsibility towards the kidnapped);
- an agreement on the overall strategy to be pursued;
- agreement on the choice of a communicator (see below).

You will also want to obtain advice from the embassy and their support for your relations with the national authorities. The same issues need to be discussed and ideally agreed with the home government. In the home country, collaboration will be required between headquarters and the home government regarding the relationship with the family.

Managing the press

You will need a proactive strategy vis-à-vis the press. Do not get overtaken by the media.

Guidelines for Managing the Press

Generally speaking, try to exclude the press as publicity renders the captors more nervous and suspicious and can complicate negotiations. Contact the national and international press and ask them not to report the story, or not to provide any details, as this puts the life of the captives at risk. However, there may be circumstances when you want to seek publicity: if your colleagues have been captured by a group that is concerned about its international image then a high-profile publicity campaign will help in persuading them that retaining the captives is not in their long-term interests. On the other hand an aid worker could be kidnapped with the deliberate intent of the captors getting attention from the international media. It may therefore be the captors who bring in the press. This is highly dangerous; it turns the situation into an international spectacle with the killing of the captive as a possible 'dramatic climax'. To counter this strategy you need to persuade the press not to go along with it.

If the story is out and you cannot avoid questions, limit what you say to basic, minimal facts. Always assume that the captors monitor the news and may hear what you are reported to have said in the home country, thousands of miles away. It is not advisable to try and communicate, let alone negotiate, with the captors through the public media. Media messages get distorted and undermine 'genuine' messages as well as the negotiation process. Engage with editors and journalists so that they work with you rather than against you. The family may insist on making a public appeal through the press: manage that request constructively.

There may be indications that the captives are allowed to read the newspapers or to listen to the radio or watch television. Under these circumstances you may consider using the press to try to send a supportive message to the captives. Various examples show that morale is boosted if captives hear themselves mentioned in the news.

13 Detention, Arrest, Abduction, Kidnapping & Hostage Taking

> ## Case Study: Irresponsible and Dangerous Press Coverage
>
> Unfortunately not all journalists follow professional ethics, and news today is a commercial and competitive business. This can lead to unpleasant surprises as this example shows.
>
> In 1998 a number of Red Cross workers were kidnapped at Mogadishu airport in Somalia. As their captivity continued and they were increasingly intimidated by the kidnappers, their emotions and their ability to cope became more volatile. One day the group were unexpectedly taken out of their room and forced in front of the camera of an international press agency, which must have paid the captors to be allowed to film the hostages. The hostages refused to issue a declaration. The cameraman then aggravated the situation by turning the machinegun of one of the guards towards one of the hostages to get a more dramatic pose. The guard became agitated and more aggressive and on the spot demanded US$100,000 per person. The images caused the agency and the relatives deep distress. The event increased the risk and imperilled the ongoing negotiations.

Attending to your other staff

Internal communications with other agency staff are important and need to be proactive and well-managed. You will need to anticipate questions and maintain staff morale and confidence in the agency, while at the same time avoiding everyone else getting 'involved' and constantly commenting.

Managing relationships with other agencies

Kidnap situations carry a high-risk, are highly sensitive and need to be handled discreetly. As with sexual assault and rape, however, the need for discreteness needs to be balanced with responsibility for the security of all aid workers, including those of other agencies. Case analysis indicates that this is not generally understood.

As already noted kidnapping is a crime that inspires others to imitate the initial perpetrators. The kidnap of an aid worker signals risk for other staff members of the same agency as well as of other aid agencies. The immediate reaction should therefore entail a review of the agency's security measures as well as informing other agencies to put them on alert.

Discussions may arise between the various agencies about risk-control strategies and about aspects of the management of the situation, especially the role of the authorities and the issue of ransom. It is difficult to be prescriptive for this type of situation, but guiding principles could include:

- Every agency remains responsible for the security of its own staff. This also involves giving staff the possibility of making an informed choice: if individuals prefer to leave a high-risk area that wish should be respected.
- What one agency does has implications for the security of all others. There is therefore a need for collective responsibility for security.
- An agency whose staff have been kidnapped retains the responsibility to choose its own approach. Yet it may be sensible to listen to advice from others with experience in the area, especially with regard to the possible security implications of certain strategies.
- In principle no ransom should be paid as this increases the general risk: while it may obtain the release of one person it certainly sets a precedent and creates the risk that many others will be kidnapped. In reality there have been instances when agencies have paid ransom and denied doing so. The reluctance to admit that ransom has been paid is understandable, but paying ransom also dramatically changes the overall situation. Even though what ultimately counts is not so much what agencies do but what potential kidnappers believe they did or will do, it is advisable to inform others in strict confidence. At the very least, if a staff member of another agency is subsequently kidnapped that agency should be informed that a ransom has previously been paid, as this will be a vital element in their analysis and the development of their strategy.

13.4.3 Communicating and Negotiating with the Captors

Communicating with the captors

Kidnapping, as understood here, is deliberate and for a purpose. Normally the captors will establish contact to make clear their demands and conditions. The following box summarises key principles for communication with kidnappers.

Negotiating with the captors

The crisis management team should retain control over the negotiations. They should not have therefore be in direct communication with the captors. The decision making power should be withdrawn from the incident management team at field level and a 'communicator' posted between the field team and the captors, the purpose being to create a time lag to allow for internal and external consultation, reflection and analysis before responding. Competent communicators and outside experts working with you will help retain this control.

Guidelines: Communication with Kidnappers

- **Logbook:** As soon as a kidnapping is suspected a logbook should be started at field level and at HQ in which full details are kept of the time and means of communication, those involved and the contents of the communications. The authorities may advise you to try to tape communications as the choice of a particular word, the tone of voice, and background noises can all provide certain insights. At the same time if the captors become aware that you are taping communications they will lose trust and may become nervous and angry. The communications logbook needs to be expanded, or complemented, with a crisis management logbook that records who agreed to follow up on what, what feedback may have been received, and what key arguments and considerations informed the decisions taken.

- **Proof of identity:** You may be approached by someone pretending to be the captor. Therefore you first need to obtain confirmation that your interlocutors do indeed hold the kidnapped person. Ask for details of proof that this is the case.

- **Proof of life:** You want to be certain that your colleague has not been killed during or after the kidnapping. A cassette with his/her voice, a picture or a video is no absolute proof as your colleague could have been killed afterwards. Check by obtaining from the family or a close friend an intimate detail that the captors cannot possibly know (eg, the name of the closest school friend of the kidnapped person during his or her teenage years, or the identification of an event during a memorable family holiday many years ago). As the situation continues you may want to check in this way regularly to remain sure that the captive is still alive. The best proof is to directly hear the person kidnapped. If no proof of identity and life is provided you should not pursue the negotiations.

- **Proof of identity of captors:** Agree a code word with the captors whereby they identify themselves so that you are sure you are continuing to be approached by the right people and not by impostors.

- **No decision making authority:** Make it clear that you have no decision making authority and need to consult with others whom you might not be able to reach immediately. You are not, therefore, in a position to agree any demands right away. This gives you time to reflect and room for manoeuvre.

- **Agree communications times:** Try to get agreement about the next contact; ask how you can contact the captors, for example through a third party or a message in a specific newspaper, etc.

- **Humanise the captives:** Always refer to the captives by name. Encourage good treatment: indicate any special needs they may have, for example, spectacles or special medical treatment. Signal their human concerns: family, children and whether a way can be found to arrange an exchange of messages.

- **Do not agree to go to a specified place for an encounter:** If there is very strong pressure to do so, insist on detailed guarantees for your own safety. You may be kidnapped as well.

- **Listen carefully to the demands of the captors, and also their style:** What seems to be the motivation behind the kidnapping, and how do the captors appear: aggressive and threatening, rational and factual, highly emotional, etc? What tone of voice and style of speech is most appropriate to defuse the situation and establish some 'rapport'?

- **Language problems and translation:** If the captors do not have a good command of English, for example, then communication will be difficult and frustrations on both sides may render the situation more tense. You will need a communicator with local language skills.

13 Detention, Arrest, Abduction, Kidnapping & Hostage Taking

The communicators

The position of the communicator is a tactical one: he/she is the screen between the incident management group and the captors. As kidnappings can last a long time, over time you may need more than one communicator. Their task is simply to convey messages. In order to fulfil this task, however, they will need to be well prepared through, for example, simulation exercises, as inevitably there will be unexpected demands and pressures from the captors. The communicators are not party to the discussions of the crisis management team, which considers scenarios and hypotheses and formulates responses. Clearly good communicators are intelligent, verbally skilled, stress-resistant and disciplined. They should also have good knowledge of the local language (dialect) and local area.

Outside experts

'Experts' in kidnap management may present themselves spontaneously, be proposed by the host and/or home government, or sought out by the agency which has no in-house expertise. Such 'experts' can play a useful role by offering an objective perspective on the analysis and the crisis management approach, by anticipating scenarios and ensuring preparedness, and by confirming that what is done is done well and that the 'ups and downs' are 'normal'. However, they become a problem if they pursue someone else's agenda rather than the agency's, start imposing strategies, and/or force themselves onto you as 'negotiators'. They are also a problem if they are not highly sensitive to the local context and come with ready made approaches from totally different situations and scenarios.

The 'local' negotiator

An intermediary can be also come forward 'spontaneously' from within the community, can be sought out by the agency, be proposed or approached by the authorities, or even put forward by the captors.

It is not uncommon for locally respected and influential people to get involved in kidnap-resolution. Elders have often played an influential role in Somali and Afghan society, for example. In the Caucasus, influential local business people have played catalysing roles. In a situation of high acceptance, and where the community retains a measure of influence over the captors, a trustworthy local person can secure the release of the captives. It should be made quite clear, however, that they cannot make commitments on your behalf without your prior consent. In the face of a well-organised criminal element that is more autonomous from the community, on the other hand, traditional leaders may be fairly powerless.

The question of trust is crucial, and can be a problem. There may remain uncertainty about on whose behalf the intermediary is acting? Are they on your side, or do they perhaps have hidden connections with the captors? Whose game are they playing? Who controls the negotiations?

The official negotiator

In siege situations (see below), and sometimes in the management of a kidnap, the authorities will put forward an official negotiator. The negotiator's strategy will be to try to build up a process that moves from stabilising the situation, towards 'rapport', and eventually to compromise. The situation will be framed as a problem in need of solving, and the emphasis will be on reaching a solution through dialogue.

The first step will be to establish a climate for dialogue. The use of 'we' rather than 'me and you' in the conversation will be balanced with an explanation of the constraints on the agency/authorities. Initially, the focus will probably be on some minor issues on which agreement can be reached. This will establish firm ground on which to base the discussion of more difficult issues. Throughout the negotiations it is generally advisable to allow the captors not to lose face; also when they agree to release the captives. The situation will remain delicate throughout and any sense of humiliation or defeat could trigger violence. If the negotiator is fielded by the authorities there is always the risk that other, more political, considerations than the concern for the safety and release of the captives, may influence the decisions. Sometimes a prestigious non-governmental entity may propose an envoy to try and mediate the release of the captives. A risk for the envoy/negotiator is that s/he will be lured into a trap and also kidnapped.

13.5 A Hostage/Siege Situation

As mentioned earlier it is not uncommon for the security forces to try to trace the captives and attempt either their release by force or the creation of a siege situation to try and force the captors to surrender. This is a high-risk strategy as the captives may be killed by their captors when the latter find themselves (virtually) trapped. The captors may even commit suicide, killing the captives at the same time. Alternatively one or more captives may be injured or killed in the confusion and crossfire that often accompanies a forced release. Siege situations or attempts at forced liberation should not be tried without the agreement of the family and of the agency. However, the approach should not be totally rejected: if the captors start maiming or killing captives to step up the pressure, or if there is a risk that the captives may die through weakness and exhaustion after a prolonged captivity, a rescue attempt by force may be the option of last resort.

As an aid agency representative you will generally not be allowed to be present during a siege situation. Case analysis points to a number of reasons why siege situations can go wrong. From the agency's point of view there are perhaps three elements to watch and try to influence:

1. Whether or not those carrying out the siege have a clear overall command. If not, uncoordinated actions will occur that can imperil the lives of the hostages.
2. Whether or not the commander has a balanced attitude to the two-pronged approach of persuasion (negotiation) and pressure (threat of forceful intervention). Both build on different attitudes to the captors which can be potentially contradictory and therefore difficult to reconcile.
3. Whether or not the troops have a clear description of the hostages in order to be able to differentiate them from the captors, and whether they have been given clear instructions only to fire on those firing at them. (It is not uncommon for captors to dress the hostages in clothes similar to their own, which increases the risk of the hostages being shot during a rescue operation.)

13.6 Managing the Return of the Abducted/Kidnapped

The return of an abducted/kidnapped person also needs to be fully managed. Several competing demands will have to be taken into account simultaneously:

- the emotional and communication needs of those released, and their family and friends;
- the need for rest, tranquillity and possibly medical care;
- the wish of the authorities (host and home governments) for urgent debriefing of those released;
- the desire of the press to get hold of the story.

Other agencies also need to be informed that the situation has been resolved. These different interests can lead to conflicting pressures which might harm the released and threaten to overwhelm the agency.

Case Study: Overtaken by Rumour

During the final phase of negotiations with the kidnappers of an aid worker in Somalia the need to control rumours became a real challenge. When the situation was still tense another aid agency, without cross-checking, unexpectedly announced that the captives had been released and had left on a plane the previous day. This rumour circulated immediately within the aid community and was taken up by the local press. It took the agency two frantic hours to find out where the announcement had come from, and to issue a correction.

The crisis management teams, at both field and HQ level, therefore need to prepare themselves to:

- attend to the needs of the released, and to effect communication and, if feasible, reunion with loved ones, as a priority;
- provide accurate information rapidly to other agencies with, if deemed necessary, a request to abstain from public comment, and an indication of when further information will be provided;
- manage the press and retain control over the organisation a press conference with the released and/or the family (eg, how long the interviews last, how many questions to be allowed, etc);
- arrange for the authorities to meet and interview the released.

The needs of the released and their family must come first. But you may not be able to withhold others from seeing the released for a prolonged period of time. The situation will need to be proactively managed in consultation with the released and their family: determine the circumstances in which others can have first contact indicating, if need be, that more extended contact can follow later. At all times accompany the released and the family, including when they are interviewed by the authorities. In consultation with them intervene to conclude an encounter if it is becoming too much of a strain.

Surviving a prolonged and tense abduction and/or arrest, and certainly a kidnapping and hostage situation, is a traumatic experience. It takes a long time to 'fit' such an event into one's life experience, self-image and worldview. Survivors will need long-term accompaniment and access to professional support; so may their loved ones, who also have lived through a very anxious experience and should not be overlooked. As with rape survivors, the agency will have to find the 'right' professional counsellor. The wrong one or the wrong type of 'counselling' can itself become a stressful and disorienting experience, as some aid workers who have been kidnapped have discovered.

13.7 Preparation and Training

At organisational level
- identify who would be a competent member of a crisis management team;
- train the crisis management team, including using simulations of kidnap scenarios and involve operations, personnel, finance, press, and legal department staff as well as senior management;
- discuss with the Ministry of Foreign Affairs what help you can expect if a staff member is kidnapped overseas;
- identify qualified external expertise for the crisis management, and for post-crisis support to the family and the released;
- keep a record of all international staff involved, including the contact details of close relatives, and a record of special medical conditions/attention points;
- kidnap insurance is sometimes taken out by business corporations for top executives. It may be considered null and void if the fact that someone is insured becomes more widely known. It is probably too expensive for aid agencies;
- it should be clear who is responsible for what in case of an

Continued...

Detention, Arrest, Abduction, Kidnapping & Hostage Taking

13

abduction/arrest/kidnapping under collaborative agreements with other agencies that involve staff secondments;

- articulate an internal policy that spells out clearly what responsibilities and obligations the agency assumes with regard to staff abducted/kidnapped or arrested and their relatives. Such a policy will not only clarify mutual understanding and expectations but also legitimise internal resource allocation and skill development and enhance accountability when an incident occurs;
- create a policy that staff should be not be deployed in high-risk areas without being fully informed of the risk in advance, and without their explicit consent;
- constantly monitor high-risk zones.

At field-office level

- establish and maintain contact with the embassy and other diplomatic presence such as the UN or the Organisation for Security and Cooperation in Europe;
- in a high-risk environment, know whom to contact in the ministry of the interior;
- identify the structure of command of the national security forces in your area of operation;

- identify and get acquainted with a reliable and competent local criminal lawyer;
- learn about the legal procedures for arrest in the country;
- learn about the government's policy on contacts with kidnappers, if any;
- constitute a competent crisis management team, and provide specialist training;
- keep a full record of staff details, including ID and family contact details;
- deploy a low-profile 'monitoring/witness car' to follow vehicles carrying persons at risk of kidnapping (to observe details during a kidnap and see in what direction the captors disappear; it should not intervene and try to prevent the kidnap or follow the captors to the ultimate hide-out as this might endanger the life of 'witnesses' and deprive you of their information).

At the individual level

- prior to deployment make sure your domestic affairs are in order. Ideally the following should be readily accessible: birth certificate; marriage/divorce record; insurance policies; medical/dental records; naturalisation papers; adoption/guardianship records; military record; power of attorney; key financial papers; list of names and contact details of doctor, lawyer and other key professionals;
- be aware of the risks and of the approaches to try and control it;
- maintain constant alertness, pay attention to small signals, to what s/he hears people talking about;
- read, and reflect for a while, on the guidelines for survival in this Good Practice Review;
- know the physical environment, carry a map if possible/appropriate, but also develop a mental map;
- carry a 'constant companion' – a list of key telephone numbers/radio frequencies of agency and other resource people; also memorise some key numbers in case of loss;
- carry a blood group card and a note on special medical requirements, also in the local languages;
- carry family pictures, including children;
- if on medication, carry a small supply; carry a spare set of contact lenses or spectacles in a high-risk environment;
- wear good walking boots;
- have a small amount of money hidden in boots/belt.

13 Detention, Arrest, Abduction, Kidnapping & Hostage Taking

14 Withdrawal and Hibernation

14 Withdrawal and Hibernation

14.1 Planning

14.1.1 Assumptions and Basic Scenarios

Evacuation is an important part of an agency's security planning. It is important, however, to be aware of three common but often misleading assumptions:

1. **Gradual deterioration:** Evacuation is conceived as the ultimate step in a gradual reduction of exposure – from suspension of movements of certain types of staff, to suspension of operations, to partial withdrawal of staff from a site, to total withdrawal of staff from a site, to closure of activities. This logical progression is reflected in different security phases or 'alert states'. These range from 'normal' to 'acute crisis', with full evacuation taking place in the last 'state'. Bear in mind, however, that testimony and case analysis provide ample examples of aid agencies being overtaken by events in a very rapid deterioration of the situation.

2. **Evacuation according to plan:** These assumptions lead to a concentration on and investment in detailed planning. This may also be the wrong thing to do. Testimony and case analysis indicate that not infrequently:

    - staff do not refer to the plan in a sudden and acute crisis;
    - important elements have been overlooked and not planned for;
    - things simply don't go according to plan because of external actors and factors.

3. **Evacuation possible:** This again may be a wrong assumption. Testimony and case analysis offer ample evidence of situations in which evacuation routes were blocked, where the logistical capacity for evacuation was insufficient, or where it simply became too dangerous to try and evacuate so that staff had to stay put and 'weather the crisis' (hibernation).

Certain elements in evacuation and hibernation can be systematically explored and planned:

- Where will you go to?
- Who goes and who stays?

- How will you go?
- What goes and what stays?
- Will you exit on your own or with other agencies?
- Will those who stay continue to manage the programmes and if so, how?

Other key questions, however, cannot be answered with absolute certainty. For example, whether you will be able to go will depend on situational factors not totally under your control. In addition, when you go may be a matter of very difficult situational judgement.

The three basic scenarios to be thought through are:

1. **Evacuation:** the physical withdrawal of staff from a crisis spot across an international border.
2. **Relocation:** the physical withdrawal of staff (and assets) from a crisis spot to a safer location within the same country.
3. **Hibernation:** staff staying behind in one or more concentration sites in a crisis spot because evacuation is impossible or too dangerous.

14.1.2 The Limits of Planning Through 'Security Phases'

Many agency security guidelines refer to three to five security phases or states of alert, with a number of prescribed actions to be initiated as one or the other is declared (Annex 3). A security phase may cover the whole country; alternatively different areas of a country may be given a different security phase status.

Thinking about security phases and planning mandatory action for each is a useful planning exercise. But it is important to understand the limitations of this approach as a crisis management tool. Some of these are:

Lack of linear progression

Real-life situations do not necessarily gradually deteriorate and/or gradually improve. A situation can suddenly deteriorate from conditions corresponding to Phase 1 to conditions corresponding to Phase 5 – in other words, you may be overtaken by events.

A false sense of control

Identifying what security phase you should put yourself in does not guarantee that you will be able to implement the plan, especially in more acute crisis situations.

Interpreting the situation

Even if you develop a set of indicators that signal that a certain state of alert has to be declared, incomplete information and the difficulties in correctly interpreting a messy reality may still make it difficult to decide whether you should move to a different state of alert. In short, reading risk involves interpretation and judgement, which means there may be differing opinions. Some will err on the side of caution; others will not want to 'overreact'.

Interagency differences

Different agencies may interpret the same situation differently, and consequently put themselves in different security phases with correspondingly different security measures. For example, in Angola in November 1992 when UN agencies were effectively implementing Phase 3, the UNAVEM II mission (military observer/peace keeping) was technically still in Phase 1. This sort of situation might happen for a number of reasons:

- different lines of command and decision making, leading to different speeds in switching from one phase to another;
- different interpretations of the situation and therefore different risk assessments;
- different mandates: an agency with an emergency response mandate, for example, the ICRC, MSF or UNHCR, will appreciate risk differently from a development NGO, or for example, the World Health Organisation.

Given the above, you should bear in mind the following:

- if you have chosen to be a formal part of the UN security umbrella you will be obliged to adopt the mandatory measures that come with the UN 'security phases' (Annex 3);
- evacuations in serious crisis moments usually require interagency collaboration, which may be complicated by different appreciations of the risk;
- the fact that some agencies evacuate while others do not (yet) may actually change the risk and increase the vulnerability for those remaining. There may no longer be a 'critical mass' of agencies present, and not only armed groups but also local people and local authorities may want to get hold of the assets of those remaining before they too pull out. The risk of looting, theft and attack may increase.

The politics of 'security phases'

The presence of the UN, of NGO aid agencies, and of diplomatic missions sends political signals that the security situation is tolerable and that the local and national authorities are in sufficient control to maintain security for international actors. An evacuation will obviously send the opposite signal,

14 Withdrawal & Hibernatoin

something that political actors, whether the local and national official authorities or an armed rebel group, may be keen to avoid. Diplomatic missions will be very cautious about such political signals, and this may influence the nature of their travel advice and other security-type recommendations. If the international presence withdraws, this changes the overall perception and could seriously (further) destabilise the local authorities. Thus the perception of various international NGOs after the breakdown of law and order in Albania in 1997 was that the embassies had waited too long to raise the 'security alert phase', and advise evacuation. In contrast, more recently (1997-1998) international NGOs have suspected that the embassies and their home governments overstated the 'security alert phase' in Sierra Leone and Afghanistan, for example, for political reasons.

Motives other than security

Aid agencies can also hesitate to declare a state of alert that would initiate partial or total withdrawal because of considerations other than those of security. Common arguments are that they want to demonstrate solidarity with an endangered population or retain a 'monitoring' or 'witnessing' presence, or that, once evacuated, it becomes very difficult to return. The danger is that some staff remain exposed beyond the threshold of acceptable risk and/or that the situation suddenly deteriorates into one where it is no longer possible to relocate/evacuate.

14.1.3 Planning Through Scenarios

While you can develop an ideal-type 'plan A', good practice requires that you question the assumptions on which this is based and think through a number of 'what if' scenarios; and that therefore you should also prepare for 'plan B' and 'plan C'.

Case Study: Unrealistic Planning of a Withdrawal

In the spring of 1999 several aid agencies working in refugee camps in Kukes, north-east Albania, on the border with Kosovo, were concerned about cross-border artillery fire and a possible incursion from Serb security forces. Informal discussions revealed that their one crisis plan envisaged their escape by car over the main road towards Shkodre. What was completely overlooked was the likelihood that thousands of Kosovar refugees might do the same and so block the road. Alternative routes to central Albania or a safe relocation spot in the mountains outside Kukes were simply not considered.

The ideal-type plan does not automatically have to be evacuation. It is not by definition the safest option: the exit roads may be mined, the port could come under fire, and looters and bandits will anyway expect the expatriates to use the road from the city to the airport and therefore put up roadblocks. Too many 'security plans' only consider evacuation, neglect the relocation option, and fail to consider forced hibernation.

Case Study: Relocation into a Country at War

The outbreak of the Gulf War in 1991 caused great agitation in Pakistan. There were daily pro-Saddam and anti-Western demonstrations in all towns. The US, as leader of the Allied Coalition against Iraq, perceived all US citizens to be at risk and advised them to leave the country. Conversely, Scandinavian aid agencies working across the border in Afghanistan decided, by and large, to evacuate family members from Pakistan but to retain their international staff for the time being. In contrast, one French organisation decided that if Peshawar became high-risk it would 'relocate' its assets and international staff to east Afghanistan and put them under the protection of local people with whom it had close relations. Various considerations influenced this decision: the desire to maintain programme activities in Afghanistan, the perception that the roads from Peshawar to Islamabad might be cut off by violent mobs, and the knowledge that at the time the Afghans were adopting a fairly 'neutral' position despite their sympathy with the Iraqis as fellow-Muslims, because the mujahedin were very dependent on Western military and other aid. It also knew that the Pushto laws of hospitality oblige a host to take full responsibility for the security of his guests.

More flexible scenario thinking would first consider relocation and then 'evacuation' (each with different possibilities), and then 'hibernation'. Preparedness measures can thus be developed for the different possible scenarios.

14 Withdrawal & Hibernatoin

14.2 Preparedness: Management and Practical Steps

14.2.1 Decision Making Authority

It needs to be clear not only under what conditions you will withdraw/evacuate, but also who has the (ultimate) authority to make that decision.

- Is it international HQ or the resident representative? What happens in the case of divergent opinions?
- Can a programme or office manager in a provincial base take the decision to withdraw without prior approval from the agency representative in the capital?
- If you rely on the UN or embassy/international government support, for example, to mobilise planes or a ship, how does this fit into your decision making?
- Is it clear to all staff that the decisions taken by management are mandatory?

14.2.2 Crisis Management Team

While a forced relocation or evacuation can occasionally take place under smooth circumstances, often it occurs in an atmosphere of crisis, chaos and confusion. Many people and tasks need to be attended to. Good practice suggests that a crisis team should be identified and tasks and responsibilities allocated in advance; also that a central coordinating function be established. Decide who, and at what point in a crisis, will be in charge of what. For example:

- monitoring situational developments via the telecom system, local and international radio broadcasts, etc;
- the logistical arrangements for, and security of, the exit;
- the assembly and organised movements of all staff to be withdrawn;
- the assets to be taken along;
- the management of financial and administrative matters;
- securing essential and sensitive documentation;
- communications with headquarters, other agencies, the national authorities and the embassy;
- public relations (communications with local people, the local and international press);
- the attempted continuation of the programme;
- the internal coordination and monitoring of the various tasks being implemented.

A crisis management team may very well include nationally recruited staff.

Note that staff turnover will require that these responsibilities are covered in a handover, or that the crisis management team as initially established will be reviewed. Note also that the crisis management team cannot include any who might be considered non-essential staff who would be withdrawn earlier.

14.2.3 Logistics and Reconnaissance

How do you get out of the danger spot? The key issues to consider are:

- the routes and means of transport under different scenarios;
- what transport you will require if you take more people and assets; alternatively who and what you take in view of the transport capacity is likely to be available?
- who provides the transport? (if it is not your own agency then you will need to discuss logistics with the organisation providing the transport.) Alternatively, if you are a potential transport provider, then you will need to discuss in advance your capacity, procedural requirements and the limits of your responsibility and liability.

Many evacuations depend upon the collaboration between different organisations. Don't draw up an evacuation plan in isolation.

In certain relocation or evacuation scenarios staff may have to drive or even walk a long distance. In others they will need to make their way from the assembly point(s) to a port or airport. Good practice suggests that you undertake detailed reconnaissance in advance using, or sketching, maps. This will probably involve exploring alternative routes if the preferred one is blocked or considered too dangerous. Good scenario thinking also requires that you consider the requirements of different routes and the potential impact of different climatic conditions. It may, for example, not be possible to drive all the way to the border, so that you may have to walk for two days. Therefore be prepared in terms of supplies and walking equipment.

14 Withdrawal &
Hibernatoin

14.2.4 Detailed Preparation

Sites

Assembly points
Identified sites from which those qualifying for relocation or evacuation proceed, to the (air)port, for example, or where a convoy will be constituted. The assembly point needs to be accessible, secure, large enough to accommodate many people and several vehicles, have reliable communications and emergency stocks (including medical supplies and fuel) to take along in the evacuation, or so that it can develop into a 'hibernation point' if evacuation proves impossible.

Retreat/hibernation facilities
Retreat and hibernation facilities (in plural: give yourself options and alternatives) should be identified and equipped in advance. Typical basic facilities and supplies include a stock of food, water, essential medical supplies and fuel, sleeping and toilet facilities, lighting (candles/hurricane lanterns), power supply (for the radio, and communications). In high-risk areas where evacuation is likely or has happened already, more advanced preparations can be pursued. An agency operating in Kosovo prior to the NATO action, for example, anticipated the possibility of evacuation and rented a flat, opened a bank account, and set up email in Macedonia.

Communications

The communications tree
Many people and organisations may have to be informed very quickly at a time of crisis. Rather than have one person try to do this, establish a reliable communications tree or network in which each 'node' has the responsibility to pass on information to three or four other nodes. A 'warden system', if in place, can be integrated into this. The same communications tree can function to pass on incident alerts (Chapter 16).

Crisis communications
You will need multiple channels, all of which should be constantly monitored during a crisis: one channel will be for internal, another for interagency crisis management communications. You may need a separate 'emergency channel' for acute emergency calls (Chapter 17). You will also need to agree, internally and probably on an interagency basis, code words for places, routes, actors, movements, etc (Chapter 16).

Vital documentation and authorisation

The agency headquarters, the embassy and the central logistics provider need to have accurate and regularly updated information in terms of how many of your staff (and their dependants) qualify for international evacuation. Special requirements should be indicated, for example, of a medical nature or if there are infants, etc. If it is likely that international evacuation will be to a neighbouring country, explore the possibility of maintaining valid visas for that country for all those qualifying for evacuation. All those eligible should ideally have one or more credit cards to cover initial expenses until the agency's cash flow has been re-established.

Staff matters

As the employer, you need to make clear to all staff who qualify for international evacuation or assisted in-country relocation and who do not, and what those not qualifying can expect from the agency (see below). A priority list should be drawn up which should distinguish not only between essential and non-essential staff, but also who will go first, second, third, etc, if all cannot be evacuated at the same time.

In times of forced exit qualifying individuals are typically allowed only one piece of luggage or luggage of a maximum weight. In times of high tension, such staff should always keep their 'evacuation bag' and vital documents ready. Passports should be kept with individuals, not in the office safe. If the programme continues (run probably by national staff), the 'terms of reference' for that delegated responsibility should be clarified in advance (see below).

Key records, essential and sensitive information

You will need certain essential information in terms of being able to report to donors after the evacuation and to return properly informed to your operational base when the danger period has passed. This will include inventories of assets, accounts, bills paid since the last financial report, payroll details, contracts and outstanding liabilities, memoranda of understanding, and registration and tax liability correspondence with the national authorities. What constitutes sensitive information will depend very much on the context and will be information that could be used or abused politically, thereby endangering the staff or the return of the agency. It should only be taken if there is absolutely no risk that it will be intercepted during exit, otherwise it should be destroyed (Chapter 15).

14 Withdrawal & Hibernatoin

Stocks, assets and liabilities
Stocks and assets
Using different scenarios, clarify in advance which assets are to be taken and which left behind and what will be done with the remaining stock.

Liabilities
Keep track of outstanding financial obligations, for example, to landlords, suppliers, contractors, staff, owners of rented vehicles, etc, and consider the possibility of clearing these prior to exit. If this is not possible, take the up-to-date records with you for later reference.

14.2.5 Simulation and Rehearsal: Advantages and Disadvantages

A team that is prepared is less likely to undergo chaos and confusion than one that is unprepared. Even if things do not go as planned, the planning exercise will have familiarised people with the external factors to take into account and the operational principles to apply. In principle at least all senior and mid-level staff, both national and international, should participate in and therefore know about the details of plans. If properly conducted the planning exercises should have increased team cohesion and trust in the crisis management team.

The planning exercise should ideally be reinforced with an (indoor) simulation, and even with an (out of compound) rehearsal of aspects of the evacuation movements. This will increase the speed and effectiveness of implementation when the need arises. The exercises are also an opportunity to get a feel for individual competencies and therefore the strengths and weaknesses in a particular team. No less importantly, they reinforce the crisis management team's confidence.

The disadvantage of team planning and outdoor rehearsal is the loss of confidentiality: whether deliberately or accidentally someone 'in the know' may reveal your planned responses to someone else with malicious intent. Wider team planning may thus increase risk. In addition, it may alert the local authorities to the fact that under certain circumstances you may try to leave the area. This they may consider against their interests and, although generally respectful or at least tolerant of your presence, they may plan to ensure that in times of crisis they keep you where you are.

The advantages of team planning and rehearsal therefore have to be weighed against the risk of losing the element of surprise. This will be a situational judgement and will depend on the trust you have in your team members and your assessment of your operating environment.

Another possible, unintended, side-effect of an outdoor rehearsal could be to create panic as it could be interpreted by the local population as indicating deteriorating security. In some countries, for local populations the 'foreigners leaving' has become a major indicator of high insecurity. They may take your rehearsal for real and start fleeing in the belief that you know about some imminent danger. This happened in Dushanbe, Tajikistan, when the UN carried out an evacuation drill.

14.3 Preparedness: Staff Policy

Staff policy with regard to relocation and especially evacuation needs to be elaborated and communicated clearly to all in advance.

14.3.1 Essential and Non-essential Staff

In times of rising tension, and as part of the procedure associated with a specific security phase, non-essential staff should be relocated in-country or to another country. The purpose of this pre-emptive measure is to reduce overall vulnerability by reducing the number of people at risk and thereby making a crisis relocation or evacuation more manageable.

Who constitute 'non-essential staff'?

- All dependants of international staff and all international staff not in senior management positions?
- International staff not essential to the continuation of the programme? How likely is it that certain programme components, or any programme at all, could be maintained?
- Staff having difficulty coping with tension? A staff member may be in a key operational position and have important technical skills but find it psychologically difficult to deal with the rising insecurity. Maybe s/he should be withdrawn, as maintaining such people in a deteriorating situation may eventually cause more problems than their earlier departure.
- Staff at higher risk? Certain nationalities may be a potential target because of resentment over their government's international policies.

When considering relocation to a safer area, the withdrawal of 'non-essential staff' also includes national staff. This raises practical questions; for instance, where do you draw the line regarding 'dependants', where one staff member may have family responsibilities well beyond the nuclear family unit? In addition, how do you identify which national staff are at higher risk?

14.3.2 Internationally Recruited Staff

Relocation or evacuation is mandatory for all international staff. This should be clearly articulated in a policy statement, and possibly written into the individual's contract or in accompanying written agreements with the agency. An individual refusing to obey a relocation or evacuation order should be made to sign a statement to that effect, confirming that s/he understands that the agency will no longer be responsible for his/her security.

Equally clear, however, should be the right of an individual to demand to be withdrawn from a risk area for relocation or repatriation on the grounds of a profound feeling of insecurity. This too should be made explicit in the agreement between agency and prospective employee.

14.3.3 Nationally Recruited Staff

In practice, nationally recruited staff can seldom expect to be evacuated across international borders. This may mean that they remain in a danger zone. As international agencies rely increasingly on nationally recruited staff for reasons of capacity-building and cost-reduction, the question of their security will become more acute. There are no simple solutions to the gap between what an agency wants to do and what it can in practice do in view of the financial, legal and practical constraints it faces.

Nevertheless, key principles of good practice can be identified:

Distinguish among national staff
Local and relocated national staff
National staff members may be working at an operational base in a different part of the country from their district of origin and thus, in times of crisis and danger, in unfamiliar physical and social territory and without the normal support mechanisms. Relocated national staff can therefore be at higher risk. If the relocation was a consequence of employment by the agency, the agency should take responsibility for moving these staff members to a safer area. If the relocation took place prior to employment with the agency, efforts should be made in line with agency capacity.

Staff wishing to be relocated or not
It would be wrong to assume that all national staff want to leave. A number may want to stay to protect their dependants and assets. You need to ask who wants to leave, also if dependants and personal assets cannot be relocated by the agency.

Staff wishing to be evacuated

Certain staff members may genuinely fear persecution and therefore request evacuation. This should not be automatically dismissed: there are international legal instruments and national procedures to provide asylum to people with genuine fears of persecution. The UN, for example, though afforded a different international status by governments than NGOs, is prepared to consider the evacuation of nationally recruited staff if their life becomes endangered as a consequence of their employment by the UN. You may therefore find it useful to discuss this in advance with your embassy.

This issue becomes more complex when a category of people is threatened. In the 1994 genocide in Rwanda, many Tutsi and moderate Hutu staff of international agencies were killed; the international staff, far less at risk, were evacuated. In 1996 when Iraqi troops made an incursion into the northern governorates, the US government evacuated Kurds who had been working with them. Albanian Kosovars who had been working with the Kosovo Verification Mission and with aid agencies prior to the NATO attacks of early 1999 were not evacuated and subsequently found themselves targeted by Serb security forces. As the number of potential asylum seekers grows the politics surrounding this issue will become more dominant. However, this should not make you shy away from it.

Domestic staff

Are domestic staff on the agency payroll logged as 'staff' or are they contracted by individuals (mostly international staff)? There may be strong emotional ties, but what responsibility can and will the agency take?

Contractors and consultants

Again the situation may arise that you employ someone who is not on the payroll but who you have hired for a medium-term period, for example, a driver, a builder, or a local analyst. In general these people will expect you to take responsibility for their security. You should clarify what they can/cannot expect.

Local partner organisations

You may be working closely with a local organisation in a contracting or 'partnership' relationship. Again you need to clarify what you consider to be your responsibility and what people can realistically expect from you.

Allow staff to make an informed decision

The most systematic complaint and cause of resentment among national staff is that the agency does not allow them to make an informed decision. Common causes of this resentment are: that the agency has always maintained a rhetoric of equal care for all of its staff; that the limits of responsibility assumed towards national staff are not made explicit until the last moment; and/or that international staff suddenly withdraw without advance notice, leaving national staff shocked and bewildered. None of this is necessary. Good practice requires you to discuss and clarify these issues in advance. For example, clarify:

- what the practical, financial and legal/diplomatic limitations of your agency are;
- who in principle qualifies for evacuation and for relocation;
- what is possible and not possible with regard to dependants and personal assets of national staff needing or demanding relocation;
- what the status of the contractual employment relations is after prolonged relocation or evacuation and possible suspension of operations, and for how long.

Staff should be clear what they can/cannot expect, so that they can start planning their own arrangements for their security and that of their dependants.

Provide some practical support

In most circumstances the most practical support you will be able to provide, short of evacuation/relocation, will be financial. If there is an option discuss whether the choice would be for local or hard currency or a mix of both. The calculation of a lump sum for staff who are not formally being made redundant but who will cease work because of security risks can be phrased in terms of ongoing payment during annual leave and/or 'extraordinary leave', 'severance pay' and/or extra payment 'in lieu of notice'. Depending on your means, the salary scales, and the cost of living, an amount in the order of two to three months salary will provide staff and their dependants with some financial reserves to help them find security. Alternatively, if you consider the risk to be equal, you could provide everyone with the same lump sum and not differentiate between salary scales. In order to effect these payments you may need to bring in large sums of cash, which is itself a risk (Chapter 11).

14.4 Programme Continuation

National staff can be asked to continue the programme. It is imperative that this situation is planned for in detail in advance. You will need to pay attention to the following areas:

- the allocation of tasks and responsibilities: key areas are financial management, administration, security, internal and external communications, personnel management, logistics and programme activities, etc.;
- the allocation of authority in line with responsibilities;
- the limits of responsibility: it should be very clear that staff well-being comes first and that they should not put themselves at risk in trying to protect agency assets;
- the clear demarcation of the limits of authority: can staff acting in charge purchase or sell assets; hire and fire personnel or take disciplinary action; enter into new contracts; liaise with the authorities; decide on changes in the programme, etc? What do they need prior authorisation for, and what should they do if communications are interrupted for a prolonged period of time?
- the communication of the new arrangements: as well as informing all remaining agency staff you will need to tell other agencies, perhaps the embassy, the local authorities, the bank (alterations in who is authorised to sign cheques, etc) and so on. How widely and publicly the new arrangements are communicated will depend on the context and the size and visibility of the ongoing programme. National staff may be more vulnerable to pressure, intimidation and threat, in which case discreteness might be more advisable;
- a protocol of communications with agency representatives abroad.

14.5 Crisis Management

Notwithstanding preparations, any rapid deterioration in a situation will create confusion if not outright chaos. Things never work as planned, and situational judgement and initiative will be required at all times. The following are some key areas for attention:

14.5.1 Timing

The two most difficult questions are whether to withdraw and, if so, when?

As already mentioned, relocation and especially evacuation are difficult decisions – not just from a programmatic but also from an ethical point of view. If your mission is the provision of services then a criterion will be whether you are still able to do this in a meaningful way. If your mission is also to provide a 'witnessing' role, or if solidarity and market-share considerations come into play, the hesitations about your withdrawal will only increase. On the other hand, you may be putting staff lives at risk by staying.

14 Withdrawal & Hibernatoin

The temptation will be to postpone the decision until the last moment, when the situation has become so clear that there is no room for hesitation. This is a high-risk strategy as you may be overtaken by events and no longer be able to withdraw – a common occurrence according to case studies.

The 'humanitarian logic' and the 'security of staff' logic do not go easily together. This GPR urges that you err on the side of caution, as nobody is helped by aid agency staff being aggressed, wounded or killed. Good practice in this regard therefore holds that you set the 'triggers' for withdrawal before the situation 'boils over'.

14.5.2 Key Principles

In a crisis situation the key management challenge and priority will be to maintain discipline, orderly communications, and interagency coordination.

Maintaining discipline

Individual staff members may be tempted to take all sorts of unplanned initiatives and go to places other than the planned assembly points. The net effect is likely to increase confusion, delay the evacuation and heighten the risk for everybody. No individual initiatives that deviate from the plan should be taken without prior authorisation by the crisis management team.

Maintaining orderly communications

It is vital that communications with one's own staff as well as with key external actors are maintained. To this effect the allocation and preservation of a means of communication are a priority. In an acute crisis, however, the amount of information flowing from a variety of sources can be overwhelming and can contribute to the chaos. Discipline is therefore required among the information providers and receivers and any report coming in by telephone, radio, messenger, etc must be communicated in a disciplined way. In your communications be clear about:

- who reports (on behalf of whom);
- of the urgency of the communication;
- the basic facts/messages;
- on the reliability of the information (source of the information/information confirmed or not);
- planned movements of the reporting person/group (if applicable);
- planned time of next communication.

Those receiving the many reports – normally the resident representative and the crisis management team – should organise themselves so that they can maintain an overview rather than become overwhelmed by the possible bombardment of messages. A possible plan would be for some staff members to monitor telecommunications and any messages coming in, with others designated as interlocutors for people coming in person with requests for information or of another nature. In a complex operation, an additional staff member could plot the evolving situation on a map. The leader of the crisis management team is thereby screened off from the immediacy of the information flows and can keep sight of the overall picture.

Maintaining coordination

If you are involved in an interagency exit operation, there should in principle also be a central coordinating point which you will keep informed about your movements, any problems you encounter and possible changes of plan.

14.5.3 Delicate Decisions

Depending on the context, additional key decisions may present themselves:

Whether to travel high or low profile

What, during the evacuation, is likely to reduce risk most: moving in high profile with logos, flags and HF mobile radio antennae prominent, or low profile with all of these removed?

Informing the authorities

Do you inform the local authorities before exiting? If you don't they may be upset and your relationship will be compromised when you to return. If you do, they may want to stop you because of the value of your assets and your presence.

Whether or not to use an armed escort

A crisis can trigger chaos and unleash looting. Looters and even members of the security forces may try to stop you moving to your assembly point and exit point, by force. Do you ask the local police or army to provide an armed escort?

> **Case Study: Evacuation from Uvira**
>
> In October 1996, all remaining international staff were evacuated from Uvira in south Kivu, shortly before Burundian and Rwandan refugees were forced back from what was then east Zaire. The local authorities did not want them to leave, and delayed authorisation for a plane to land. When permission was finally granted the internationals organised an escort from Mobutu's Presidential Guard, which had been hired by UNHCR to provide security in the camps. A number of Zairean civilians put up a barricade on the exit road. The Guards opened fire and two civilians were killed.

14.6 Hibernation

Good practice recommends that you also plan for hibernation. Hibernation in a danger zone can be voluntary or forced. Voluntary hibernation is the result of your decision to stay confined in a very high danger zone on the assumption that, although violence may be unleashed around you, your staff are unlikely to get hurt. This is a very dangerous assumption. Past experience should not be taken as guidance: just because armed groups or local people have respected your assets and staff in previous crises does not mean that they will do so now. Voluntary hibernation is a decision that consciously puts staff at high risk. It cannot be imposed and requires fully informed consent. Even then, you expose the agency to serious allegations and liability claims from relatives and friends should something go wrong.

Forced hibernation, on the other hand, can result from a rapid unfolding of events that could not be anticipated, or can be imposed by external factors outside your control that make withdrawal impossible (eg, the scheduled plane does not arrive).

Forced hibernation is high-risk. It could mean that staff are confined to the same building for hours, days or even weeks on end. In Angola, for example, non-essential staff of an agency had to live for weeks in a bomb shelter in a town under artillery fire until the negotiations for permission for a plane to evacuate them finally succeeded. Anticipatory planning is required:

- **Long-term physical requirements:** food, water, medicine, fuel, lighting, cooking, sleeping, washing and toilet facilities, power supply (battery recharging), air circulation, etc.

- **Long-term psychological requirements:** books and games, daily physical exercise and also stress management, team management, and mutual psychological support.

You also need to prepare for:

- **Looting:** the most precious item to preserve is your means of communication. Hide a radio and aerial or satphone where it cannot be found, even if the whole site is being stripped down to the door frames. Negotiate to be left other vital items such as food and medicine, but anticipate waves of looters who in the end may take everything (Chapter 10).
- **Aggression against one or more team members:** with no short-term possibility of back-up and support from the agency, or the possibility of leaving the site (Chapter 12).

14.7 Post-evacuation Steps

There are a number of post-evacuation steps to be considered:

1. Contact headquarters: At the first opportunity you should provide a detailed update on staff, security, finance and expected imminent movement plan to HQ; which should immediately contact the families of all evacuees.
2. You will also need to contact officials in the country of arrival, including the embassy, the lead UN agency, and the local authorities if it is likely that you are going to stay for some time and are not merely in transit.
3. Establish or try to re-establish contact and communications with staff left behind and continuing to run the programme.
4. Consider scenarios and who can usefully stay in the region (typically in a neighbouring country) and who should go home (on 'annual leave' or 'end of contract').
5. Organise medium-term accommodation and access to finance.
6. Prepare a report for headquarters and donors with detailed updates on personnel, assets, stock and finance, outstanding liabilities, etc. at the moment of evacuation.
7. Debrief evacuated staff and provide psychological support, as evacuation is likely to give rise to a variety of disturbed feelings: emotional exhaustion, a sense of failure, anger, guilt towards those who were left behind, etc.

14 Withdrawal & Hibernatoin

227

14.8 Exploring Return

The key question is: how are you going to find out whether it is safe enough to return, and who in the agency will take the responsibility for the decision to conduct an exploratory mission and subsequently to return all evacuated staff?

Key information for assessing the security situation for an exploratory mission can be:

- the actual security situation;
- the existing military/political situation, which may have changed;
- the status of logistics (airports, roads, etc), communications and service (banks) infrastructure following the crisis;
- the whereabouts and status of staff not evacuated;
- the status of property, assets and stocks left behind;
- the movements of local people;
- the availability of essential provisions, especially food, water, perhaps fuel.

14.9 Preparation and Training

At organisational level
Evacuation and return involve both headquarters and field-based management. Preparedness can be increased through the detailed and critical analysis of past evacuation experiences and through simulation exercises, for headquarters staff and for (prospective) field-level managers. Include exercises which alternate roles so that both sides understand each other's realities and possible functions.

Such simulation exercises need detailed preparation. They require time (easily three hours) to enact. It is also advisable to prepare simulations that, as the play unfolds, bring in various elements not anticipated by the participants and that effectively force them into hibernation. The participants need to be closely monitored by external observers who take notes. The exercise needs to be followed by an emotional debriefing and a critical review of the actions and decisions taken and responses to events.

A further step in training can be to involve field managers in the development of a simulation exercise. This gives them a more 'Olympian viewpoint' on the situation, and provides an exercise in imagining scenarios.

At field level

Ideally you will conduct simulations and possibly rehearsals at field level, but in practice the time may not be available. Good practice recommends that you devote time with a team to discussing this in some detail, using maps, possible scenarios and possible responses for your particular location and situation. It is also general good practice to give people 'tangible knowledge' of key sites or locations (eg, assembly points) and key routes likely to be used in the event of an evacuation. 'Visual memory' may be stronger than an abstract reference in a discussion or on a piece of paper. New arrivals should be briefed in detail about scenarios and plans and about their responsibilities and obligations, and as quickly as possible should become 'visually familiarised' with their new surroundings, key routes and key locations.

14 Withdrawal & Hibernatoin

PART V
INFORMATION AND COMMUNICATION MANAGEMENT

15 Protecting Information

15 Protecting Information

15.1 Key Records

The decision as to what constitute key records that will need to be kept at hand, and what is to be kept in duplicate, will to a degree depend on your situation. A minimum would be:

- copies of passports including visas of international staff;
- updated list of international and national staff;
- individual health records, including blood group types;
- list of next of kin or others to inform in case of an emergency;
- updated list of agency ID cards and their details;
- inventory of assets, kept up-to-date;
- vehicle chassis and engine numbers, and copies of purchase/import documents;
- office equipment identification numbers and copies of purchase/import documents;
- radio equipment identification numbers and copies of purchase/import documents;
- list of keys of houses and cars, how many duplicates exist and who has them;
- staff contracts, contracts with suppliers or service-providers, lease agreements;
- updated list of telephone numbers (residences, offices, emergency contacts) and radio frequencies.

This should all be readily available at the field office and at headquarters, with up-to-date details of international staff on file with the respective embassies.

Make sure to keep track of agency ID cards and get them returned when someone leaves your employment. You do not want people no longer in your employment to present themselves under your name.

Whether of not international staff carry their passports on them depends on the situation. In principle you want to avoid this; rather, provide them with an ID card with their details, also in the local languages, and perhaps photocopies of their passport. Passports are a valuable commodity and may get stolen. Only carry them when the local circumstances require it.

Generally speaking staff should also carry on their persons and in their vehicles a list of emergency contacts including, for example, radio frequencies, local authority, embassy numbers and, unless this is seen as increasing suspicion and thereby risk, maps. Documents, however, can always be confiscated so staff should have a mental map and memorise some key contact numbers.

If your warehouse is looted, or if cash or computers are stolen from your office or you have to evacuate very quickly, it will be handy to have copies of key records to hand. Where these are computerised it is easy to have back-up discs and perhaps also to send key records to headquarters. These will include stock records, accounts, latest payroll details and a list of contractors/people you rent assets from, and copies of the contracts with them.

Case Study: The Importance of Back-up Files

In 1996 Iraqi troops, at the invitation of one of the Kurdish parties, made a brief incursion into the mainly Kurdish northern governorates that were nominally under UN protection. An aid agency rapidly evacuated all its international staff and destroyed all sensitive files. The loss of some key records, for example, related to staff employment issues, later proved a problem once they had returned. The field office now sends regular back-ups of vital records to its headquarters and only keeps very recent ones in the field.

15.2 Sensitive Records

What is 'sensitive' information depends very much on your particular context and the possible scenarios that can happen. It is up to you to identify it, for which good contextual knowledge and scenario thinking will be a great help. However, a record of special medical conditions and requirements of staff, including national staff, will certainly need to be kept. This record will be confidential.

In principle you will have nothing to hide and your activities will be transparent. But in a politically charged and conflictual environment information can be abused, for example, to identify and target staff working for international organisations or to find out the residential details of staff of a particular ethnic or social identity. Other records, such as situation reports that document and/or comment on political and military developments, reports on security incidents and human rights abuses, records of meetings with people who are influential in a conflict, etc, can also raise suspicion and be seriously misconstrued by those with malicious intent.

Access to sensitive information needs to be restricted and protected. Key files should be kept under lock and key and/or electronically protected by passwords. But passwords are not fool-proof, so you should also lock away the laptop and diskettes If you are in an environment where there is concern about 'infiltration' you should ensure that sensitive records cannot be secretly copied in your office.

Destroying files is difficult. Papers torn up into large pieces can easily be reconstructed. A shredder does better and files can be burned, but this takes time. In a sensitive environment, you may want to consider the following:

- do not keep on paper what you can store electronically;
- do not keep in your office what you can keep overseas, for example, any sensitive records more than two months old. You should be able to transfer them abroad safely.

The drawback is that there will be no deeper institutional records at hand for your successor. This means that HQ will need to provide time for file study prior to departure.

15.3 Discreteness and Encoding

15.3.1 Discreteness

As an aid agency you will not want to be secretive. Openness and transparency can themselves be part of an acceptance strategy as they put you above suspicion. In most circumstances it will be sufficient to be discreet in terms of your everyday formal and informal meetings and discussions, in communications that can be overheard or intercepted, and with regard to what is documented in writing.

You will need to find a balance between openness and discreteness within the agency – ie, towards your staff. Shying away from any discussion with or statements to your staff about the developing situation around them may leave them uncomfortable and concerned, and it certainly offers no guidance in terms of what to say to outsiders about the role of the agency. The challenge for you is to be able to refer to developments in an informed and non-partisan manner and to articulate the arguments for the role the agency plays and the position it adopts. This requires good contextual knowledge, monitoring and analysis.

If the circumstances should arise of there being sensitive internal matters with potential security implications (eg, suspicion of corruption or theft by a staff member or suspicion of a staff member providing 'insider' information to criminals) you will want to be very discreet. Find one or two colleagues you can fully trust and with whom you can openly discuss possible approaches and tactics. If national staff are involved, ideally include a national staff member in this trusted group as they may have access to certain information and a sharper awareness of sensitivities and perceptions than international staff.

When you need to have sensitive conversations with people or over the telephone, do it in a separate room, after hours in the office, or in a residence. If you have to do it over the radio during office hours and the conversation can be overheard, either change the time or perhaps ask neighbouring staff to leave. If you have to send a sensitive fax call first to ensure that the designated recipient is at the other end when it arrives.

In general you must assume that you can be 'overheard': telephone conversations, by landline or mobile phone, and radio conversations can be intercepted, as can satphone communications which are often considered safer (although the technology may not be so widely available). If you suspect that you are being monitored but you have to relay sensitive information, consider finding a 'safer' channel, such as a public telephone or a friend who will carry mail, etc. Emails can be intercepted, and letters and pouches sent by commercial courier can be opened. In general it is wise to express yourself in a moderate, factual and non-partisan way. In times of stress this will require self-discipline.

The 'need to know' rule

A stricter way to secure information is to limit knowledge of sensitive matters and the circulation of/access to key documents to a restricted number of 'need to know' people.

15.3.2 Encoding

If you are in a situation where you might be the target of criminal, terrorist or military acts, you may have to encode certain information that could give away your position or movements. There are various ways of doing this. Choose the one that is effective for your situation. Some possibilities are:

• Use code words to designate offices, people, routes and route points, vehicles, types of cargo, etc. This is popular but seldom well-managed and therefore not very effective. It requires careful briefing and agreements in advance. You can use metaphoric expressions to refer to politically sensitive events, for example, 'The sky is overcast' to indicate that the place is under air or artillery attack. Ideally the code words/phrases are known by heart (you don't want someone at the checkpoint to confiscate your 'code book'). You will need to change the codings every so often because monitors will break your code after a while. For politically sensitive events your metaphoric expressions will give you room for 'plausible denial', but for more direct security threats a code that is broken without your realising it can constitute a major vulnerability. Note also that if you have too many code words some staff will get confused .

- A more sophisticated version of this – which is also more confusing for those trying to monitor you – is to introduce a system with internally agreed temporal and spatial references. For example, you might agree that 14 hours will be the internal reference time (TEMPUS) and any communication about time is subsequently expressed as 'TEMPUS plus 3' or 'TEMPUS minus 6.45'. Spatial locations can also be disguised, for example, by agreeing that you will always add 50km to the real distance, for example, 'I am 75km from target' really means that you are 25km from target.
- Use a language that those who might be listening in are unlikely to understand, for example, Norwegian, Dutch or Hindi, or a very idiomatic English in strong dialect. This only works, of course, if both ends of the line understand each other!

15.3.3 Encrypting

It is possible to send encrypted messages, though this is likely to draw attention and arouse suspicion. You would need special components for the emitter and the receiver. In many environments this will require formal permission which may not be available if you do not have diplomatic status.

15.4 Dealing with the Media

In Chapter 3 it was suggested that you monitor the media. However, journalists may approach you and/or you may want to approach the media, for example, in politically charged environments you may want to consider contacts with the media not only from a 'visibility' and 'advocacy' perspective but also from a security point of view. If your HQ is involved in public relations with and through the media, it will be important to ensure close consultation between field and HQ about making public statements and the nature of those statements.

Protecting
Information

15

Key questions to consider include:

- **Do you want to get a message across in the media?** From a security point of view you may prefer to keep a low profile and therefore limit your contact with journalists to providing only background information. Make sure you do so only to the professional and responsible ones who will not use it directly in their reporting. Note that certain common forms of 'light disguise' in media reports, such as 'a senior UN source' or 'aid agencies operating in the conflict zone', may not be very effective. There may be only a few such agencies, and local authorities may have a good idea of who the 'senior source' is likely to have been.

- **What message?** Think carefully about the message you want to convey, how you phrase it, and how it might be misunderstood or misread. If you are commenting on a particular event consider how much factual and confirmed information you have, how much is based on eye-witness accounts or on hear-say, how much is interpretation and allegation and how much your own opinion. Think also about protocol: if you voice criticism about another party, it might be more diplomatic to speak to them face-to-face before going public, or at least give them advance notice that you are going to make a public statement.

- **What channel?** TV and radio may devote less space and perhaps analysis to an issue than a newspaper. But TV comes across more directly and strongly. Think about who has TV, and/or the access to TV and/or radio, especially among the local population. If you wish to target the international media note that the military and political operators in your environment will probably have access to satellite TV and world radio services and will see/hear your messages. The local intelligentsia and educated middle class may also have access to international TV and radio world services, and/or read the national English/French national language newspapers. However, the majority of the population will get its news from the local language media which it may trust most.

- **How to control the press event and the editing of your message:** Inquire into the perceived professionalism and objectivity (or not) of the press you are interested in and get to know journalists and editors. Do they have the same understanding of 'off the record' as you? Can you cultivate their understanding of your work by taking them to see some of the work you do? What kind of communication will you choose? A press conference or a live interview gives you less time to choose your words; a written press release is easier to keep under control although it may still be edited or 'hidden' in the back pages. The shorter and simpler the statement, the less editing it 'allows'.

16 Incident Reporting and Analysis

16 Incident Reporting and Analysis

16.1 Crucial Good Practice

There is significant scope for improvement in current agency practice in reporting incidents. Evidence suggests that not all incidents are properly reported, that reports may not contain essential information, and that many aid agencies fail to keep easily retrievable records of security incidents, either in the field or at HQ.

It is important to report incidents in order to:

• inform decision makers in the agency and obtain an appropriate response;
• alert others to potential threats and risks;
• create an information base for incident mapping and analysis in the context of operations;
• have a full institutional record in the agency. (Keep a designated file for security incident information for reference by new managers following staff changes. Restrict access to this 'sensitive information'.)

Incidents should be analysed to:

• deepen the understanding of why an incident has happened;
• assist in reviewing critically your threat and risk assessment, security strategies and specific operating procedures in a given field location;
• review critically whether there are structural deficiencies in security management at the overall agency level;
• learn from identified weaknesses and so improve security management.

16.2 Incident Reporting, Inquiry and Analysis

16.2.1 Incident Reporting

When a staff member is implicated in a security incident or observes one, an immediate report should be sent to the field office/interagency emergency channel. Key information in this report should include:

• who is reporting;
• what happened;

- where it happened, as precisely as possible;
- when it happened, as precisely as possible;
- who was involved, with details of the victims of the incident;
- what the impact is on those affected, with details of their current condition;
- who perpetrated the incident, with brief details of numbers, weaponry, apparent affiliation, post-incident actions;
- summary of the current situation and whether there are problems and, if so, what;
- decisions and actions that the rapporteur proposes to take/has taken;
- decisions and actions requested from the country office.

At the receiving end, the information is written down as reported and further questions may be prompted if the rapporteur has not covered all these points, or in sufficient detail. If the recipient, for example, a radio operator, has no decision making authority s/he should clearly signal the steps to establish contact with a decision maker, eg, 'the country representative is out, but I will call the deputy in the office, so stay on standby'.

Depending on the gravity of the incident the country office may pass on a similar report to HQ with further indications of the actions it has decided or proposes to undertake, and a clear indication of what is expected from HQ. Upon return to base, those affected by the incident will be verbally debriefed after which a written, factual report may be produced. You could develop a standard incident report form.

Report of a Landmine Incident

A staff member comes running into the office to report that a colleague, with whom he had gone out for a walk, has stepped on a mine. It happened an hour-and-a-half ago, on the hilltop left of the pass, a few kilometres from the town where the project office is located. The victim is unconscious. On the way in the staff member has already alerted the local UN head office, which is contacting the military for a rescue operation. The staff member wants someone to contact the surgeon of the medical agency nearby, and get further support for a rescue operation.

16.2.2 Incident Inquiry

Just as the police would do after any serious accident or incident, it is recommended that you conduct a further inquiry into the incident as this may yield more detail and provide a more complete picture. An inquiry can consist of more detailed interviews with those affected by the incident, potential and actual witnesses (neighbours of the residence burgled, villagers living close to where the ambush took place, etc) as well as an inspection of the site where the incident took place. Local staff often have access to networks of information or will come to hear of rumours and information circulating among local people that international staff would not pick up, so you may want to involve some of them. In drawing upon a variety of sources your report should clearly indicate differences in information or interpretation, the degree of confidence attached to different sources, and the reasons for the assessment put forward by the rapporteur.

Inquiry into the Above Mine Incident

It turns out that the staff members had gone for a picnic in the hills that Sunday. They had invited others to join them, but in the end no one else came. They had driven halfway up the hill to where the dirt track ended. They had then decided to climb to the top for pleasure, not knowing that at the top were the remnants of an abandoned defensive position, and that the hill had been the scene of fierce battles during a war 15 years earlier. Presumably the mine was a relic of those years. There were no mine warnings. Only one dirt track provides access to the top for motor vehicles, and they had not known or discovered it. The military had extracted the victim but he was already dead.

16.2.3 Incident Analysis

Too often this is overlooked, yet it is vital for understanding why an incident might have occurred despite your preventive measures. The following are key areas to investigate:

The motives

You may not be able to determine the motives with any certainty and over time new information may come up that sheds more light on the incident. Your report should indicate the degree of confidence you attach to your own interpretation. It is important, though sensitive, to recognise that another aid agency, your own aid agency or one of your staff members, may in fact have 'provoked' the incident. This should be acknowledged and taken up in the analysis, although the inclination will be not to do so for reasons of liability. But one cannot learn from mistakes if they are not first acknowledged.

Were you targeted?

This could happen for criminal reasons because you are a 'wealthy' and 'soft' target, or for political reasons. The most common reasons for political targeting are to drive an aid agency out, to influence the actual humanitarian programme policy, or to obtain status and concessions from an actor other than the humanitarian agencies.

Surviving and managing the incident

In reviewing the incident, what good actions did those affected carry out and what could have been done better? In terms of those managing the incident or its aftermath at the country level and at headquarters, what was done well and what could have been done better?

Surviving the Mine Incident

When the explosion happened the surviving staff member who had been some 20 yards ahead, ran back to the victim, ignoring the risk that he might step on another mine. Realising it was getting dark and that he could not easily carry the victim, he ran down to where they had left the car, presumably through other mines, jumping from stone to stone in a high-risk manoeuvre. The army rescue team, which knew the path to drive up to the top of the hill, made its own way there. However, the rescue operation was then held up because the surviving staff member did not know the road to the hill top where the rescue team was waiting in the dark for detailed guidance on where to search for the victim. In the end someone had to drive down again to the foot of the hill to show the survivor the safe way. In short the rescue operation was poorly coordinated and much time was lost. On the other hand communication with HQ and the physical and religious care of the body and its repatriation were handled well.

The adequacy of your security management

Again it is sensitive but vital to review your security management at field level: why did the incident occur or why did it have the impact it did, in view of your security measures? There are various overall possibilities, each of which can be explored in more depth:

- no security measures in place;
- security measures in place but not properly communicated to staff;
- security measures in place and communicated but not understood;

- security measures in place but not followed;
- security measures in place and followed but not appropriate to the threat and risk pattern of the situation;
- warning signs of impending threat not observed, or observed but ignored;
- no warning signs of impending threat and incident not foreseeable.

Security Management Review following the Mine Incident

The analysis revealed serious deficiencies: the agency had not identified mines as a possible threat; the medical agency working in the hospital nearby occasionally saw local mine victims but never reported this at interagency security meetings; the local army knew about three other areas with mines but had never alerted the aid agencies; some local staff knew that the hills were mined but had not thought that expatriates would go there for a leisurely walk.

Structural deficiencies at agency level

Broader organisational practices complicate security management at field level, and their weaknesses may be revealed by a security incident. Some examples are:

- lack of security culture in the organisation;
- lack of security training for those charged with managing security;
- inappropriate recruitment or redeployment of staff;
- lack of mission-specific security briefing pre-departure and/or upon arrival;
- inadequate resources of finance or material;
- major situational mistakes, such as HQ deciding to maintain its field operation when withdrawal or perhaps evacuation would have been the prudent decision.

Organisational Deficiencies Revealed by the Mine Incident

The local project manager responsible for staff security had had no security training. Security had not been addressed in her pre-assignment briefings or during the handover from her predecessor. There was no record on file of past security incidents. The resident representative in the capital city had classified the event as a 'tragic accident' and left it at that. International HQ had also not pressed for an analysis and review. This had been left to the initiative of the local project manager who concluded that it had been an avoidable death.

16.3 What Is an 'Incident'?

Staff perceptions of what constitutes an 'incident' vary: an experienced aid worker may feel that soldiers at a checkpoint who point their guns threateningly, or a short exchange of gunfire 400 meters away (neither of which create any further problem for the passing aid agency vehicle) do not constitute an incident worth reporting. A newcomer to this sort of environment may perceive this differently. Clearly in an environment where violence and intimidation are daily occurrences it ceases to be practical to report every single incident. Recognising the 'significant' event is not easy; part of it consists of 'sixth sense', and part of it is close monitoring of the context and constant alertness.

Two areas require special attention, however: the narrowly avoided incident, which should always be treated as a full incident, and the 'warning signal' – any casual or more explicit 'hint', 'advice', 'message' or 'warning' given to a staff member or to the agency, or that should be interpreted as such. This can be an ambiguous remark, a message from a 'friend', a phonecall or letter, or evidence that suggests that someone is watching a residence or office, has been trying to tamper with windows or locks, or has been asking questions of guards or domestic staff, etc. This has to be reported and attention paid to it unless there is sufficient evidence that it is a false alarm.

You therefore need to discuss matters explicitly with your staff and give them clear guidelines on what you want to see reported. In turn they may have to give similar instructions to junior staff, such as drivers, guards, domestic staff, etc.

16.4 Interagency Collaboration on Security Information

16.4.1 The Obligation to Share Incident Reports

Case analysis reveals that the failure of aid agencies to share security information and to inform each other adequately about security incidents is a major contributory factor to higher risk, and has at times been the key factor in avoidable injury and death.

> **Case Study: Failure to Alert**
>
> In early 1993 two UN vehicles were ambushed on the road from the Pakistani border to Jalallabad in Afghanistan, and all staff but one were killed by gunfire. They had received security clearance for the journey. However, some weeks before two Afghan staff from an international NGO had been killed on the same road. This incident had been interpreted as a 'tribal' killing. Shortly afterwards some international trainers in de-mining had narrowly escaped when shots were fired at them, again on the same road. They had subsequently recounted the colourful story in the bar but had not reported it formally. Consequently no pattern was identified and no wider alert given.

The earlier example of the mine incident also indicates the importance of actively inquiring into clinic and hospital records, and of medical agencies examining the medical records and what they may tell about the security information (for example, mine casualties, patients with gunshot wounds or from car accidents, etc).

16.4.2. Centralising Security Information Management

Case analysis indicates that efforts to establish better interagency communications related to security are poorly managed and therefore of limited effectiveness at best.

> **Case Study: An Overdose of Under-exploited Security Information**
>
> During the spring of 1999 in Albania, security information was collected on a regular basis by a variety of aid organisations – UNHCR, the OSCE, and the European Commission – all of which had field monitors in the various districts. The various international military contingents also obtained information about security threats and incidents in their area of deployment. In addition, there was a contingent of international police officers under the name of MAPE that worked with the Ministry of the Interior to strengthen the capacity of the Albanian police corps. UNHCR, together with representatives from the military, organised weekly security briefings and sent out updates by email. A quick review revealed, however, that:

- the various security reports were not centralised;
- quite a number of NGOs didn't know about the weekly security briefings and/or the email updates;
- the security information disseminated did not contain any incident analysis, and did not always report on how incidents were responded to, managed and resolved;
- there was no attempt at incident mapping or pattern analysis.

Although there were many resources and presumably expertise that could have been combined, the potential for quality management of security-related information was not fully realised.

Common objections and reservations about sharing security-related information are:

Confidentiality

This may relate to protecting the identity of the victim, a key concern, for example, with regard to sexual assault and rape (Chapter 12). But confidentiality also extends to other aspects of a security incident. Analysis of the incident may reveal shortcomings in the agency or its performance, which it does not want to publicise for reasons of image but also of legal liability. Confidentiality is often also a key element of incident resolution. Many incidents are resolved (the stolen car returned, the kidnapped person released, etc) in discreet ways, and with the help of people or through channels of communication for which confidentiality and trust are essential. Excessive confidentiality, however, can have serious drawbacks, for example, the failure to alert others to a new threat or an increased risk, or to the fact that you have created a potential precedent (for example, paying for the return of the car or the release of the kidnapped staff member). You also deprive other agencies, and possibly your own or your successors, of an opportunity to learn from your experience. You need to consider how the advantages and disadvantages weigh up against each other and how much you can disclose.

Trust

In all probability you will be sharing information informally with certain individuals from other agencies whom you know and whom you trust not to misuse the information or give it undue publicity. You may not feel comfortable with a more formal information sharing system, with more organisations involved you do not know and are not sure you can trust. It might be possible, however, to create a smaller group of agencies who are willing to collaborate

16 Incident Reporting & Analysis

on security. Participation in this would be subject to a number of agreements about providing and using the information.

Perceived 'intelligence gathering'

If you are operating in a context where other actors are highly suspicious of aid agencies and their 'hidden agendas', then any formal interagency setup around security information may be construed as 'intelligence gathering'. There may also be strong sensitivities about any formal or public mention of perpetrators of violence against aid agency staff or assets being related to official or de facto authorities.

Clearly the need for confidentiality and trust is even greater in this context. Yet your own security management and that of other aid agencies will still benefit from a more complete picture of the threats and incidents and their (non-)resolution. Rather than not sharing any information, you may want to do it face-to-face in informal meetings.

Whereas these, and perhaps other, reservations are pertinent, the obstacle in many situations is not so much contextual but a problematic culture of 'secretiveness' in aid agencies with regard to security information. This is dangerous. *Failing to alert others to a serious identified threat or to an incident that has taken place or has narrowly been avoided can put other people at risk.*

The advantage of improved collective management of security information is the potential for incident mapping and pattern/trend analysis, identified in Chapter 4 as a useful tool for initial and on-going threat and risk analysis. Such analytical work is not possible unless there is good and fairly detailed reporting of many, if not most, incidents.

16.4.3 The 'Security Information Cell' (SIC)

The following offers an overview of the potential roles of a 'collective' security information cell. Centralising security-related information does not mean centralising security management. Each agency will in any case retain the ultimate responsibility for the security of its staff and assets. But all (participants) will benefit from a comprehensive security picture. Certain contexts may not allow you to set this up in too formal or visible a way, or involve all agencies in it. What matters is whether an interagency mechanism can be found to perform certain beneficial functions:

- **Record keeping:** Depositing all information related to security at a central point.

- **Security alert dissemination:** Incidents are immediately reported to the SIC which sets in motion the wider alert – a cumbersome task that can be facilitated by the use of email Listservs if you are confident that emails are quickly picked up, and/or by a 'communications tree' (Chapter 14).
- **Screening/qualifying of reports:** Where an incident report does not indicate the level of confidence regarding the information or certain details (verified or not?), the SIC may decide to add these reservations before passing it on. In practice central security officers spend much time quashing rumours and sending out messages to that effect. The more disciplined everybody's reporting, the easier the task for the SIC.
- **Incident mapping and pattern/trend analysis:** This requires the sharing of all incident reports and the outcomes of the incident inquiry. Ideally SIC staff are informed about (some of) the outcomes of your incident analysis and the strategy that resolved a security-related problem (or failed to do so).
- **Security guidance:** Providing general security briefings and specific security advice to incoming organisations seems an acceptable role, but providing advice on request to individual agencies will be possible only if and when there is enough staff capacity and time.
- **Security focal point meetings:** A useful way of working can be regular meetings of the focal points for security/security officers of different agencies. The resulting personal networks will facilitate interagency exchanges of information and provide an opportunity for broader sharing of advice, guidance and expertise, and regular, collective re-assessment of threats and risks. It is imperative that you designate a security person to participate who is not constantly replaced by someone else without that responsibility and knowledge.
- **Liaison with the authorities:** The SIC can develop contacts and relationships with counterparts among the 'authorities' in your operating environment. This should remain a 'resource' and not turn into a 'management' role on behalf of the agency collective, unless specifically agreed to by all the participating agencies.

Case Study: Centralising Security Functions

In the mid-1990s, the OCHA office in Angola fulfilled several of the above functions rather well. In another country, however, an NGO attempt collapsed. When the security situation deteriorated, some 20 international NGOs agreed to the deployment of a collective 'security officer' to work under the supervision of the NGO security task force which itself was part of the larger NGO coordinating structure. An evaluation after six months was highly positive: the security officer had

Continued...

provided high quality situational updates, helped sharpen the security management of several agencies, and catalysed interagency interaction on security issues. Shortly after this, however, the security officer received clear 'unofficial' warnings that the government wanted him to leave the country. A contributory factor was the fact that the post had not been established with prior government approval. Two months later an assessment took place to see whether and how a replacement should be deployed. This revealed a rapid deterioration in security collaboration among the NGOs, mainly because of the change in expatriate personnel who had been instrumental in developing the earlier initiative.

In order to function properly, a SIC needs to be well designed and adequately resourced with:

- workspace for meetings and briefings;
- maps and possibly (access to) a photocopier to reproduce maps;
- excellent communications infrastructure: long and short-distance radio, mobile phones, fax, email;
- staff with expertise in security but also excellent interpersonal skills;
- a team with a good mix of language skills, technical expertise, analytical skill and experience with a diverse range of organisational types and cultures;
- enough staff capacity to man the centre on a 24-hour basis at times of high tension and crisis;
- a clearly circumscribed mandate/task description, ideally guided by an interagency steering committee rather than a 'lead organisation'.

17 Telecommunications

17 Telecommunications

17.1 Telecoms and Security

A radio does not automatically mean security.
More radios do not mean more security.
Radios can reduce but also increase the risk.

Radios, and more recently satphones and mobile phones, are increasingly in use by aid agencies operating in violent environments. Yet as assets they are poorly managed. Many aid staff with years of experience in using radios still have basic questions. Field managers are not trained about the technical, and especially the managerial, aspects of telecoms.

This chapter reviews some key managerial aspects of telecoms from a safety, and especially security, point of view. From a security perspective the first question will be not only how you can establish effective communications in a given context, but also how you can maintain communications in a crisis scenario. This is not only an internal but also an interagency question. A second question is whether the prominent use of telecoms assets is likely to reduce or increase risk. Indeed, there often seems to be an assumption that telecoms are an effective security measure; on their own they are not, and are simply a channel of communication. If warnings are not communicated in good time, a team can still walk unknowingly into a risk situation; if a team in danger can send a distress message but no help is available nearby, they will remain on their own. Thus while radios and mobile phones can be psychologically reassuring this does not mean that they effectively reduce risk. On the contrary, they can increase it as they may increase your 'visibility' as an outsider and attract criminals or armed groups who want to steal them from you.

17.2 Choosing Telecoms: Cost and Performance Criteria

The main telecommunications systems (telecoms) are telephone, fax, email/internet, telex and radio. Your choice of these will depend on a combination of criteria. The key performance questions are: What will be the nature and volume of the traffic? What do you want your telecoms to be able to do?

Generally, telecommunications serve the following functions at field level and between the country office and the international headquarters:

- maintaining managerial contact;
- administrative reporting;
- security.

You will need to consider if you want to transmit data or voice only. Systems are increasingly being developed that allow the transmission of data. Bear in mind, however, that when your system is busy transmitting data it may not be open to receive distress calls and security notices. This can constitute a risk. Do think about how you can maintain an emergency channel open at all times.

Another aspect is the number of users. An integrated network typically has at least three channels. One is the call channel to which all are tuned and where two stations can make contact to then switch to another channel for the communication. The same channel is also used for sending and receiving, and while someone is talking other communications have to wait. This can become burdensome when you have a large or very dispersed agency team, and are on an interagency network. You will then be looking for systems with a larger number of channels.

The most common transmission mediums are high frequency (HF) and very high frequency (VHF) radios and landline, mobile and satellite telephones. It is important to know what you can expect from your equipment.

17.2.1 High Frequency (HF) Radios

The advantages are:

- short- to extremely long-range communication without a relay station;
- less affected by topographical variation;
- high degree of independence;
- easy to network, with multiple stations sharing the frequency;
- messages can be sent simultaneously to multiple destinations;
- constant monitoring is simple to perform;
- well-adapted for vehicle use;
- adaptable to changing operational conditions;
- relatively cheap to purchase; no call charges;
- well adapted to vehicle use;
- relatively easy to diversify functions of network (voice, fax, Global Positioning System tracking, SITOR or PACTOR data transmission);

17 Telecoms

- possible to integrate with other networks (phone/email);
- requires limited maintenance.

The disadvantages are:

- requires registration and licensing in most countries;
- transmission strength varies during the day depending on solar activity;
- 'skip zone': no reception between maximum extent of direct wave and longer radius starting with the closest reflections from the ionosphere;
- full-time radio operator needed for adequate message handling;
- training of staff needed to take full advantage of the network;
- technical expertise needed to install, and can interfere with other electronic equipment if not installed correctly.

Consider whether a radio set has the following capabilities. This is directly relevant from a security management point of view:

- **Remote diagnostic:** one unit can interrogate another to get details on operational factors such as power output, signal strength or battery voltage. This allows for diagnosis of potential impediments by a technician who does not have to be physically present at the unit.
- **Emergency call:** distress signals are automatically sent out to a number of pre-programmed stations, prioritising the urgency of the call for the receiver.
- **Global Positioning System:** a GPS connected to a personal computer with tracking software installed can interrogate a GPS connected to a mobile unit without the persons in the vehicle being aware. Vehicle movements can thus be monitored.

The most commonly used brand of HF radios are Codan and Barrett.

17.2.2 Very High Frequency (VHF) Radios

Advantages are: hand-held portable or mobile installed; fairly inexpensive; user-friendly; sturdily built: can be dropped, withstand rain, etc; well-positioned repeaters can increase area coverage; and 24-hour contact if users are monitoring.

Disadvantages are: limited battery life (need for spare batteries/ongoing recharge); inappropriately placed repeaters greatly limit the utility of the network; hand-held units are frequently lost or stolen; repeaters are very vulnerable to intentional damage; and very dependent on topography of area (handset-to-handset, 2–5km; handset to base, mobile or repeater, 7–15km. Obstacles in between, such as high buildings or hills, will interfere). Positioning yourself on a high point can increase your range.

The most commonly used brand is Motorola.

17.2.3 Mobile Telephones

Mobile telephones rely on the distribution and interconnection of a number of transmitter/receiver sites (cell-sites), which in turn are connected to a telephone switch and for most purposes work like a normal telephone. Each cell site has an area of coverage where service is available; outside the service area it will not be possible to use the phone. Cell-sites are generally clustered around population centres, and in most developing countries service will not be available in rural areas. As with all telephone systems this is one-to-one, ie, you can only talk to one person at a time which may not be suitable for the rapid dissemination of emergency or security calls.

Advantages are: highly compact and mobile; reliable communication when within service area; fairly confidential; and easy to use.

Disadvantages are: expensive (transmission costs money depending on transmission time); vulnerable to theft; dependent on third parties; and can become 'over-loaded' with users (especially in times of crisis).

17.2.4 Satellite Telephones

Satellite telephones rely on the global system of communications. The largest and most popular system is managed by the International Maritime Satellite Organisation (INMARSAT; headquarters in London) which is a partnership among a number of countries. With their most popular 'M' service it is possible to have voice, fax and data (including email) transmission capability. Fax and data functions require external IBM-compatible computers and standard fax machines. The system essentially relies on four satellites, each covering a so-called 'Ocean Region' with terrestrial so-called 'Land Earth Stations' that perform a national routing function, and mobile stations, of which your satphone is one.

Advantages are that they are: compact and mobile; reliable when properly set up; and fairly independent.

17 Telecoms

Disadvantages are that they are: expensive (transmission costs money depending on transmission time); vulnerable to theft; require technical expertise to set up data services; require user training; and can become 'over-loaded' in times of crisis.

Different systems have different start-up and operating costs. Satphones, for example, are reliable but relatively expensive to run; HF radio communications are less reliable but free once the investment has been made. Where call charges apply, obtain details about the composition of the costs, ie, the charge rates that apply to different links in the chain. In situations where there are no functioning state authorities or national service providers there may be no 'billing authority'. This can lead to problems in using certain telecoms, notably satphones.

Different types of equipment also have different life-spans. The average life-span of a base station radio can be more than five years, of a mobile radio two or more years (typically the life of the vehicle), of a radio battery about 18 months if used everyday. The life span of a particular piece of equipment can vary depending on whether you go for the cheaper 'Amateur Radio' (Ham) versions – not recommended – or for sturdier 'heavy-duty' commercial equipment. A consideration in the cost calculation can be the risk of losing the equipment due to theft or looting, or because you have to leave it behind during an evacuation or hand it over to the government when closing the programme. Finally, remember that all your equipment needs to be of good quality: a radio set, for example, is only as good as its aerial!

Certain systems, especially VHF repeaters, require technical expertise to install and to a lesser degree to maintain. You should not, as often happens, opt for a telecoms system without having the technical know-how in-house or knowing where you can contract it.

These days almost everyone has access to, and makes use of, a computer to carry out normal administrative routines and reporting. It is becoming more convenient to execute transactions electronically and the integration of telecommunications with computer networks, whether landline, radio or satphone, is developing rapidly. A skills shortage exists in this area and contracted technical assistance can be at premium rates.

From the perspective of an international organisation, you may want to rationalise the use of telecoms equipment among your global operations. This will reduce logistics overheads and lead to discounts on volume purchases. Standardisation will allow the transfer of resources between projects and has the benefit of reduced maintenance supply, training requirements, technical back-up, etc.

17.3 Choosing Telecoms: Contextual Criteria

The general costs, and standardisation criteria, however, will have to be weighed against contextual criteria. The key questions are:

1. What are your operational requirements?
2. What facilities exist in the context where you operate? How independent or controlled are the existing systems? What are their vulnerabilities in times of crisis?
3. How can you maximise compatibility and network possibilities between agencies? Will the equipment be used as a stand-alone system or can it be integrated with other agencies at the scene? Will you need to share facilities with other agencies, eg, repeaters?
4. What is administratively and politically possible?

17.3.1 Operational Requirements

Your communication requirements will depend on the type of programmes/ projects you are running. They will vary, for example, between a large-scale food aid operation with a trucking fleet and several distribution points and a psycho-social trauma counselling service or a family tracing programme. Take into consideration the number of project areas and the distance between them, the type of project activities, the number of personnel envisaged in each project area, and the facilities already available.

Also consider programmatic scenario changes: what might be the future needs as programmes expand or adapt? Anticipate programme developments with staff changes, office/base scenarios and changing travel needs between local bases.

Finally, consider local/national/regional/international reach or 'coverage'. What distances does your telecoms systems cover, and how well does it cover it? This is especially relevant for radios (HF/VHF; see below) and mobile phones. A standard target is that cover is available 90 per cent of the time over 90 per cent of the area. You may find this insufficient, in which case you need to consider how you can increase the coverage.

17.3.2 Vulnerability

The advantage of certain systems, such as HF/VHF radios and, to a large degree, satphones is that they are under your control and make you independent of public facilities which can suffer from technical failures or political control. Relying fully on public facilities for international communications can mean that you get cut off in times of crisis. Similarly, mobile telephones and VHF networks that rely on repeaters for range/coverage are very vulnerable. In times of crisis the repeaters can easily be put out of order; this is what happened, for example, in Albania during the breakdown of public order in 1997. Telephone landlines can become inoperative when the telephone exchange is sabotaged. You also want your own power supply as back-up, since electricity supplies are often a military or terrorist target. There are also technical dimensions to the vulnerability: can you get hold of spare parts, and can you get the technical expertise to carry out repairs?

17.3.3 Network Compatibility

There are two dimensions to this:

1. **Internal compatibility:** Can you connect your various pieces of equipment, eg, telephone with HF radio, computers with radio, etc?
2. **External compatibility:** What choices would make your telecoms compatible with the existing public facilities and/or those of other agencies? What keeps them compatible with telecoms within your agency (regionally/globally)? The question of 'networking' is very important but is seldom asked. Yet the 'one organisation one network' practice is not efficient from a technical, economic and security point of view: although they require a little more practical planning and organisation, interagency networks offer substantial advantages in all these respects. This is not an either/or question: you can have some intra-agency capability and share other telecoms facilities on an interagency basis.

17.3.4 Administrative Permission, Licensing and Ownership

Each country is sovereign in internal communications matters and will exercise control to a larger or smaller degree, in the first place through licensing. You will need to consider what equipment you can legally obtain/import and operate in-country. Normally permission to use radio equipment, under specified conditions, is granted by the national post and telecommunications office. In times of conflict, however, other governmental authorities, such as the Ministry of Defence, can take overriding authority. Where there is no functioning government a lead agency, usually the UN, can become the controlling authority.

Before you purchase and try to import equipment, you should be clear about: permission to operate (operating licence); allocated frequency; call-sign; and import licence.

The authority granting the operating licences is typically also the one allocating frequencies. Note that its remit will typically be for in-country communications; for international radio communications the authorities in other countries may have to be contacted. The authority may allocate you an individual 'call-sign' and you will have to pay a licence fee.

Find out about the application process. Some of the issues that are likely to get raised are:

• what equipment you intend to use, sometimes including details of manufacture, technical specifications, model numbers, height of the aerial above the ground, etc;
• number of base and mobile stations and location (including perhaps the specified vehicle);
• what functions the equipment will have (eg, voice only, or also fax/data transmission etc);
• the hours you intend to operate it;
• language(s) to be used in the communications;
• encoding or not of communications;
• frequency: ideally you want the use of several frequencies, exclusive to non-aid agencies, but with a common interagency channel;
• end of project ownership of the equipment (this can depend on whether you pay import charges or not).

An operating licence may be a pre-condition before you can obtain an import licence. Inquire in advance about import duties and import and customs clearance procedures. Inform your headquarters about these as failure to observe them may mean that your equipment is held up at the port or airport for many months.

Telecoms equipment is a valuable asset. Establish at the beginning of a project where these assets will be disposed of at its conclusion. Some countries make a point at the importation stage (especially where an agency has asked for tax relief for 'aid' material) of insisting that at the conclusion of the project assets will be gifted to the host government. An understanding of your agency's mission or mandate will allow you to choose whether the host government may be allowed to receive these items (for possible inclusion within its military

17 Telecoms

potential?) or whether it would be better to pay the appropriate taxes on importation so that you can dispose of these assets – maybe to other agencies with a similar mission or mandate to your own.

17.3.5 Political Permission

It is often easier to obtain permission at the beginning of a relief operation as over time the authorities may become more sensitive and difficult. It may therefore make sense to get clearance for additional capacity in the initial stages to allow your programme to expand.

Case Study: The Politics of Radio Licensing

When Eelam War 3 broke out in Sri Lanka in April 1995, the government only allowed the humanitarian agencies already working in the Liberation Tigers of Tamil Eelam (LTTE)-controlled areas to scale-up their relief operations; it did not grant them permission to deploy more radio units even though they had radios in their bases in LTTE-controlled areas and in the existing aid agency vehicles which crossed the lines. This was perhaps not so much to prevent the LTTE from abusing aid agency radios – which, with its own telecoms, the LTTE had no need for – as to constrain the scale of the relief operation which could help to consolidate the displacement of civilians in LTTE-controlled rather than government-controlled areas.

17.3.6 Risk Management

You may consider telecoms an important component of your operational security management. However, you may not have the desired telecoms available because they are too expensive, the authorities refuse to grant permission, or the equipment has not yet arrived in-country. If this is the case you will need to evaluate the risk of proceeding with operational deployment without this component. Can you reduce the risk by emphasising other security measures? If not, are you prepared to wait or to abandon your plans?

Also consider carefully if and when telecoms may actually increase risk. As aid agencies perceive an increased security risk and telecoms become cheaper and more multi-functional, there has been a proliferation of telecoms gadgets. There is an element of conspicuous consumption about this; it portrays an image of wealth and arrogance to local people which may create jealousy and resentment and decrease your acceptance. It may also turn you into a more attractive target for militia and criminals.

17.4 Operating Radios

You need technical expertise to install your radio equipment properly at a base and mobile station, and to train users in correct handling. There is no need for a radio technician per agency, and agencies can work cost-effectively by sharing this expertise. There is also not, per se, the need for an expatriate expert; technically competent people may very well be available nationally. In any case, always check and follow the instructions that come with the equipment! This GPR is not a technical manual, so we only give some pointers to indicate where technical competence is vital.

17.4.1 Effective Radio Communications: Proper Installation

Locating the base station

You will need to consider ease of access to/from the office but far enough away to avoid the noise disturbances from the radio room as well as interference from office equipment such as computers and photocopiers, or from satphones. You will also want a convenient link to the (back-up) power supply, and easy access to the outside for your cables. In a high-risk area where 24-hour radio monitoring is envisaged you need to think about the comfort of your radio operator(s). For safety reasons all equipment should be supplied from one isolation switch. This can make the whole station safe in case of malfunction or fire.

Choosing and setting up the aerial

You need to know about antenna characteristics such as polarisation, bandwidth, effective height and impedance, as well as being able to select the right type of antenna (dipole, vertical, inverted V, broadband). Generally, aerials function best when installed in open terrain and as high as possible, eg, on the roof top. Setting up the antenna correctly is crucial for the performance of your radio system.

Installing a radio unit in a car

The radio unit itself may consist of a separate control panel and main unit; the control panel must be fitted where it can be used easily, the main unit can be mounted in the glove compartment or under or behind a seat. It is important that the radio is properly earthed and that no one steps on any part of the installation

17 Telecoms

when entering or leaving the vehicle. A crucial factor is the location and mounting of the antenna. Faulty mounting is often the cause of equipment failure. It is recommended that the bracket holding the antenna be well bolted or even welded to the car chassis to guarantee good earthing. The main part of the antenna needs to be clear of the vehicle framework. For safety and security purposes you would do well to remove the antenna when not in use. It can be stored in the vehicle. Note that you should not be transmitting with the engine switched off as this will quickly drain the battery.

Power supply

No radio system works without power, with generators and batteries normally providing the back-up. Common operational problems are poor maintenance and servicing of the generator, and poor storage and discharging/recharging of batteries. This needs to be addressed by management and through training.

17.4.2 Safety

Electricity

Remember that throughout you are dealing with electricity, and that electricity is dangerous. All items of equipment must be separately earthed and terminated in suitable plugs and sockets. Check that fuses and circuit breakers are in good condition and have not been overridden or bypassed. Always use double insulated cable. Cables should not pose a tripping or overhead hazard.

Radiation

Antennae emit electromagnetic energy in the form of radiation that can affect the human body. You should not use hand-held radios with damaged antennae or with the 'bobble' at the top of the antenna missing. You should not use hand-held radios too close to the face (6 inches or 18cm away is adequate). There is a particular hazard with satellite terminals, whose energy density is very high and also focused in one direction: while operating a satphone, you should observe the radiation hazard notice and position yourself as required, but you should also ensure that nobody else walks past in the danger zone.

Lightning hazard

Remember that antennae can be a lightening hazard. Dangerous static voltage can build up and there is the risk of a lightening strike. Some technical precautions can be taken to reduce the risk. In the event of a thunderstorm, the safest move would be to abandon the radio room.

Electric shock

If someone receives an electric shock, never hurry to touch or try to release them. The first step is to try and switch off the power. Only when that fails should you try to pull or push the victim clear, using non-conductive material such as dry rope, a dry stick or dry clothing. Obtain medical help as soon as possible.

Radio frequency burn

When fixing or removing the vehicle-mounted antenna, the car engine should be switched off to avoid receiving a radio frequency burn from an aerial during transmission. These burns are particularly painful as they appear under the skin and can take a very long time to heal.

17.5 Operational Discipline

The key requirement, often difficult to sustain, is discipline.
The key principles are clarity, brevity and security.

Guidelines: Clarity and Discipline in Communication

Clarity and brevity are achieved through the mode of communication and the use of procedural words and communication signals (such as 'over', or 'repeat'). Clarity is also enhanced when:

- you prepare your message in advance;
- present your message point by point;
- stop talking when you have nothing to add;
- speak in short sentences, using plain language, and standard 'broadcasting' language rather than your local dialect;
- speak not too quickly, especially when the recipient needs to write the message down;
- speak in a normal tone of voice (shouting will negatively affect the quality of reception).

If users chat on endlessly instead of making their point clearly and concisely, or if they do not observe basic rules such as identifying themselves or engage in 'social chat', this 'clutters' the radio space and impedes important and perhaps urgent messages from getting through.

There are ways of imposing discipline, such as automatic identification of the caller through the use of ID codes in a VHF, limiting the use of radios

Continued...

17 Telecoms

263

to authorised personnel only, and withdrawing an operating licence for consistent abuse. These are usually measures of last resort and harm can have been done before they are undertaken.

Message logbooks are an essential element of good radio management. The basic components of the log include: time of transmission, time of log in, source of the message and/or of the transmission, person filling in the log to whom the message is ultimately addressed, the key points of the message (verbatim for important ones), follow-up action to be taken by the radio operator/others and whether action has been taken or not, and equipment faults or problems. A good radio operator is someone with good technical knowledge but also with a very good ear, a clear voice, a clear and structured mind and clear handwriting, with an ability to concentrate and a strong sense of discipline. In recruiting, therefore, personality characteristics are as important as technical qualifications.·

For security reasons it is advisable always to keep the radio on 'ON'. Turned-off radios are not able to receive emergency calls or other security-related messages.

Distress and security calls

There is an internationally agreed radio protocol for emergencies (with many local variations). The caller seeks clearance on the channel by repeating three times 'MAYDAY MAYDAY MAYDAY' or 'PAN PAN PAN', usually followed by 'ALL STATIONS'. There is an absolute obligation to accept emergency calls and to interrupt ongoing conversations.

A security message that does not indicate a threat to life or property (eg, notice of civil disturbances in a town that therefore needs to be avoided) can be initiated by repeating 'SECURITY, SECURITY, SECURITY'.

Emergency calls must be responded to, ie, reception must be confirmed and the identity of the receiving station given. All stations receiving the emergency call must confirm, even if other confirmations have already been heard. Steps must be taken to respond to the emergency.

Normal radio communications should not be resumed until the emergency has been cancelled. It is normally the responsibility of the station issuing the emergency call to indicate the end of the emergency.

Security messages do not require confirmation unless that protocol is established. They can be repeated at intervals to maximise the chances of everybody picking them up.

During times of crisis, decision makers can be bombarded with so much information that it is impossible to differentiate fact from rumour. To be effective at these times it will be important to minimise communications to only those matters of direct importance. Again this can be achieved through training and discipline.

17.6 Preparation and Training

Many experienced aid workers who have used telecoms for many years still express a need for more precise information about telecoms and for practical training. This suggests that current practice can be improved. A sensible approach would be for HQ to ensure basic training for all internationally recruited staff, with the country office providing training for nationally recruited staff and refreshment/context-specific training for international staff.

Written guidelines on the standard radio language and radio-operating procedures cannot substitute for practical training. As with all training the first question management needs to answer is: who needs to be trained, for what (hardware care and operation; competence in communications) and to what level? Clearly radio operators need training/refreshment; so too do all staff who will normally be using a radio (eg, project managers at field bases, or every staff member with a VHF). Should drivers of vehicles with a mobile unit be trained, and in what: technical maintenance and/or radio operating procedures? There are no standard guidelines. What competencies you would like different people to have will depend on the scenarios you are likely to face. If a project vehicle travels for days on end in an environment where its radio is the only means of communications, you will want to ensure that at least one member of the team can undertake basic radio maintenance and repairs, and that essential spare parts go with the vehicle. If in the course of their work expatriate staff move away from the vehicle, perhaps in risk areas, the driver needs to know how to operate the radio in case of an accident or security incident. If expatriate staff come on short-term contracts you may want to hire-in/develop technical expertise among nationally recruited staff.

17 Telecoms

PART VI
PERSONAL AND PERSONNEL DIMENSIONS OF SECURITY MANAGEMENT

18 Personal and Team Competence

18 Personal and Team Competence

18.1 The Relevance for Security

Reducing risk and managing security is an organisational but also an individual responsibility.

It is the organisation's responsibility that all staff are familiar with:

- the agency and its mandate;
- the agency's specific mission in a certain operating environment;
- the responsibilities of the agency and the individual with regard to security, and the extent of the agency's authority and responsibility in that regard;
- the context in which the individual will operate;
- the threats and risks in that context;
- the security (and safety) measures to be observed to reduce the risks.

It is also the organisation's responsibility to see that staff have the appropriate awareness, knowledge or skill required to avoid, survive and/or manage particular types of incidents and crises. Finally, the organisation has to monitor stress levels, promote – and practice – policies that limit the build-up of stress, and intervene in a responsible and sensitive way when an individual is having difficulties coping with stress (Chapter 19).

Individual staff members have to be mentally prepared in order to operate effectively in an insecure environment. They need to be responsible and disciplined about observing organisational security measures and competent to the extent that they can make situational judgements and retain self-control during moments of crisis. An effective team is an overall support, not only for general management and programme requirements but also in maintaining security. Dysfunctional teams are likely to increase risk.

Managers have the responsibility of helping individual staff members gain and maintain an appropriate level of personal competence in risk reduction. They also need to maintain their own personal effectiveness. Finally, they have a role to play in creating and maintaining effective teams.

Personal
& Team
Competence
18

18.2 Personal Competence

18.2.1: Guidelines: Behavioural Self-discipline

Good practice in personal responsibility for security suggests the importance of the following:

- **Maintain constant situational awareness:** At all times you should remain aware of the broader context you are working in, and how you might be perceived or portrayed. Keep your eyes and ears open, listen to people's opinions and be aware of local perceptions through the local press and through listening to/talking with national colleagues and local people. In the actual location, maintain 'terrain awareness': know where you are, scan the environment for potential threats and for where you might find help or cover or in what direction evasive action might be taken.

- **Remain security conscious:** Understand the agency's security guidelines, rules and rationale, and accept that in violent environments it is insecurity and danger rather than organisational measures that generate the constraints on personal freedom. Understand that your risk-taking behaviour can put colleagues at risk and affect the image or actions of your organisation. Remain aware that no civilian in need is helped by your getting injured or killed. Feel responsible for security and act when security measures are seen to have been neglected on the road, around the office, or during and after working hours.

- **Maintain contact and communications:** Always let someone know when and where you are going, and when you expect to be back. Do not just 'disappear' without anybody knowing where you are. Don't go without knowing key telephone numbers and perhaps radio codes. In high risk-environments don't move around without means of communication.

- **Maintain a low profile:** Do not ostentatiously display your wealth, foreign status, personal opinions about social and cultural issues. A quiet and unassuming individual is less likely to be spotted as a good target.

- **Move with self-confidence and determination:** You should not appear arrogant, but also not timid and uncertain or lost. This may be perceived as a weakness and vulnerability, and show you to be apparently 'easy prey' for the opportunistic criminal or soldier at the checkpoint. Walk as if you know where you are and where you are going even if you have lost your way, and show self-confidence and appear composed in your body posture, facial expression and eye movement even if you don't feel it.

- **Be tactful and diplomatic:** Avoid getting into disputes with local people and displaying anger or arrogance. Avoid arguments about sensitive cultural or political issues with people you do not know well. Refrain from making disapproving or even derogatory comments about local customs and habits. Always be respectful, while making yourself respectable. In programme matters, make time to listen to people's concerns, priorities, complaints. Don't make promises you can't keep or leave disputes unresolved.

- **Manage your stress levels** (Chapter 19).

- **Be a constructive team member** (Section 18.3).

- **Be prepared to face a threat:** In practical terms this means knowing the basic principles and/or procedures to follow in the case of specific threats/incidents as reviewed in this manual. It also includes mental preparedness to maintain self-control to help you respond constructively and effectively to a situation of (potential) danger, or cope better with what you are forced to undergo.

18.2.2 Skill: Defusing Anger and Hostility

Cultural expectations

Different cultures and social sub-cultures have different 'codes' with regard to displays of anger and hostility. International staff come with their own. It is advisable to discuss this informally with colleagues and to consider potential implications. In Indonesia, for example, as in many other South-east Asian cultures, there is a strong emphasis on formal politeness, respect for elders and superiors, and self-control that disapproves of the expression of irritation or anger. International staff unfamiliar with the culture may not realise when they are provoking anger or hostility as they do not notice cultural signs and expressions. National staff, on the other hand, may have difficulty responding firmly if suddenly confronted by an expression of strong hostility that they are not used to (for example, at a checkpoint). Both may have to learn to adjust their habits in order to deal optimally with situations.

From an immediate security point of view it is useful to learn the skill of defusing anger and hostility in yourself as well as in the one or more persons facing you:

- When faced with a clear threat or crisis our natural physiological reaction is flight or fight. There is a close connection between fear and anger and fear can easily transform into anger and therefore violence. This is because both fear and anger create adrenaline flows – a transformation of our biochemistry that can affect our mental clarity of judgement.
- Sometimes tense and potentially threatening situations are partially open to influence, depending on how one behaves; the ability to maintain self-control and a clear mind is therefore an important part of self-protection. There are then two simultaneous challenges: controlling one's own reactions and defusing the hostility in another person.
- The key rules are: remain patient, do not be provoked, listen and say little, watch your body language, and gradually shift the dialogue from that of personal confrontation to one of the issue as a problem for which there is a mutually acceptable solution.

Guidelines: Diffusing Anger and Hostility

- Beware of your facial expression and body language: 90 per cent of communication is non-verbal. Stand at an angle to the angry person rather than facing them fully.
- Watch the tone of your voice, and keep it calm.
- Listen without interrupting as interrupting will only increase anger (when the angry person starts repeating him/herself learn to gently paraphrase the message so as to signal that you are listening but have also received the message).
- Listen to the 'real' message and try to steer the communication towards the real issue and check if it is being understood correctly.
- Become a curious listener and ask for clarification and information in order to understand what really upset the other person or caused their hostility. Do not contradict/correct an angry person before they have finished venting their anger.
- Focus on the issue and not on the person: do not confront the other personally and avoid openly judging him/her; do not respond to provocative judgements about yourself or your organisation; always shift dialogue onto the issue; if the main message of the angry person is to express objection to your being there, then say that you have got the message and will comply, and leave.
- Maintain your own dignity, but also allow the angry and hostile person to save face too.

The appropriate application of defusing tactics

It is a situational judgement whether or not you should try to control anger and defuse hostility. Such an attempt is most likely to be effective with somebody who is hostile and angry but not at the point of preparing to cause harm. If somebody becomes very threatening it will be important either to disengage or to comply without delay or verbal resistance; there may be a moment when the hostility is no longer at boiling point when you can try to engage carefully as described above.

Other situations are best managed by making an assertive request. This allows you to confront the problem behaviour and request, with authority but without aggression, a change in the other's behaviour. You need to be able to appear totally calm, confident and clear about the source of your authority. Be careful, however, not to personalise the problem by challenging the other person: be hard on the problem, soft on the person. Responding to anger with more anger only leads to escalation.

18.2.3 Skill: Incident and Crisis Survival Techniques

Part 4 on threat management has mostly focussed on behavioural do's and don'ts. However, competence in survival requires first of all strong mental preparedness and self-control. Confrontation with acute danger causes shock, fear and terror. This can be overwhelming and can lead to behaviour that increases rather than reduces risk. The purpose of prior exposure to threatening situations through training and in simulations and role plays is to reduce the element of surprise and help the staff member retain mental control.

The key elements of mental control are:

- don't panic;
- act or react quickly but with situational awareness;
- don't show anger or fear to your attackers; retain your dignity;
- preserve your life.

It may be impossible to avoid or restrain the aggression against you, and you may be overwhelmed by force. This can happen, for example, in the case of sexual aggression, detention or kidnapping. Under such circumstances the emphasis will shift from behavioural to mental survival techniques. You must come to terms with the serious reduction and violation of your freedom and personal boundaries, and readjust to the new situation. Additional elements of mental control are now required:

Personal & Team Competence 18

- don't despair, and maintain hope that the situation will be reversed in the future;
- maintain confidence that the organisation, friends and loved ones will help you regain your freedom and personal boundaries;
- try to put yourself mentally 'outside' the situation into which you have been forced;
- draw on your personal values and spiritual beliefs.

18.3 Team Competence

18.3.1 Why Teams?

Effective teams are an important contributory factor in risk reduction and incident and crisis survival. Good team work means that:

- everybody is security conscious and contributes information;
- everybody helps to maintain a high level of security awareness;
- team members support each other in coping with stress and fear;
- at the time of an incident those caught up in it can concentrate on the attackers and the do's and don'ts, knowing that the others present are also reacting competently;
- crisis management is smooth, efficient and competent because different team members know their roles and tasks;
- team members know the hierarchy and also each other's respective strengths and weaknesses, and can temporarily switch roles if the situation so requires.

18.3.2 What Makes an Effective Team?

The elements that make for effective teams are no different in the aid world from elsewhere, namely:

- a clear identity (know who you are; see Chapter 3);
- clear roles;
- overlapping responsibility and authority (no authority without responsibility; no responsibilities without authority);
- clarity about how decisions are made and what decision making processes apply when (consensual when the circumstances and issues allow; consultative, but not necessarily so, when decisions need to be made; centralised with regard to mandatory rules and orders and in times of crisis management);

- good information sharing;
- high awareness of the value and importance of team functioning;
- constructive interpersonal approaches and relationships;
- effective conflict management approaches.

A team has a 'horizontal' ethos to it: everybody in the team has equal value. At the same time teams operate within organisations with a line-management structure. Different aid organisations tend to have different emphases. In general the UN is more hierarchical while international NGOs are more 'egalitarian'. In practice all organisations need to combine both.

It is not uncommon for both managers and managed to be confused sometimes over the fact that everybody has equal value but not always an equal vote. There is also sometimes confusion about whether teams are a means or an end, and who has the responsibility for creating and maintaining an effective team.

18.3.3 Teams and Leadership

The key elements that help to bind everyone together are leadership and management style. It is important not simply to be aware of these concepts, but to understand what they mean in practice. Box 18 spells out the principles that would inform one particular management style. You may disagree. If so, articulate your alternative principles and think through what the implications are for your security management.

Principles of Leadership and Management Style for Team Functioning

- Authority is allocated, leadership is gained.
- A leader is respectful and is respected.
- The respect of team members comes from the perception of the leader as:
  - responsible, competent and skilled;
  - making his/her case based on arguments rather than on authority;
  - aware of his/her own weaknesses and willing to ask for and listen to advice;
  - fair, just and evenhanded, and ready to change a decision if more information or better arguments are presented;
  - allowing everyone a valued space and place in the team;
  - consultative when possible, decisive when it matters;

Continued...

Personal & Team Competence

18

- addressing the professional problem rather than judging the individual person.
- Different members of a team can demonstrate leadership in their own field of competence.
- Team members have trust and confidence in what they perceive as 'quality leadership'.

Leaders encourage team work but not to the point that the management line and the allocation of responsibility and authority becomes blurred. Ultimately, organisations exist to fulfil certain functions and specific objectives. While teams are an important and vital means to that end they are still only a means. Managers should encourage and foster good relationships with everybody but not to the point of shying away from perceived problems with professional responsibility, performance and discipline. Effective team work and staff morale can be seriously undermined by allowing a non-performing staff member to get away with it for too long.

18.3.4 Who Makes Teams?

Managers have a responsibility to stimulate effective team work by showing leadership. But this responsibility cannot be solely theirs and every staff member shares this responsibility – all the more so in unstable and dangerous situations. This is especially the case as staff turnover and many other pressing obligations make it humanly impossible for a field manager to bear this responsibility solely and completely.

18.4 | Preparation and Training

At organisational level

- Make sure that all staff know the organisation and its mission in context.
- Make sure that all staff are familiar with the context, the risks and the commitments of the organisation in terms of risk reduction and security management.
- Make sure that all staff are clear about their individual responsibilities with regard to security and to team functioning and discipline.
- Advise and assist staff to sort out their medical, financial and personal insurance matters prior to deployment in a high-risk environment.
- Be clear about the expectations of managers and management styles under normal and under high stress high constraint circumstances.
- Run personnel management and leadership training.
- Run general security training with an emphasis on awareness, knowledge and incident and crisis survival practices for all staff in high-risk areas.

At individual level

The reality of violence: The confrontation with and experience of violence do not leave our spiritual worldview unaffected. It is helpful to interrogate yourself consciously about the reality of aggression and violence in human beings in your world view: is it something that you accept or that you try to ignore and push to the margins? Not being able to 'understand' it one way or another may leave it as a profoundly shocking and disturbing reality which, over a period of time, may negatively affect your personal effectiveness.

Personal fears: How does the fact that the threat might be directed at you, or that you might be confronted with it, make you feel? Where are your own personal vulnerabilities; how can you be most deeply hurt? What causes you to feel fear, what can make you panic? Recall past experiences and reflect on them. How do you deal with humiliation and a deep sense of powerlessness which is often a part of the experience of being victimised? What are your impulsive emotional and behavioural reactions to being confronted with anger, pain, fear, and humiliation?

Continued...

Personal & Team Competence

18

This self-awareness of your own emotional dynamics is a first step in strengthening your self-control in situations of future crisis.

Personal style: You also need to understand your own impulses, and control your expressions of frustration and/or fear in the form of anger. Both can be an obstacle to building good relationships with others. Strong expressions of frustration and/or anger can provoke hostility in someone else or may escalate a tense situation. Look at yourself and learn about your own emotional dynamics and how you express yourself, and consider how you can control and defuse yourself so that you can deal with situations in less tension-creating ways. Think about a few situations in which you have actually got angry, and the sequence of events; then honestly review your behaviour and try to see the assumptions that 'justified' and drove you into an angry escalation. Consider how you could have dealt with the situation differently.

Team behaviour: Reflect on your experiences and your own behaviour in teams. What do you see as the function of teams in organisations in general and with regard to security in particular? What do you expect of teams? What do you expect of the manager with regard to team work? How strong are your leadership qualities? What are your areas of leadership? Are you a responsible and constructive team player, and if not, why not and when not?

Role plays and simulation exercises, perhaps captured on video so that afterwards you can review the situation and your own behaviour in that situation, can be a useful learning and competence developing tool.

19 Managing Stress

19 Managing Stress

Managing stress is an individual and an organisational responsibility. There may be cultural differences in the experience of stress and the ways of coping with it, and national staff are not immune to it. Organisations and managers need to talk about stress, and organisations need to have an appropriate rest and relaxation policy.

19.1 The Relevance for Security

Stress and security are related in various ways:

- living in a dangerous environment contributes to stress;
- when we are stressed our professional effectiveness and our situational judgement are affected and we may start behaving in ways that increase the risk to ourselves and to others;
- when we are directly affected by, or witness, an incident in which our own physical integrity or that of people around us is threatened or violated, we can come to experience acute stress disorders.

The management of stress is therefore a dimension of security management.

19.2 Who is Affected by Stress?

All field staff

Not only international but also nationally recruited staff are vulnerable to stress. National staff may have the advantage of being in an environment that they know intimately and of retaining their social support networks. However, they are often not 'outsiders' to the conflict as expatriates are and they may have been exposed to danger for months if not years, which can add to stress.

Field-level managers

A major unrecognised problem in field situations is that of who supports the manager. Personnel management is part of the responsibility of the field manager who is therefore expected always to be a pillar of stability, support and sound judgement. Clearly this is not realistic but, certainly in more hierarchical organisations, it is not clear how the manager manages his/her own stress levels.

Managers at headquarters level

Some desk officers with many years of field experience may bring cumulative stress and some of its living and working patterns to the job at HQ. In times of tension and risk in the field some may feel very responsible and feel they have to be on-call constantly and are unable to 'switch off' until the crisis is resolved. In addition, there may be significant amounts of stress generated from workloads, divisional rivalries and organisational crises at HQ level.

Men and women are equally susceptible to stress

Women can experience heightened stress because of fears about gender related violence. Women in management positions can also experience heightened stress because they may feel – or imagine themselves to be – under greater pressure to prove themselves, or because they feel their authority is more quickly challenged. Uncertainty and lack of confidence in one's management abilities and position can equally affect men, however, and men may have greater difficulty admitting that they have reached the limit of what they can handle and are in need of a break. Some research suggests that women tend to respond differently to stress than men, seeking more social contact and support from others and intensifying a protecting and caring role.

Professional counsellors and mental health professionals

These staff can also become affected by the stress of ongoing exposure to the problems and stresses of those they are trying to help.

The family and loved ones of the aid worker

The separation and reduction in communication, the experience of different realities, the feeling that loved ones were not there when support was needed, the perception that the other is interested only in his/her problems, the confrontation with changed behaviour, perhaps substance abuse (such as increased alcohol consumption), and perhaps a change in 'character' or outlook on the world and on life resulting from intense experiences can all affect family relations and friendships. The proactive and retroactive management of stress therefore needs to involve the family.

19.3 Types of Stress

It is useful to recognise that there are different types of stress and that not all stress is debilitating:

- **Positive stress:** Stress is a natural reaction and it can be positive and stimulating. For example, quite a number of people need a 'deadline' to get a task completed. Positive stress helps us focus on the task or situation at hand, mobilises energy, and prepares us for action. In that sense stress can contribute to our safety and security in a situation of tension or risk.

- **Negative stress:** Stress uses energy. When it occurs too often, is too intense or lasts too long, it turns from positive to negative. A never-ending series of tight deadlines, just like continued exposure to risk situations, depletes our energy reserves. Less easily recognised or admitted and yet very much present among many professionals, including aid workers, is so-called 'cumulative stress'. Prolonged stress eventually leads to physical and emotional exhaustion or 'burn-out'.
- **Traumatic stress:** This results from the direct experience of, or close exposure to, traumatic events or incidents that are life-threatening or involve death, and involve physical and emotional loss. A term often used here is that of 'critical incident'. Mental health experts further distinguish here between acute stress disorders, which occur a few hours or days after the event, and post-traumatic stress, which can occur after several months or, sometimes, years.

19.4 Symptoms of Negative Stress

There is quite a range of possible symptoms of negative stress, and individuals differ in terms of which symptoms they exhibit:

- **Physical:** Continuing fatigue and a sense of exhaustion are common symptoms, yet these may very well go together with hyperactivity and overwork and/or with sleeping difficulties. 'Flame-out' is expressed in maybe 24-hours continuous sleep, often with slight flu-like symptoms that can occur after critical incidents or can be a sign of more general burn-out; other symptoms can include headaches, backache, or gastro-intestinal disturbances. Cold sweats, heightened blood pressure and heart rate, general trembling and nausea to the point of vomiting can all occur in situations of acute stress disorder.
- **Behavioural**: Substance abuse, notably caffeine, alcohol, cigarettes and perhaps drug abuse; a series of 'one-night stands' or short 'flings', and unprotected sex; also dangerous driving and more risk-taking in general.
- **Work-related:** Workaholism, tardiness, absenteeism, lack of concentration and diminishing productivity or poor work performance.
- **Emotional:** Low morale, pessimism and cynicism can be symptoms and expressions of coping strategies, as can feelings of anxiety, guilt and depression. However, excitement and a feeling of power and invulnerability can equally be symptoms of excessive stress, as can irritability, a constant tendency to pick a quarrel, and aggressiveness. Another expression of emotions can be that of over-identification with the target beneficiaries, and of excessive

empathy leading to a loss of perspective. Nightmares, 'flash-backs' or intense emotions surrounding anything that evokes a critical incident, and therefore often a tendency to want to avoid and repress any thought or feeling about it, are among the symptoms of post-traumatic stress disorder.

• **Relational:** Relational symptoms of stress include 'distancing' of oneself from the beneficiaries of aid by intellectualising or dehumanising them, or constantly making jokes about them; poor communication with colleagues and with family; withdrawal into oneself.

19.5 Contributory Factors

Stress is often a combination of various contributory factors. Analytically these can be grouped into four categories: situational, job-related, organisational, and personal.

1. **Situational Factors**
   Exposure to misery and suffering, and especially to violence and abuse, is certainly stressful. Exposure here not only means seeing and being confronted with the situation, but can also include listening to stories of violence and abuse – for example, while visiting prisoners or receiving fleeing refugees. Moving and certainly living in a risk environment, or coming under fire or being intimidated, humiliated, threatened or aggressed are all stressful experiences.

2. **Job-related Factors**
   These are often a major cause of stress. Potential job-related stress factors can include poor accommodation; lack of privacy; poor hygienic facilities; a monotonous menu; on-going problems with colleagues; difficult relations with one's supervisor or manager; difficult and expensive communications with friends and family far away; excessive workloads and unrealistic deadlines; repeated reassignments to stressful environments; job insecurity.

3. **Organisational or Management-related Factors**
   Among these factors are: lack of adequate pre-departure briefing, training and/or preparation, including about the work context; the complexities of the tasks and the stresses that the assignment is likely to bring; poor leadership and lack of supportive supervision; poor security management; poor communications between HQ and field and between field offices and within teams; organisational conflict or crisis; lack of clear situational updates and guidance, and of supportive organisational policies on rest and relaxation and family contact; no or poor post-assignment debriefing; an organisational

19 Managing Stress

'macho' culture that denies stress, hardship and emotional difficulties and that, implicitly, completely personalises all stress-related problems and treats the acknowledgement of stress as 'failure' or 'weakness'.

4. **Self-related factors**

These include a 'macho' attitude of not knowing or admitting our limits; unresolved problems from the past or from home that are taken along into the field; an idealistic identification with those we want to help beyond our means; moral conflict over our role in a particular situation; a misfit between the personal and the organisational mission; excessive demands made of ourselves.

Some of these are within our own control, others less so. It is important to try to see which elements contribute most to our stress, and which we can reduce.

It is also important to realise that the degree of stress is partly dependent on our own personal disposition. Stress is the result of a combination of objective pressures and the importance we attach to the need to meet a demand, or to the failure to do so. This means that not all of us will react in the same way in the same situation. It also means that we can learn to develop our own personal coping mechanisms.

19.6 Managing Stress

The proactive and retroactive management of stress need to take place at various levels: organisational, field-level management, and individual.

19.6.1 Organisational Level

Whereas more aid agencies are beginning to pay attention to safety and security, few as yet recognise staff stress as an organisational concern. This is despite the fact that far more staff experience stress than security threats. Stress affects performance, morale and motivation, and possibly the length of time a staff member is willing to remain in place. It therefore affects staff turnover.

Organisations can help to manage stress by recognising it as an organisational responsibility, by talking about it, and by developing general and situation-specific rest and relaxation policies. Stress levels and stress resistance should also be explicitly taken into account in recruitment and re-deployment decisions.

Organisations need to review what they expect of field-level managers in complex, volatile and highly constraining environments, and the practical support they offer them. Maintaining expectations that would hold for a 'normal', 'stable' environment is unrealistic and sets a manager up for failure.

A regular cause of stress in aid agencies tends to be poor relations and communications between HQ and the field. Field staff tend to feel that HQ makes unrealistic demands and time-tables and does not understand the constraints of their situation and local-level priorities. HQ sees the field as not responding adequately to changes in the theatre of operations, or 'out of control' and insensitive to wider organisational management and information needs. The more centralised an organisation and/or the more ambiguity there is about the division of authority between the field and HQ, the greater the likelihood of a stressful relationship between the two. The solutions lie largely at the level of the organisation, but mutual respect between the desk officer and field representative, with regular and structured communications between them, is strongly advised. Even though the financial cost may be higher, communications by telephone and visits from and to HQ are recommended because they give each a first-hand understanding of the working environment of the other. Written communications are devoid of non-verbal signals and can easily be misinterpreted. It is also much harder to interpret difficult exchanges constructively when they occur in writing rather than in direct talk.

19.6.2 Field Management Level

There are various things that the field manager can do and encourage to help stress management:

1. **Briefing and familiarisation:** Newcomers are likely to experience the initial stress of having to adapt to a new environment. This goes for national as much as for international staff. Even if HQ has organised a pre-departure briefing, further briefing and introductions at field level are recommended. These should cover the context, the mission, the programme, the nature of the organisation if the person is new to it, an introduction to the existing team in their formal roles but perhaps also at an informal event.

   It is advisable that a senior manager spend time with a new staff member so that there has been a personal exchange. This is an opportunity to talk to the individual about security issues and to signal that stress will be a part of his/her experience, and that it is a normal phenomenon. Encourage people to be attentive to it, and to talk about it when they feel it is turning into distress. It is also an opportunity to establish some personal 'rapport' and to give the staff member the feeling that you are accessible if there is a problem. After an initial period of about three weeks it is good practice to organise another meeting with the new staff member to talk about her/his experience of settling in, and what is going well and what appears more difficult – not only on the professional but also on the personal level. Newcomers sometimes see a situation with more clarity than those who have been in it for a while, and it might be worthwhile asking for their impressions and observations.

2. **Delegation after training:** It is impossible for a senior manager personally to attend to sometimes several hundred staff. Mid-level managers and supervisors have a role to play in this regard. This means that nobody should be appointed to a mid-level management position without some briefing and training on the basic principles of personnel management. On-the-job learning can also take place by discussing personnel concerns in a management team and making explicit the principles of good practice that you want to see applied. Consider the possibility of hiring someone, perhaps on an interagency basis, to run some training sessions for mid-level staff.

3. **Leadership and team building:** The importance of effective teams and of respected leadership for overall management, but also for security and stress management, was elaborated on in Chapter 18. There should be sufficient trust in the management team for a staff member to be able to come and say that s/he has reached her/his limit and needs to get out of the stressful environment without fear that this will be held against them on a personal level or in terms of work opportunities. Good management means that you will intervene, sensitively and respectfully, when you see a person showing symptoms of excessive stress. This is not an easy task as the staff member is more likely than not to deny it, and may become defensive and even more upset by your demarche. Prepare yourself, therefore, before undertaking it, and think about what you want to say and how. It may be necessary to 'extract' an overstressed person from a difficult environment, for his/her own wellbeing and for the safety and security of the whole team. As a manager you should have the confidence to take that decision, after consultation with your desk officer at HQ and the human resource department or medical division. The approach should be firm but supportive, and should not stigmatise the person concerned.

4. **Talking about stress:** Introduce discussion about stress in staff meetings, and encourage its recognition and admission by talking about it.

Guidelines: Talking About Stress

Encourage teams to take on stress concerns more actively by asking every member in the group to list the three things that, in general, tend to cause them most stress; also which are their most typical symptoms of stress and finally what are the three things that help them most to relax. Then ask them to exchange their observations about themselves with their neighbour; there could even be an open discussion about them. Lead the discussion to an identification of the most stressful factors in the situation you are all in, and facilitate a group discussion about what could be done to reduce factors that are under your control. Introduce the notion of the 'buddy' system. This is a common technique among civil defence rescue workers, fire fighters or ambulance staff, etc, and consists of two colleagues who get along with each other talking about their stress and relaxation patterns, and agreeing to watch each other for symptoms of stress. The two will provide each other with support and perhaps sympathetic advice when one or the other is reaching their limit. You can do some role play to demonstrate this. It is not easy to point out to someone that s/he is perhaps drinking too much, or that they should take up sports again to unwind, but if 'buddies' have a prior agreement to look after each other's wellbeing it will be a lot easier.

5. **Policy adjustments:** In highly stressful situations it is good to review, in consultation with HQ, the policy on rest and relaxation and on family contacts for national staff as well as international. This may have short-term resource implications but it will yield long-term benefits as staff stay longer in an assignment or with the organisation, and as risk is managed better by everyone. The challenge then will be to put policy into practice.

6. **Practical adjustments:** Try to do something to reduce staff stress if and where you can. If a team is stressed because of its living conditions, try and improve them. If an individual does not fit well into a team, see whether s/he can be moved to another team. If work demands are unrealistic, discuss together and establish priorities.

7. **Pre-task briefing and post-task debriefing:** Prior to a stressful or distressing action in the field, such as driving through a dangerous area, recovering the dead from under the rubble of houses following an earthquake, or bringing in the first supplies to a group of displaced people who are acutely malnourished and have suffered abuse, the team leader may hold a short pre-departure briefing in which

Managing Stress

19

the fact that the action involves exposure to stressful factors is acknowledged. Upon return to base the team can again sit together for 20 minutes or so for a short 'defusing' exercise – a review of the day's experience and the activities undertaken but also the emotional reactions of each team member.

8. **Traumatic stress support:** When a staff member shows symptoms of acute distress after having experienced or witnessed a critical incident, and is therefore vulnerable to post-traumatic stress disorders, you should call in specialist expertise. Be aware that the survivor may deny the depth of the distress and oppose the calling in of a specialist, for example, following a relatively short period of abduction without serious mistreatment or after a rape that the survivor does not want other people to know about. You will need to make it clear that at that moment the person involved may not be the best judge of his/her own state of well-being and that it is better to get special care for his/her long-term health.

Critical incident debriefing and follow-up requires special training and preparation. It is best undertaken by someone who understands the context but also who stands outside it. Do everything possible to create a protective and supportive environment for the person(s) concerned while you wait for the specialist to arrive: create a place where they feel safe, have access to communications with loved ones, and physical comfort. Two points are important for you to follow in these circumstances:

i. Limit yourself to factual debriefing: Let people reconstruct what exactly happened. The versions of different people involved in the incident may differ and it will be important for the survivors to get the right picture. The factual debriefing will touch upon the emotions the survivors experienced and now feel. You should not, however, go into an 'emotional debriefing' such as accompanying the survivor further into the exploration of these emotions. This should to be left to those who are better qualified.
ii. Emphasise that the distress experienced is a perfectly normal and healthy reaction, that there is nothing wrong with the person and that, with time and rest, s/he will regain physical and psychological equilibrium.

The 'stressed-out' manager

In volatile environments, expectations of field-level managers tend to be unrealistic – probably in terms of the many tasks that need to be performed with skill, and certainly in terms of what can be done in a working week that more often than not amounts to 55 hours and more. Overall authority also brings overall responsibility which in itself can be a source of significant stress, as the responsibility does not stop at night or weekends or during official holidays. The staff need to feel that their manager is strong and solid and reliable, and therefore a source of stability. A senior manager who shows signs of severe stress, or who continues in post although burned out, is likely to demoralise staff and add to their sense of insecurity and stress. But the expectation that the manager will always be sound and solid, and his/her attempts to meet that expectation, adds to the stress.

Guidelines: Tackling Managerial Stress

- Acknowledge your own limitations to yourself and to your staff. Admitting that you too are not immune to stress does not need to undermine your authority if you are managing according to principles and arguments that are defendable. Invite everybody to take their share of responsibility.
- Develop a good relationship with your own manager, probably a desk officer at HQ. Ask that s/he come and experience at close hand the realities you are facing. Ask that s/he protect and screen you from unnecessary pressures from HQ.
- Delegate or share your tasks with a deputy representative, an office manager, a senior medical officer, or a security focal point. This will be a great help if the people in these positions have the experience and ability rather than themselves being on a learning curve. Insist on appointing a high quality person when the post needs to be filled.
- Try to create and stimulate a 'senior management team' around you that shares in the responsibility, although you remain the ultimate decision maker.
- See if you can find a 'sounding board' or possibly a 'buddy' in one of your peers from another agency.
- Manage yourself the way you recommend that your staff manage their stress levels.

19.6.3 Individual Level

Individual staff must also try and manage their own stress levels. Factors that play a role here are personality characteristics, realistic expectations, lifestyle, and knowing one's limits.

19 Managing Stress

Guidelines: Managing Individual Stress

Personality characteristics
A number of personality characteristics help us to resist the negative impact of stress, namely, a positive self-image or self-esteem; realistic self-confidence; a vision of a moral order or a personal philosophy; the intellectual ability to see a situation in its various dimensions and not just through the filter of our own emotions; a good physical constitution; the ability to be constructive and see the positive elements; above all a healthy sense of humour. All of these give us emotional strength and therefore resilience.

Realistic expectations
It is helpful to realise, and therefore to expect as normal, that humanitarian work, conflict mediation, human rights or social change work are full of frustration and failure. Many factors are beyond our control, so we just must try to develop a level frustration tolerance in order to continue to do our job well. More difficult to anticipate is the spiritual pressure that one is bound to experience: the confrontation with gratuitous violence, unimaginable cruelty and unending destruction is likely to disturb our spiritual outlook on life and on human beings, either through 'shock' or more gradually. Try not to neglect the human, moral, social and spiritual values of life.

Lifestyle
Make sure you sleep well and eat healthily. Control your use of substances such as alcohol which only give a superficial sense of relaxation and add to the stress on your body and your nerves. Create a 'nest', a space you can call your own where you have a stronger sense of privacy and relaxation. Do regular physical exercise especially if, as a hostage, you are confined or when you have to spend days in a bombshelter while the city is under attack. Staying in touch with close friends and relatives is important and becomes easier and cheaper by email including email attached to satellite phones. Seek out colleagues or friends in your own environment with whom you can talk about things other than work. Use your free time for relaxation and plan it in advance so that you use it constructively.

'Know thyself'
Know your own limits and the limits to your self-sufficiency. In other words, acknowledge that you don't have unlimited reserves and that

when your reach the limit it is wise to call upon others for help and support. Distress does not disappear because you keep it bottled up and denied. It is a perfectly normal human reaction from which nobody is immune, so talk about it and ask for help when you feel you need it. Watch yourself, recognise the factors that cause you stress and your symptoms, and take timely preventive action. Nevertheless, over the years stress may accumulate. Make it clear to the organisation that you now need an assignment in a less stressful environment; end a long-term contract in advance if you feel you have reached your limit, or take a longer break between stressful assignments. And if there is no other option, change job.

19.7 Cultural and Situational Experiences of Stress and Stress Management

The above reflects mainly white Western ideas about personnel and stress management. The validity for people from other cultures, mostly nationally recruited staff but also 'non-white' expatriates, cannot automatically be assumed. For example, there are cultures where managers are expected to exercise authority and not be supportive and attentive to personal distress. There are cultures where speaking about emotions is not done, or where admitting to levels of stress which are no longer manageable would constitute a 'loss of face'. In others, people cope with stress-related disorders through a social ritual.

Case Study: Searching for an Appropriate Stress Response in Cambodia

In July 1997 heavy factional fighting erupted in Phnom Phen, the capital of Cambodia. After two days the airport re-opened and expatriates were able to leave. After a relatively short time the city returned to an uneasy calm, although members of the losing side continued to be assassinated. An aid agency decided to deploy a team of mental health specialists for its returning international and its national staff to help them cope with what it had identified as a 'traumatic event'. Interestingly, the Cambodian staff asked for some changes in the proposed team, choosing people they knew because they had earlier lived and worked in Cambodia and were

Continued...

19 Managing Stress

personally known and respected. More importantly, however, the team soon discovered that their individual mental health approach and the assumptions on which it rested, were not valid for the national staff.

First, it proved difficult to demarcate a 'critical event': for the Cambodians who had been living in a violent environment for decades, this eruption did not have a clear beginning and end, nor was it 'abnormal'. The 'debriefing' environment therefore could also not be called 'post-traumatic'. Second, the national staff were 'neutral outsiders' but they were also part of the factionalised environment with different political perspectives. The experience of violence would therefore be given meaning in social and political as well as psychological terms. Third, 'employment status' as agency staff was not necessarily the best way of identifying the group boundaries of a 'collective' experience: the national staff had experienced the event as part of the general city population not as 'agency staff'. Why would a 'group' approach based on staff status be more relevant than one based on family or neighbours, for example? Fourth, the national staff did not share the implicit understanding of 'stress' that the foreigners introduced. Fifth, traditionally Cambodians would not seek out 'mental health' professionals for a 'state-of-mind'-oriented 'talk-therapy', but use other resources such as monks or traditional healers and other methods of coping. Finally, 'coping' could not be simply a matter of psychological reframing; for national staff effective long-term coping had other significant dimensions of justice, reconciliation, compensation, etc. In short, an initial 'psychological' approach quickly had to develop into a more exploratory 'anthropological' one, and the original intention of 'delivering' an (outside) support service had to turn into another, more in line with the principles underpinning 'community development'.

It seems advisable, therefore, to discuss with some sensitive and trusted local staff members the following types of question:

- Is there a concept of stress and trauma in their culture; how do they experience it, identify it, and describe it?
- How has it been dealt with traditionally and historically, and who would deal with it?
- What is the nature of stress and trauma today and how has it changed from before?

- What coping strategies are currently being pursued and why, and how effective are they perceived to be?
- What resources can be recovered, remobilised or developed to address current needs?
- Is there a role for an international agency, or is it rather a role for the local community, for example, and/or indigenous social institutions?

The nature of the response may be more important than its speed.

Resource:
ICRC (no date), Le Facteur Stress / Stress (English version) Geneva.

19 Managing Stress

20 Staffing and Personnel Management

20 Staffing and Personnel Management

Death threats and shootings, court summons, imprisonment, burglaries and mob demonstrations have all occurred to aid agency staff due to poor personnel processes.

20.1 Differential Risks

In theory all staff in violent environments are at equal risk. In reality this may not be the case. There are no good statistics on aid worker casualties and fatalities, but the impression given by the available evidence suggests, for example, that certain types of staff are at more risk from car accidents than from intentional violence, and that international staff appear more at risk of kidnapping (Annex 1). There are contexts where the presence of an international staff member has reduced the risk for the national staff, and others where accompaniment by national staff is suggested to reduce the risk for international staff. There are also contexts where male staff are more at risk than female staff, and vice versa.

A first management requirement, therefore, is to refine your threat and risk assessment with a consideration of which categories of staff are more at risk from what type of threat. Reflect on, and discuss with staff members, the risk they may run while working in a violent environment: are national staff more at risk than internationals and if so, why? Are there particular categories of national staff more at risk, such as women, young men of fighting age, staff of a particular ethnic identity or political affiliation, relocated national staff from another part of the country and with no connections in the province where they are working now?

What can be done to control the risks for them, and what security support can your agency provide for them? There probably are security measures, such as restrictions on movement after dark, that you can impose on international but not on national staff. What does this mean in terms of agency responsibility for their security? What about stress in national staff resulting from prolonged exposure to high-risk environments: how do they experience it, how do they manage it, and what can you realistically offer in terms of support?

20.2 Staff: The Source of Problems, the Source of Solutions

20.2.1 The Source of Problems

Disgruntled staff

Disgruntled staff feel less loyalty and may create security problems within the agency. Much of this has to do with personnel management. Proper personnel management requires respect for existing employment and contract law. (Because of conflict, state institutions may not be functioning but employees still have 'legal rights'; moreover 'employee rights' are probably one of the issues that your agency would advocate). As a minimum, your employment and personnel policies should be clear, consistent and transparent. Your being perceived as a fair and just employer will strengthen loyalty among your staff.

Disloyal staff

National staff can be a source of security problems within the agency: they could be seen to be hiring too many of their own relatives or friends, thereby affecting the image of the organisation; they may provide 'insider information' to criminals in exchange for a share in stolen goods from the agency; or they may pass on real or false 'sensitive information' to the authorities or non-state actors which compromise the agency's image and security procedures. Care in recruitment, transparency about who you are and what your mission is, staff supervision, internal checks and balances, and security alertness will reduce the risk.

Dishonest staff

Financial checks and balances, stock control or incident analysis may suggest that an international or national staff member has been dishonest. Just as with the suspicion of staff disloyalty, this is an extremely difficult situation that requires careful but also determined action. Care is required to avoid false accusations but also a perhaps violent escalation if a dishonest staff member becomes aware of being investigated and feels under threat. Yet action is necessary or the atmosphere becomes one of pervasive mistrust which affects everybody. As long as there is suspicion but no clear circumstantial indication, let alone proof, of the involvement of a staff member, the investigation will have to be discreet. Evidence suggests that international staff take the lead and responsibility in these investigations as national staff may be more vulnerable to retaliation. If you have no absolute proof but enough circumstantial evidence you will want a quick dismissal, though you will have to think carefully about the grounds for it.

Offending staff

Incompetent, arrogant, corrupt and/or careless staff may create resentment, anger and irritation among outsiders in your working environment. All your staff, therefore, need to be instructed to adopt a correct attitude to all outsiders in your operating environment – be they target beneficiaries or not. Remember that it is not only programme officers who interact with outsiders but also drivers, purchase officers, receptionists, guards, etc. All of them can benefit from a clear understanding of the agency's values, mission, principles and objectives, and an appropriate sense of what is sensitive and confidential.

Complacent staff

A difficult situation, from a management point of view, is one in which there is a perceived risk but no actual incident. As a manager you will have to confront people's 'personal sense of security' and the complacency resulting from it. It is difficult to adopt a policy that prefers to 'err on the side of caution' in the aid environment where international staff in particular seem not infrequently inclined to 'throw all caution to the wind'. The challenge for the manager will be to demonstrate competence in security management and the soundness of the risk analysis, and involve the team in the security planning and reviews. That way staff get to understand the logic rather than reacting to what they perceive as senseless administrative edicts.

20.2.2 The Source of Solutions

This GPR holds that good security management is a team task, and that national staff should be part of that team. The question is, who among the national staff?

The answer may depend on what function of security management we are talking about: monitoring and situational assessment, adopting preventive security measures, or solving a security crisis?

In order to get security measures adopted, implemented and observed, all staff with management responsibilities have to play a role, including the office manager, storekeeper, logistics manager, programme supervisors, etc.

National staff in particular can contribute to ongoing monitoring and situational assessment, but perhaps in an 'outer' and 'inner circle'. The outer circle of staff that contributes to information gathering can involve drivers, programme officers, guards and others who move around and see and hear what goes on in the operating environment. Bear in mind, however, that staff members may be reluctant to mention security problems for a variety of reasons: they may simply

20 Staffing & Personnel Management

not want to bring them up for fear that the agency will stop its programme and they will lose their jobs, or they may not want to mention a perceived risk or problem in front of others whom they do not trust sufficiently. As a manager you will need to create an atmosphere in which staff trust you sufficiently to bring something to your attention, and feel confident that you will handle it sensitively and discreetly without implicating them.

An 'inner circle' can be a few select staff with a demonstrated loyalty to the agency, good contacts, a demonstrated skill in contextual and situational analysis, and a more extensive and in-depth understanding of the dynamics of your operating environment and the potential risks resulting from these. They will be well-informed and trustworthy; people with whom you can discuss highly sensitive and confidential matters. They may not be formally in senior management positions but are identified on the basis of their individual competence in this regard.

At a time of high risk or crisis it is members of the 'inner circle' that you will probably involve. Note that in tense or crisis situations national staff are usually more vulnerable to outside pressure from those to whom they owe social loyalty, and/or to retaliation. A careful allocation of tasks and good role play are therefore required, with international staff being seen to be handling the affair, leading the negotiations, and taking the difficult decisions.

Competent and mature international staff can play a vital role in security management. By being perceived as 'neutral' and outside the local conflict arena they can sometimes build up more broad-based relationships and obtain agreements that local people, whatever their integrity and skill, would find more difficult to realise because they are embedded in the social and political arena. Their presence can sometimes have a protective influence for local people, and the example of their commitment to non-violent values and social work can be an inspiration and confidence booster to national staff.

Case Study: Balancing Competence and Social Vulnerability

An international agency, implementing programmes on behalf of internally displaced people in a Latin American country, appointed a trusted, competent and very well informed national staff member as security manager. Soon afterwards warnings were received, apparently from paramilitary groups, that the agency was not acting in a neutral way but taking political sides. It turned out that not the national security manager but members of her extended family had contacts with the guerrillas. The agency decided to withdraw the formal responsibility for security from the staff member.

You may also consider employing nationals with security expertise as members of your staff in conjunction with, or even without, an internationally recruited security officer. This national could be a former policeman, for example, who might be in charge of the security of premises and the training and supervision of guards. As always, 'technical' expertise in security management should not be confused with the social and political astuteness that is an equally important component of security management.

When evacuation takes place, especially of international staff, national staff may continue to run the programmes (Chapter 14).

20.3 International Staff Issues

20.3.1 Recruitment and Preparedness

As a field manager of an international organisation you seldom have a voice in the recruitment of international staff members, which is undertaken by HQ. What you want, however, are people who have more than just technical competencies.

Tact and interpersonal skills, cultural sensitivity and a mature sense of responsibility and self-discipline are important contributory factors to security (and programme) management. A number of years' experience in the field is no guarantee of maturity: quantity does not automatically guarantee quality, certainly not in the humanitarian sector where personnel management tends to be hasty and references given are not always frank or are not taken up. The shortage of 'experienced' aid workers also means that agencies may recruit whoever they can get rather than who they want.

Whereas you may want someone with experience, you don't want somebody still half burned-out from a previous demanding posting.

HQ should assume certain tasks for pre-mission preparedness, but inevitably the best 'learning' takes place in context. If the record shows a heightened risk in the first three months of an assignment (Annex 1) then it is imperative that intensive briefing is provided to newcomers upon arrival. This should include detailed contextual orientation and explanation of the logic behind the security measures in place.

20 Staffing & Personnel Management

20.3.2 Authority and Credibility

More often than not international staff are automatically put in senior positions. This practice is often justified on the basis of technical skill, although there may be elements of 'bias' and 'prejudice' as well.

National staff tend to be keenly aware of potentially problematic dimensions to this practice: lack of knowledge of the working environment and of the culture, social habits and language; not infrequently lack of the 'age' and perceived 'experience' to have credible authority in the eyes of local people and local staff. Younger and older expatriates can create dysfunctional teams, especially when they are perceived as being both ignorant and arrogant. This may directly or indirectly contribute to resentment, anger and threats, and therefore to security problems. It may be good practice to discuss honestly and openly, with newly arriving expatriates, the need for sensitivity, tact, listening and consultation, and to take up concerns in this regard before problems crystallise.

20.3.3 Discipline

A security strategy that relies on acceptance as well as preventive measures will be undermined if staff are undisciplined in their speech and behaviour. Ideally you want staff to demonstrate common sense and self-discipline. In practice that will not always be the case.

The reality is that not infrequently managers in international organisations are stricter about enforcing discipline among national staff than among international staff; also with regard to security. There are a variety of reasons for this:

- the awareness that international staff can be more susceptible to stress because they are further removed from their normal environment;
- the realisation that it is difficult to attract and retain international staff in difficult environments, and that there is a high financial cost to staff turnover;
- a fear that international staff will initiate a formal complaint procedure more quickly than national staff;
- the inclination of expatriate managers to socialise more with other expatriates, which makes it difficult to call to order someone whom you regularly have a beer with in the evening or even share a residence with.

Understandable as these reasons are, they cannot become reasons for allowing international staff to get away with behaviour which is irresponsible from a security point of view. Managerial practice of 'two measures', one for national and one for international staff – as if the latter were 'above the law' – would be completely unacceptable. In higher-risk environments you may have to make security procedures mandatory and breaches of them a 'disciplinary offence'.

20.3.4 The Private Sphere

Another difficult area is the 'private sphere'. During a security alert phase it may be easy to keep international staff from visiting bars and discotheques or going on picnics, etc. However, it will be difficult to explain that releasing stress by, for example, heavy drinking in public (with rows of agency cars lined up outside the bar every evening), too many liaisons and affairs that are not kept discreet, or arrogant behaviour and improper dress, affect the image of your agency and of international aid workers as a whole. Doing aid work does not require one to live like a saint, but it does require social and cultural sensitivity and does not offer a licence for total personal freedom and liberty.

This is a difficult and sensitive issue that can best be raised proactively at HQ and at field level. Managers should lead by example and persuade by argument and should not shy away from confronting an international staff member whose behaviour is considered offensive and dangerous, to the point of ordering early repatriation. At least one major international organisation has had extensive discussions about this which resulted in an internal 'code of conduct' about good behaviour and staff attitudes which new staff members have to sign as 'read and understood'.

20.4 National Staff Issues

20.4.1 Recruitment

Failing to invest time in careful recruitment and subsequent staff monitoring can cost you dearly, not only in terms of job performance but also security. Recruiting the right staff is crucial but also difficult, especially when an agency comes new to an environment and needs to respond urgently to an emergency. The first few national staff recruits will be influential, since at least, for a while these staff may acquire a strong influence in the agency management which may be difficult to reverse. The following principles of good practice arise from many cases:

20 Staffing & Personnel Management

Professional and social references

Technical job qualifications are a necessary but not sufficient criterion for recruitment. In theory professional references should be taken up about an applicant, but in practice agencies do not do this even if a national has worked for another aid organisation in the same environment. It would be further good practice to take up what might be called 'social references' – ie, identifying other people in the community, preferably with standing and authority, who are prepared to vouch for the integrity of the applicant. Certainly in more traditional social environments these people can come to act as the 'guarantor' of a staff member; in return they may challenge the aid agency over perceived poor personnel policies and practices. Seeking out social references takes time and effort but it may prevent you from recruiting people with known bad reputations or even criminal affiliations. It can also set you on course to creating stronger relationships with your surrounding social environment. One practice, however, needs to be guarded against: the national staff member recruited on the recommendation of another local person is subsequently forced to pay a percentage of his/her salary to the 'guarantor'.

Start with short-term contracts

If you have to recruit in a totally new environment and/or in a hurry, for example, to scale up your response to an emergency, then it may be wise to issue short-term contracts with no guarantee of renewed employment so that you maintain your room for manoeuvre. At the same time you need to know and observe the national labour legislation with regard to repeated renewal of short-term contracts.

20.4.2 Staff Composition

An acceptance strategy (Chapter 5) requires you to take more than strictly technical/professional criteria into account in recruitment. What you want to avoid is ending up, unknowingly, with most national staff or most mid and senior level national staff coming from one ethnic group, political party, or social group (be they a clan, caste, occupational group, or simply mostly young urban English-speakers with totally different social habits from the people in your programme environment).

Broad-based representation

One sometimes sees aid agencies with almost a 'caste' staff system: a few white expatriates at the top, then senior national staff from urban backgrounds and sometimes predominantly from one social or political group, and then a larger complement of national staff from other social origins in the lower jobs. This can generate internal tensions and complicate the development of broad-based relationships. Good management would imply that people from different backgrounds can feel equally part of the organisation.

Balanced 'representation'

Your staff composition is a very important factor in how you are perceived (Chapter 5). Diversity of staff in a socially diverse and politically fragmented environment is generally an asset. It supports your claim of 'neutrality' and 'impartiality', can help you develop broad-based relationships, and can give you access to information and perspectives from diverse sources. The drawback is that you may import the external tensions and conflict into the agency. This creates its own difficulties, but if you can't manage to promote better understanding and constructive conflict resolution among your own staff you are unlikely to be able to succeed in the divided world around you.

20.4.3 Differential Organisational Support

The agency ethos will hold national staff in the same regard as international staff, and will accept the principle that because national staff run the same risks they have the same rights. Yet in practice there are differences in what it can and will be prepared to do at a time of acute crisis. What national staff often resent is not so much that their agency cannot provide the same security support for them as for its international staff, but that it is not honest and transparent about this in its statements and remains vague about where it sees the limits of its responsibility until the last critical moment.

Good practice suggests that you should proactively discuss these matters with national staff and in consultation with HQ. Be realistic and honest about what national staff can and cannot expect from your agency. That way they can make an informed decision before the crisis becomes acute, about how they want to try and secure themselves and their families (Chapter 14).

20.5 Gender Dimensions in Security Management

Gender issues related to security can appear among and between international and national staff. They may be anticipated or may suddenly appear in a discussion or dispute about security measures. This is a generally underexplored issue in aid agencies. The following paragraphs are therefore only introductory.

20.5.1 Gender Roles and Security Risks

Gender is a biological given but also a social and cultural construct that expresses itself in role behaviour and relationships. Power is a strong social dynamic in relationships between men and women. Possible expressions of such roles are:

Men have to appear 'strong': This may lead them to refuse to admit that they don't know how to drive a 4-wheel drive, and not to accept that they are poor drivers. It may be expressed, for example, in fast driving or heavy drinking, both of which increase risk. A 'macho' appearance in dress and behaviour may provoke anger and contribute to the escalation of a situation. In a dangerous situation, men may want to assume leadership and portray themselves as protectors of women. This can lead to team tensions which, in a delicate or dangerous situation, can increase risk. Men do not easily admit to fear and may be more reluctant to admit their stress so that they go beyond their limits, which also increases risk. Because they want to be the 'protectors', men can suffer deep feelings of guilt for not having been able to prevent the rape of a female colleague'. They may also feel humiliated and resentful.

Women on the other hand tend to be more aware of their particular vulnerabilities, especially to sexual aggression. This may influence where they live, and how, where and at what times they move, what transport they take, where they park the car, and so on. It may influence them in ways they do not necessarily express: in a high-risk environment this creates a constant additional stress and women may find they do things as part of their agency activities that they would not normally do and that in fact are against their personal judgement. This may create confusion and cause risk to be perceived differently. Depending on the environment and the attitude of their male colleagues, female staff members may have to apply real effort to be taken seriously, and may have to assert their independence and freedom of choice in ways that their male colleagues don't. This can lead to antagonistic behaviour or behaviour that is perceived as over assertive, which can affect team coherence, or to risk-taking behaviour, which can be dangerous. Of course a female staff member can just as easily take over the leadership in times of crisis.

20.5.2 Gender and Authority

Depending on their attitude, male staff may be reluctant to accept the risk assessment and the resulting security procedures of a female manager. They might adopt a macho stance and challenge her, accusing her of overreacting and panicking.

Case Study: Challenges to the Risk Assessment of a Female Manager

A female country representative in a high-risk country eventually resigned after the agency's HQ did not offer her any tangible support when some male colleagues (international) refused to accept her security guidelines which imposed certain restrictions on movement, and claimed that she was 'overreacting'. HQ told her that security management was her 'responsibility' but did not back up her authority. She felt that, with her authority challenged and undermined, she did not want to take the 'responsibility' if something happened, and so resigned.

Male staff, however, may also contest the decisions of a male manager, accuse him of being a 'wimp' and challenge his 'leadership of the pack' in a 'man to man' way. Female staff may also contest the security measures of a male manager as 'patronising' and 'male chauvinism', especially if they impose restrictions on what are considered to be personal freedoms. If this becomes an open dispute, both organisational gender and security policies are mobilised and the situation can become confusing and demoralising.

20.5.3 Gender and Negotiation

Security guarantees have to be negotiated with governmental and non-governmental actors. Security problems may require negotiation for their resolution. It is likely that the interlocutors will react differently when the negotiations on behalf of the agency are conducted by a woman rather than a man. Anticipate this and if you choose to negotiate as a team, think through in advance its composition, roles and tactics.

In some contexts women are considered less threatening to men than other men. It might therefore be a deliberate choice to appoint a woman as spokesperson when your group is confronted with hostile people or caught in an incident. But there is a risk here as well. Women are more easily prey to aggressors wanting to show off their power; alternatively if your female team member negotiates with those who arm a roadblock, the intransigents may see this as insulting and become angry. You also want to avoid a female spokesperson being taken away on her own, supposedly to 'talk to the leader' of those who stop and threaten you.

20 Staffing & Personnel Management

20.5.4 Gender and Individual Freedoms

Gender issues may emerge with regard to restrictions on behavioural freedoms, especially with internationally recruited staff, for example:

- When you try to impose what may be perceived as 'restrictions' on female staff, for example, in terms of their choice of residence or the obligation to use an agency vehicle, or to be accompanied by someone else after a certain hour for their safety.
- If you advise male staff to stay away from certain bars after office hours because it is known there is a high risk of brawls. Also if you request that male staff not visit local brothels or get involved with local women when this might create a security risk.
- If you advise female staff not to socialise too publicly with men who are not members of their family in an environment where this is strongly frowned upon and resented, of if you request female staff to dress more 'modestly' or 'conservatively' in a particular operational context which is more tolerant of how men dress.
- When international male and female staff engaged in an intimate relationship with a local person are told to obey orders without protest and dispute if a decision is taken to evacuate all international staff.

Restricting what are perceived as individual freedoms, especially after working hours and at weekends and on holidays, is always vulnerable to contestation. The contestation may, however, quickly shift from 'security' to 'gender' considerations. Discussing these issues proactively and developing an internal 'code of staff conduct' can go a long way to maintaining clarity about individual responsibilities and freedoms.

20.6 Organisational and Individual Responsibility

What are the relative responsibilities of the individual staff member and the agency as regards health, safety and security issues? This is a vital question which is very often left vague and ambiguous.

As a resident representative you need to be able to indicate clearly to your staff what their responsibilities and obligations are, but also what they can expect from your agency. However, this is not something that you can decide; it is a wider organisational responsibility.

Organisational policies on this matter are largely underdeveloped. Admittedly one cannot legislate for each and every situation but a general organisational line of deciding matters on a case by case basis is unacceptable: it is a green light for inconsistency, arbitrariness and evasion of responsibility. A general policy that is vague is also of limited use. A sexually assaulted staff member gets little from a statement that 'assistance and support will be provided' if the manager, and therefore the organisation, cannot give precise answers as to whether this includes a continuation of salary during a recovery period, payment of legal assistance, of travel expenses for treatment or legal action, specialised counselling or support services, and for how long, etc.

You should persist in demanding clarity from your HQ so that you can be clear vis-à-vis the people for whose security you are responsible.

Resources:
Macnair, R (1995) 'Room for Improvement: The management and support of relief and development workers' (London: Overseas Development Institute, Humanitarian Practice Network) Network Paper 10 <hpn@odi.org.uk> <http://www.odihpn.org.uk>.

'The People-in-Aid Code of Best Practice in the Management and Support of Aid Personnel' (1997) (London: Overseas Development Institute, Humanitarian Practice Network) Network Paper 20 <http://www.peopleinaid.org.uk> <Aidpeople@aol.com>.

20 Staffing & Personnel Management

PART VII
SECURITY MANAGEMENT

21 Security Management and Security Plans

21 Security Management and Security Plans

21.1 How Appropriate and Effective is Your Security Plan?

Security plans have been a mainstay of aid agency security in violent environments. However, more emphasis has been put on the existence of a security plan than on its quality. A quick critical examination of your existing plan, perhaps on a team basis, could be useful:

- Do you have an adequate understanding of the context in which you operate?
- Do you have a clear sense of your mission and of the 'position' you want to adopt and the role you want to play in your environment?
- Is your plan based on a systematic threat and risk assessment, and do you regularly review this assessment?
- Is it supported by clear policies that spell out the responsibilities of the agency and of individual staff?
- Do you consider programme choices and implementation approaches from a security point of view?
- Do staff understand the rationale behind your standard operating procedures?
- Are staff disciplined about the observance of these procedures?
- Have your staff been given guidance and preparedness training for incident survival?
- Do you have crisis management guidelines for different incident scenarios?
- Do you feel that the news of security incidents, also from others operating in your environment, reaches you quickly most of the time?
- Do you feel that you as security manager(s) have the required skill and competence to discharge that responsibility?

If the answer to most of these questions is 'no' then perhaps you have a 'dead' administrative document which is not very effective in controlling risk and gives a dangerously false sense of security?

This GPR recommends that the emphasis be shifted from the 'security plan' to 'security planning' and 'security management' as broader ongoing activities, that are performed on a team basis rather than by one person.

21.2 Organisational Responsibility

Security management in an international organisation cannot be totally delegated to the country office. This GPR also holds that security planning and security management are a wider organisational responsibility:

- By and large policies need to be developed organisation-wide.
- Deciding on the purpose of the mission, or reviewing it, will involve HQ.
- So too will the assessment of the risks and the requirements for risk reduction.
- The organisation as a whole has a responsibility to mobilise the necessary financial, material and also human (skill/expertise as well as time allocation) resources for effective security management.
- Organisations need to provide guidelines for incident survival, crisis management and post-incident management.
- Again HQ needs to articulate policy guidelines with regard to intra- and interagency information policy concerning security.
- HQ typically manages the personnel matters of international staff and needs to adopt a security perspective in this (eg, by addressing security issues in the recruitment interview, paying attention to personal competence and stress resistance, providing back-up to field-level managers whose authority is unduly challenged, etc).
- Finally, HQ will also play a more or less central role in the management of certain crises, such as kidnapping, sexual aggression, security evacuation, medical evacuation and repatriation of the body of a deceased staff member.

21.3 Security Planning and Documentation

21.3.1 At Organisational Level

General policy and capabilities

In principle an aid agency that deploys people in high-risk areas should have general policies, procedures and capacities to manage the associated risks. The following is a hypothetical list of documents where these policies could be spelled out. These documents have an organisation-wide remit, are developed at and by HQ, and are general reference documents, also for the field manager. Documents should always be dated and the author(s) and his/her position(s) identified:

- Agency mandate, general mission statement, values and principles.
- General agency security policy statement.
- Detailed implementation protocol for the general security policy spelling out how essential financial and material resources will be mobilised, skill and expertise obtained and retained, and who will do what.
- Detailed management protocol, spelling out the responsibilities for security management and crisis management and who makes decisions, how and about what (differentiating between HQ and field).
- Detailed policy statements spelling out agency responsibilities, obligations and commitments with regard to specific types of potential risk and suffering or loss as well as individual responsibilities of employees.
- General reference and resource documents, eg, on adequate shelter in battle zones, on radio equipment and radio use, etc.
- A list of essential external contacts (government authorities, embassies, airlines, medical and mental health back-up, specialist security expertise, etc).

Mission or operation-specific risk assessments:

- Synopsis of the conflict analysis.
- Specific mission objectives in a theatre of operations, a general risk assessment, an explicit statement of the assumptions made, an explicit statement of the capacity requirements (resources but also skills) for security management, a statement on the threshold of acceptable risk.
- Implementation capacity: essential human resources (expertise and skill, time), essential material resources, essential permissions and collaboration agreements that need to be obtained.

The issues following mission or operation-specific risk assessments should be considered by senior management (including HQ) prior to deployment/return to a risk zone (either a new country or a new geographical area in a country). The last point tends to be overlooked, which is not only bad but dangerous practice: a security plan with an intent that you subsequently cannot implement is not an effective security plan.

The documentation is a record of important decisions made and the analysis and assumptions on which they were made. It is a baseline reference for future review/evaluation.

Security Management & Security Plans

21

It is the international and specialised emergency response agencies in particular that have the concept of a 'mission'. Yet it may be equally relevant for a national organisation or for an international organisation, with a development mandate, that has been in-country for many years and now finds itself in a destabilising situation. Key questions such as: What do you want to do?, Are the risks greater than the potential benefits?, and Is the security situation such that you are still able to achieve most of your objectives? are relevant for any type of organisation.

21.3.2 At Field Level

The most common reference for security management at field level is the security plan. A review of a variety of security plans from various agencies in various countries reveals many similarities and key components. They also vary in length from anything from between five and 40 pages. What they generally have in common is that they are a mix of policy statements, management responsibilities, procedural guidelines for prevention, guidance on radios and communications, security phases, steps in evacuation, and checklists and contact numbers. Studying the security plan is undoubtedly a good exercise to focus the attention, but the end product does not generally seem to be very useable. The recommendation here is to:

- put more emphasis on briefing, competence and skill development and regular team review;
- classify the documentation into those documents that change very slowly over time (eg, policy statements and certain crisis management guidelines) and those which get rapidly outdated (this will very much depend on how volatile your context is; it may include the contact list and the risk analysis but also, depending on the situation, your context analysis and your withdrawal/hibernation plans;
- diversify the documentation according to the specific users and occasions, ie, distinguish between security documentation for all staff members (national and international) and information essentially for the crisis management team; also between guidelines for fairly 'normal' circumstances, and higher alert circumstances.

All staff members need to know about:

1. The agency they work for.
2. The assessment of the situation they find themselves in.
3. General guidance on security awareness and safe and secure behaviour.

4. Specific guidance on incident survival and evacuation/hibernation.
5. Contacts, maps.

This requires the following documentation:

1. **The agency they work for**

- agency mandate, values and principles;
- general agency security policy statement;
- mission in context statement (identify changes over time);
- identification of management responsibilities for security, agency and individual responsibilities (this may include specifics on the responsibilities of drivers, guards, the radio operators, store keepers and cashiers/accountants etc, that all staff should be aware of).

2. **The assessment of the situation they find themselves in**

- a synopsis of the general situation in-country;
- a map and short profile of key actors;
- threat assessment, perhaps on a more detailed geographical/temporal basis;
- key security strategy(ies) of the agency in response to the threats;
- known and potential indicators of a deteriorating situation.

3. **General guidance on security awareness and on safe and secure behaviour**

This will probably include:

- guidelines to maintain physical health (including protection from STDs);
- guidelines for safety while driving/in the residence;
- general good practice for security awareness and risk reduction such as:
- personal appearance and behaviour in the office, in the residence, while staying overnight somewhere else (hotel...); or while moving on foot and in a vehicle;
- with regard to cash/portable assets, ID cards and keys, and key documents/sensitive information;
- stress and self-management
- code of individual staff behaviour, disciplinary procedures and the conditions under which the agency will disclaim responsibility for incidents;

- general good practice in communications
  - within the agency,
  - with official and de facto authorities,
  - with the press,
  - with UN/non-UN peacekeeping/international police force,
  - with house staff,
  - reporting obligations and good practice in reporting on security;
- essential information/supplies:
  - to be available in the embassy,
  - to be kept in the office, the residence, the car,
  - to be carried on the person;
- security alert phases and mandatory actions resulting from their declaration.

4. Specific guidance on incident survival and evacuation

It is useful to spell out, in writing, key messages for the survival of specific types of incidents, the threats of which are identified as real in the working environment, for example, armed robbery, sexual assault, rioting and mob violence, air raids, etc. It is strongly recommended to discuss and talk these through with staff and ideally to run through simulation exercises.

As discussed in Chapter 14, individual staff need to be knowledgeable about evacuation/hibernation but they do not need to know every detail. Most nationally recruited staff need to know what they can and cannot expect and what procedures the agency intends to follow, time allowing, prior to a total evacuation but needs more detail on relocation plans. International staff need more detail about the actual evacuation plan. Senior staff in a district/province who might have to be evacuated/withdrawn within the country need to know the principles and have the skills to develop and adapt a locally appropriate plan. This again is an area where drill and skill count for more than having read the plan, so again it should be the object of discussion and ideally some simulation exercises.

5. Contacts and maps

These should not be attached to the above documents, but issued separately for easy use. The list of contacts and maps is not necessarily identical to that for the agency management team, for general staff in the capital city, or for staff in provincial offices. Contacts (and maps) should be readily available in offices and residences, but key contact numbers (and maps) also need to be carried on the person and learned by heart in high-risk areas.

Apart from the above, the field management/field-level crisis management team need a more detailed analysis on a number of issues, and checklists for quick reference.

Preparedness guidelines and protocols:

- Security management responsibilities and implementation protocol: who has decision making authority, and is responsible for the allocation of tasks and responsibilities between HQ and the field and within the crisis management team at field level in different areas, eg, in routine risk control, crisis management, or in cases of hibernation or evacuation. Summarise each in a checklist.
- Security levels and mandatory measures that follow from each, with more detail on what the field management will do in each state of alert. Perhaps event-specific guidelines for critical events with potentially higher security risks which can be anticipated, eg, elections, and which may lead to a proactive alert through the declaration of a certain security phase – though it may make sense, for the occasion, to issue all staff in advance with more event-specific security guidelines and decisions.
- Context-specific guidelines on crisis management according to type of incident (eg, office burglary, sexual assault, or forced hibernation in dangerous environments as well as evacuation on medical grounds and the repatriation of the body of a deceased staff member.
- Context-specific guidelines and protocols for post-crisis case management, ie, incident analysis, as well as staff report and security management review.
- Context-specific guidelines for information exchange and/or collaboration with other agencies or institutions.
- General crisis scenarios (as distinct from incident scenarios) and hibernation and evacuation plans (plan A and its underlying assumptions and alternative plan B?)

Reference materials and external resources:

- List of essential safety and security equipment (and emergency supplies) to be kept in the office, in vehicles and in residences, and to be carried by staff.
- Key documentation in paper and electronic format: staff details; asset details (vehicles, communications equipment, office equipment); accounts and outstanding financial liabilities (rent, leasing, outstanding

Security Management & Security Plans **21**

purchase or service fee instalments, payroll matters, etc); key project details (proposals, narrative and financial progress reports, project assets).
- Key contacts and resources: national and local authorities; diplomatic resources; warden systems; other aid agencies (including an overview of communication trees, communication channels and their times of operation); rescue services (fire, ambulance); technical expertise (eg, radio repair, car crash repairs, driver training schools); legal advice; medical support.
- Maps and sketch maps.

Detailed situational analysis:

- Detailed actor and conflict dynamics analysis including international interventions and national humanitarian, human rights and/or peace-building activities.
- Detailed threat, vulnerability and risk assessment.
- The context-specific (mix of) security strategies chosen in response to specific threats and risks, with an explicit assessment of their pros and cons.

If well developed at the outset the preparedness guidelines and reference documents will normally require only minimal updating. In a rapidly evolving situation the situational assessment and analysis may require regular review. It remains advisable to document the key elements not only to support institutional memory through staff changes but also to enable trend analysis.

21.4 Security Management

Security planning is a necessary but insufficient component of security management. Effective security management also requires constant monitoring, anticipation through scenario-thinking, and review. It cannot be reviewed, however, if there is nothing tangible or clear to review. That is why you need to develop a dated baseline and reference documentation as mentioned earlier.

21.4.1 Monitoring

The following will need to be monitored:

- situational developments in a conflict situation and/or impressions or trends of the nature and incidence of crime;
- the public image and acceptance of aid agencies in general and yours in particular;

- security incidents affecting others;
- your vulnerabilities and exposure;
- the protection of sensitive information;
- staff discipline in the observance of standard operating procedures;
- staff responsibility and discipline in the reporting of incidents and general information potentially relevant to security;
- the state of mind and stress levels of individual staff;
- team spirit and team cohesion;
- the security dimensions of programme choices or implementation strategies, etc.

When to monitor

Most of this should be monitored continuously, though closer attention should be paid in high-risk areas where events are rapidly unfolding. You will also monitor more closely after 'significant events' internally in the agency, such as changes in staff, in the programme, or in your operational location(s), as well as for some time after a significant incident that directly affected your or another agency.

Who monitors

The core management team at field level, that is, the resident representative and his/her deputy, together with a designated security officer, if applicable. You have probably organised a larger security management team which would normally include other senior managers such as the office manager/administrator, the logistics officer, as well as staff with sectoral (eg, medical, agricultural) and geographical management responsibilities. By extension, every staff member with supervisory responsibilities.

21.4.2 Proactive Scenario-thinking

The art, not the science, of security management is to anticipate and avoid, not just develop or improve risk-control measures after the incident has happened. That is why this GPR stresses the importance not only of preventive, risk-control measures but also of incident preparedness by those who might be caught up in an incident, and by those who will be managing the immediate phase of it. On a larger scale, however, this GPR stresses the importance of in-depth contextual knowledge and close monitoring of trends in crime and conflict as well as rising tensions and critical moments or events. A good security management team will therefore will regularly devote time and attention to scenario thinking.

21.4.3 Reviewing

When to review
- when there are significant changes in the external context, especially as a result of the actions of the major protagonists;
- when you have been affected by an incident;
- when someone else is affected by an incident that in its nature or intensity appears to introduce a 'new element' into the situation.

What to review
This will depend on your incident analysis. Virtually everything can be a potential candidate for review:

- your larger context and situational analysis;
- your threat assessment;
- your risk assessment;
- your mix of security strategies;
- your preventive/risk-controlling standard operating procedures;
- your crisis management guidelines and/or practices;
- the incident survival guidelines and competencies of staff;
- your recruitment criteria;
- your staffing policy;
- your rest and relaxation policies for staff;
- your communication technology choices;
- your vehicle and transport choices;
- the interagency security information-sharing arrangements/practices;
- your programme choices and/or implementation strategy, etc.

21.5 Maintaining Alertness, Discipline and Effectiveness

Effective security management ultimately relies not on documents but on skill, discipline, alertness and information exchange. Most of the time it is an interactive not an administrative exercise. There are 'natural' moments when security will be discussed: during security training, at special security meetings, or at times of incidents and high tension or imminent crisis. Remember, in a time of acute crisis people tend not to refer to 'the plan'. At such times you want your staff not to react impulsively but to use their 'common sense' and the 'instinct' they have acquired from understanding the context and from self-discipline and drill. This requires a constantly maintained high level of security awareness and security competence.

Security and risk control must be routinely and explicitly on the agenda in interactions and discussions and at key moments in the professional assignment cycle of the aid worker:

- at the time of recruitment;
- in pre-departure briefing for international staff;
- at in-country arrival/start of employment for new staff;
- prior to and after assessment missions into new territory;
- prior to programme decisions, during interim programme reviews;
- prior to travel in and upon return from any risk area;
- during regular staff meetings in risk areas;
- as part of the regular supervisory activities of mid-level and senior-level managers;
- as part of the end-of-assignment handover to a successor;
- as part of contract debriefing.

Synopsis: From the Security Plan for Management to the Management Plan on Security

1. Security management is more than a security plan.

2. The documentation related to security will be diverse:

- some will have general application eg, policy statements;
- some will be generic but require contextual adaptation eg, guidelines for prevention, incident survival and crisis management, incident follow up, checklists etc.
- some will be very context and time specific eg, the mission concept, the context and actor analysis, threat and risk assessment, situational mix of security strategies, contact lists etc.

3. The three major management questions are:

i. who needs to know what:
- what type of documents do they need?
- how to ensure that the insights are absorbed and turned into skill and discipline (briefing, training, supervision)

Continued...

Security
Management &
Security Plans

21

ii. how do you ensure that your security management is not only incident-driven (retro-active) but also driven by scenario thinking and pro-active threat and risk assessment? (the task of a small security management team)

iii. how do you integrate security considerations into:
- your programme planning and implementation;
- your personnel management;
- your public relations and advocacy work (the task of a senior management team).

4. What you need is not one security plan document for the management, but a management plan on how you will implement good practice around security and risk reduction.

22 Security Management and the Authorities

22 Security Management and the Authorities

22.1 The Responsibility of State Authorities

Nominally, state authorities are responsible for the security of their citizens and any other (law-abiding) person passing through or residing in their national territory. Under the Geneva Conventions, and the more recent Convention on the Safety of UN and Associated Personnel, certain categories of humanitarian aid workers are granted official protection (Annex 2). Both legal instruments are primarily addressed at, and discussed between states. Obviously then, they recognise the sovereignty of the state, while the Geneva Conventions also recognise the military interest of notably states involved in an armed conflict. The UN and the Red Cross and Red Crescent Movement tend to appeal to and defer more explicitly to the responsibilities of the official (or presumptive) authorities. This is not surprising given that the UN and notably the ICRC have a mandate that is recognised by states. NGOs, with a self-ascribed mandate, and who tend to argue that sovereignty is first vested in the people at large before it is delegated to a government, tend to relate less closely to the authorities with regard to security of staff and assets.

Where an authority is party to the conflict there is, in any case, always a tension between working closely together with it and maintaining a position of perceived 'neutrality'. There is also an inherent tension between the responsibility of the national authorities for security, and that of the agency as employer.

22.2 A Sensitive Relationship

Generally, where the national authorities or a non-state actor are involved in hostilities and armed conflict the relationship with humanitarian aid organisations will be sensitive, ranging from cautious tolerance to outright suspicion. The preceding chapters have indicated many moments in security management where these sensitivities can come to the foreground:

- context analysis is perceived as an 'unduly political' activity;
- security assessments and threat monitoring are perceived as implying that the authorities cannot maintain law and order, or even more problematically as 'intelligence gathering';

- the presence and programming of aid agencies in conflict zones can be perceived as affecting the balance of power or the tactics of the warring parties;
- the fact that aid agencies have to establish contact also with non-state actors, who have influence or control over their access and security can be perceived as legitimising 'terrorists' or 'rebels', and as a political act;
- government forces engaged in battlefield operations can cause security risks to aid agencies;
- the authorities may refuse an aid agency permission to deploy telecommunications equipment, especially radios, that it considers essential for its security management;
- poorly equipped and poorly paid governmental security forces may resent aid agency assets and 'requisition' or loot them; government security forces may accuse nationally recruited aid agency staff of working for the 'enemy' and persecute them; they may cause harm to aid agency staff;
- an aid agency can request, but also refuse to accept, armed protection from the authorities;
- an aid agency may question the way in which the police and judiciary deal with cases of sexual aggression;
- an aid agency may feel that the local police is not able or willing to act against criminal gangs;
- an aid agency may feel ambivalent or reluctant about involving the authorities in the resolution of a kidnap or hostage situation;
- the decision to evacuate especially international staff has political connotations which the authorities may not always feel happy about, etc.

22.3 Complex Scenarios

The aforementioned chapters have attempted to identify good practice and to give guidance on security management. It would be unfair, however, to give the impression that in reality the right course of action will generally be clear. By means of real-life cases we here need to present some profound dilemmas. The purpose is to help you think through some of the principles and major parameters that, in consultation with HQ, may shape your answer:

Scenario 1

In a clanic environment with little or no effective government presence, one of your vehicles is hijacked at gunpoint and your local driver killed in the process. Customary law means that his particular clan and lineage segment in that clan become mobilised by his death to undertake action against the perpetrators who are known to belong to another lineage segment of the same clan. The kin of your driver tell you that they will recover the car for you. It is part of customary practice for an aggrieved party to take hostages from the offending party, and also to exact revenge killing of a member of the offending social group. The person killed in retaliation has not necessarily been involved in the car-jacking; he is targeted because of the customary principle of 'collective responsibility'. Do you accept that the kin of your driver assume de facto authority to pursue the car in this manner, or not, and on what grounds? What position would you argue with them?

Scenario 2

Your agency has major assistance programmes for refugees of country Alpha, who have been in neighbouring country Beta for quite some years now. A significant number of your local staff in your office in country Beta are refugees from Alpha. One day a local staff member, your senior logistics officer, is killed in your office by a booby trap that had been attached at night to his chair. The suspicion is that it is an 'inside-job' and that he was killed because he was on the point of unearthing serious fraud involving some others of your local staff. The police of country Beta is known for its heavy-handed methods. If you call upon them, you know with fair certainty that they will arrest several of your national staff members for interrogation, and that they are likely to be detained for several weeks at least, and fiercely beaten if not tortured, to extract a confession. Will you call upon the local police or not, and what are your arguments? What position would you argue with them?

Scenario 3

During a night-time criminal robbery in one of your provincial level offices in country Gamma, one of your female international staff members is raped. You report the matter to the de facto authorities, who control much of the country but are not internationally recognised, and whose politics you do not sympathise with. You request that they take better responsibility for the security of aid agencies and their staff. Two weeks later they invite you to come to their offices, for an identification of suspects they have arrested. You realise that the de facto authorities practice their own form of justice, which you consider constitute 'executions without due judicial process'; a positive identification of the arrested suspect is likely to lead to their quick death. Will you go to the office and if they have indeed the real perpetrators will you confirm this? What are your arguments?

Scenario 4

Your agency has been working with refugees from country Delta in country Zed for some years now. You have good working relationships with the authorities of country Zed. However, one evening a senior, locally based official of the refugee administration of country Zed, together with some of his friends, rapes one of your international staff members, during what was supposed to be a 'social dinner'. Upon her own request you repatriate her two days later. Will you, as an agency, take up the matter with higher officials in the country Zed administration, and also press charges on her behalf, knowing that she would have to return to be interrogated and testify?

22.3.1 Moral and Practical Dilemmas

These scenarios highlight a number of difficult dilemmas:

You would probably accept the following basic principles:

- The cycle of impunity needs to be broken as one measure to increase security.
- You demand from the official or de facto authorities that they assume their responsibility and provide you with security.
- You are committed to respect local custom and culture.

But:

- You don't agree with the methods the authorities use to find the perpetrators and to do 'justice', even if these are part of 'customary law' (Scenario 1);
- You oppose the death penalty, even if this is part of 'customary law' (Scenario 3) or legal in some Western countries.

It is possible to argue that those perpetrating criminal acts know the environment in which they do so, and therefore the likely consequences if they are caught. It is their choice to run the risk of tribal retaliation, detention in inhumane conditions or even summary execution; against this stand Western notions of due legal process and – often – the rejection of the death penalty.

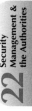

22.3.2. A 'No Win' Situation?

Not calling upon the authorities:

- may mean that in practice you allow the cycle of impunity to continue;
- will also undermine the credibility of your demand that they assume their responsibility and provide you with security. Because, from their perspective, when they are prepared to do so, you refuse their intervention (Scenarios 1 & 2) or you refuse to cooperate (Scenario 3).

Calling upon the authorities, however, in itself creates problems and potential risks:

- it may mean that an affected staff member has to return to be interrogated and perhaps to testify, which is psychologically very stressful (Scenarios 3 & 4);
- it can cause serious tension among your national staff and/or a serious rift between international and national staff (Scenario 2);
- it could antagonise the governmental administration against you if you press charges against another civil servant (Scenario 4) to the point that you may not be able to continue your programme;
- it could expose you to retaliation from friends or kinsmen of the criminals (Scenarios 1 & 3), which may force you to close your programmes.

These sorts of situations may be beyond the scope of good practice recommendations and crisis management guidelines. They will require situational judgement and an acceptance that there is no 'best solution'.

ANNEXES

Annex 1 Trends in Aid Agency Security Risks

The insecurity of aid agencies has received much attention in recent years. A seminal incident in this regard was the targeted assassination of six ICRC staff members in Chechnya in late 1996. Generally speaking, there are two perceptions that have become quite common:

1. Aid work has become more risky; more aid workers get injured and killed.
2. Aid organisations and aid workers are being targeted.

Problematic Statistics

Are these perceptions correct? This is very difficult to say in the absence of reliable statistics. Following are some of the figures that have been circulated:

• The ICRC reports an increase in the number of incidents from around 24 per annum in the early 1990s, to around 135 per annum between 1994–1997.
• Out of a total of 1074 military personnel killed in all past and ongoing missions of the UN up to late March 1994, 202 were killed in 1993 alone.
• Between 1 January 1992 and 1 March 1997, 131 civilian UN staff (ie, excluding peacekeepers) lost their lives due to violence.
• Between 1989 and 1998, 45 staff members of the World Food Programme lost their lives, of which 32 through murder, 3 due to work-related illness, and 10 through accidents.
• Between 1 January 1994 and 11 March 1997, 35 cases of hostage taking/kidnapping of UN staff involved 80 internationally recruited and 39 locally-recruited staff.
• Three-quarters of all country programmes of an experienced and reputed French NGO will face a smaller or larger security problem every year, and the organisation as a whole has to deal with at least one major security incident every year.

What does this tell us? Very little in fact. The following box summarises the problems for trend analysis:

Why we Can't Determine Larger Trends in Aid Agency Security

- **Underreporting:** Many aid agencies, especially NGOs, don't keep statistics on security incidents affecting their own staff and assets; a number of organisations do not have a policy in place that enforces incident reporting as well as incident analysis; where reports exist they may be kept confidential.

- **No common reporting categories:** There is no common use of reporting categories between and even within organisations:
  - some incident statistics do not distinguish between loss of assets, eg, from theft of looting, and incidents that affected the physical integrity of a staff member (injury and death);
  - some reports of staff lives lost do not indicate whether this was due to accident, illness or an act of violence;
  - there is no clear distinction between 'incidents' and 'casualties': with more effective security measures, eg, it is imaginable that the number of incidents would continue to rise but the number of casualties, especially fatalities, would decrease;
  - agencies use different categories in attributing acts of violence, eg, one might classify its incidents under the categories 'crime/banditry/act of war'; another under the categories 'banditism/terrorism/acts of war and of the police'. As a result many available statistics are not comparable without returning to the original incident reports.

- **There can be no valid trend analysis without a determined 'population' (demoninator):** in other words, we need to know the (changing) population of aid workers over time, per organisation, and across the sector, in order to see whether the number of aid workers injured or killed by manmade violence/1000 aid workers increases or decreases!

Some Trend Impressions

Given the problems with the data we cannot analyse trends, rather deduce trend impressions:

- **Rising criminality:** The proportion of security incidents classified as acts of crime and banditry as distinct from acts of war increased during the 1990s to 50 per cent or more.

- **Risks to local staff:** Local staff are more often victims of security incidents than expatriate staff (in a ratio of two-to-four local staff for one international staff). Whether this is only due to there generally being a larger number of local staff is unclear.
- **Risks to international staff:** International staff are generally more at risk from hostage-taking and kidnapping.
- **Trend changes are not a proportional issue alone:** An increase or decrease in the population of aid workers (ie, the total population 'at risk') does not automatically lead to an increase or decrease in the number of incidents.

Statistics of ICRC and UN casualties indicate a rapid rise in security incidents towards the mid-90s, with a subsequent decrease. The impressionistic picture from NGOs, however, does not follow this pattern and indicates an ongoing increase in incidents. It is not very clear what the contributing factors are for the decreases among UN and Red Cross/Crescent staff: a renewed respect for their staff, the agencies erring more on the side of caution and withdrawing more quickly from dangerous situations, better security skill among staff, better security strategies, or etc.

Safety or Security Risks?

It is often asserted that more aid workers get injured or killed from safety-related causes (especially car accidents and medical conditions) than from security-related causes.

Statistics on death of aid workers from medical causes seem no less difficult. There are persistent rumours that a much higher number of aid workers contract sexually transmitted diseases, including HIV/AIDs, than is popularly assumed. Difficulties related to identifying the precise moment when a disease was contracted, getting information from former employees no longer under contract, and medical confidentiality, all make it unlikely that any 'hard data' can be expected. But it is well known that 'safe sex' remains a problem and stressful and violent environments may lead to more unprotected sex. This appears to remain a high-risk factor, which needs to be more openly and vigorously addressed by aid agencies.

Car accidents are a major cause of injury and death, and assertive action by agencies and field-managers is required.

But does it matter? The question whether safety risks are greater than security risks is not simply one of statistics. Rightly or wrongly, the impact of a serious security incident on the aid agency concerned, but sometimes also on the presence and programmes of other agencies in the same environment, is much greater. For instance, the targeted assassination of an expatriate aid worker will affect your work much more than the death of three expatriates in car accidents.

From an organisational and management point of view the safety and security of all staff matters equally and merits equal attention. From a humanitarian action and impact point of view, security may be a greater concern.

A Sample Study

A recent research project funded by WHO collected information on 382 deaths among humanitarian workers between 1985–1998, from 32 organisations. Some of the conclusions are quite startling:

- Over the 13 years there was an increase in death due to intentional violence and a decrease from motor vehicle accidents. However, not all agencies contributing case material and figures gave their car accident figures, so there remains uncertainty about whether the sample was indeed 'representative'. The number of deaths increased up to the mid-90s and then fell for the UN but continued to rise for NGOs. Intentional violence accounted for 67.4 per cent of deaths, whereas car accidents accounted for only 17.1 per cent – except among UN peacekeepers where they amounted to nearly one-third of deaths. Many violent deaths are caused by crime and banditry. Only 4.5 per cent of the total sample, but nearly 33 per cent of NGO deaths, were due to 'other causes', a category in which diseases are most prominent.
- National and international staff appeared equally at risk, but national staff deaths may have been underreported.
- The average age of death for national and international staff is the late 30s - it is not only the younger and less experienced aid workers that are at risk.
- Over 30 per cent of deaths occurred within the first three months in a particular assignment. A major factor contributing to risk therefore seems to be the (lack of) familiarity with the new environment. Length of previous field experience did not correlate with the time of death. (Agencies that rapidly rotate international staff on short-term assignments therefore put them at considerably higher risk than those who encourage and support longer term field assignments.)
- Guards, medical staff and general field staff were at high risk of intentional violence. Drivers, peacekeepers and office staff were most at risk from car accidents.
- Nearly 64 per cent of deaths occurred in Africa, with the genocide in Rwanda causing a peak in 1994.

Annex 1

Annex 2 > The Legal Protection of Aid Workers

Human rights law is primarily concerned with the right of individuals, particularly in relation to the state. In times of public emergency, such as during armed conflict, states may suspend all but the most fundamental of these rights.

Protection Accorded under the Geneva Conventions

In situations of international armed conflict, international humanitarian law remains applicable. One of its strongest expressions is the Geneva Conventions of 1949 and the two Additional Protocols of 1977; international treaties which are almost universally ratified.

International humanitarian law does not give an unconditional right to receive or provide humanitarian assistance. The primary responsibility to provide such assistance in times of conflict rests with the state or the occupying power. Only when a state or occupying power is unable to supply a population's needs is it required to facilitate relief schemes by states or 'by impartial humanitarian organisations such as the International Committee of the Red Cross'. The use of 'such as' implies that other organisations can also qualify, but emphasis is put on the fact that such organisations must be impartial, neutral and have obtained the consent of the authorities. How you are perceived by the authorities is therefore important. Moreover, the Geneva Conventions, like other forms of international law, also recognise the interests of sovereign states. This means that humanitarian needs are weighed against a state's concerns with national security and its perception of military necessity. Under the Geneva Conventions, therefore, the authority which grants free passage to relief shipments has the right to regulate the times and routes of these shipments, and the right to search, so that it can be 'reasonably satisfied' that the enemy will not use them for its benefit.

Although the four Geneva Conventions of 1949 were drawn up to apply to international armed conflicts (conflicts between states), all four contain an identical Article 3 extending general coverage to non-international (intra-state) conflicts. Although not nearly as extensive as the coverage for international armed conflicts, Common Article 3 does provide basic human rights guarantees such as prohibitions against violence to life and person and the taking of hostages, as well as judicial guarantees in the passing of sentences and the carrying out of executions. The protections of Common Article 3 are extended in Protocol II of 1977; however, they only apply to states which have ratified the Protocol and to internal conflicts which have reached the high threshold requirements of an actual civil war.

Under international humanitarian law your role in an armed conflict determines your 'status'. Three distinct roles have been accepted, namely, combatant, non-combatant and impartial party (or organisation). International humanitarian law offers general protection to wounded, sick or captured combatants, and to civilians.

'General protection' means that they should be treated humanely, should receive material assistance, and can be accessed by authorised impartial relief organisations. Further provisions relate, for example, to the conditions of confinement of non-combatants and restrictions on the displacement and transfer of civilian populations.

Although 'privileged status' is granted to 'medical personnel', this category is narrowly defined in the Geneva Conventions. While military medical personnel are clearly covered, civilian medical personnel are only included when they have received an assignment from the Party to the conflict to which they belong. Privileged status confers certain rights, such as the right of access to those needing care, the right not be punished for having discharged medical functions compatible with medical ethics, generally a right not to be compelled to give information about those in their care, and the right to use the protective emblem. But it also confers certain duties, such as the obligation to provide treatment to all on an impartial basis, abstention from acts of hostility, and the need to be identifiable as medical personnel.

According to Additional Protocol I 71, which extends protective coverage during conflicts of an international character, humanitarian personnel taking part in relief operations are to be respected and protected in the following manner:

1. Where necessary, relief personnel may form part of the assistance provided in any relief action, in particular for the transportation and distribution of relief consignments; the participation of such personnel shall be subject to the approval of the Party in whose territory they will carry out their duties.
2. Such personnel shall be respected and protected.
3. Each Party in receipt of relief consignments shall, to the fullest extent practicable, assist the relief personnel... in carrying out their relief mission. Only in case of imperative military necessity may the activities of relief personnel be limited or their movements temporarily restricted.
4. Under no circumstances may such personnel exceed the terms of their mission under this Protocol. In particular they shall take account of the

Annex 2

security requirements of the Party in whose territory they are carrying out their duties. The mission of any of the personnel who do not respect these conditions may be terminated.

Note, however, that most humanitarian personnel will not fall within the narrow definition of 'medical personnel' with its attendant privileged status. As a rule, therefore, they will only receive the general protections of the civilian population and may put themselves at heightened risk by assuming protections that are not in fact granted them under international humanitarian law.

Another category of personnel entitled to be respected and protected under international humanitarian law is civil defence staff. These have to use their own international distinctive sign: a blue triangle against an orange background.

The logos and signs widely used by aid organisations are not recognised as emblems, nor do they provide any protective status from a legal point of view. Any protection gained from them is entirely dependent on the good will of the authorities or a positive profile in the community. The emblem of the Red Cross/Red Crescent, on the other hand, is recognised under international humanitarian law and does offer protection. Its use, however, is subject to very strict regulation, and misuses are considered a grave breach of law.

The Convention on the Safety of UN and Associated Personnel

In 1994 the UN General Assembly adopted by consensus the Convention on the Safety of UN and Associated Personnel. Article 1 defines who is protected by the Convention. This includes 'United Nations personnel', who are persons engaged or deployed by the Secretary General of the UN as members of the military, police or civilian components of a UN operation, and also other officials and experts on mission for the UN or its specialised agencies or the International Atomic Energy Agency, who are present in an official capacity in the area where a UN operations is being conducted. 'Associated Personnel' includes personnel assigned by a government or an intergovernmental organisation with the agreement of the competent organ of the UN and persons deployed by a humanitarian NGO or agency under an agreement with the Secretary General of the UN, or with a specialised agency or with the International Atomic Energy Agency. In other words, it covers only those non-UN staff, civilian contractors and NGOs who are engaged in UN operations through a close contractual link. The reason for this delineation is the difficulty in broadening the scope of protection to as many categories of personnel as possible, but without extending it to the point that certain states become unwilling to ratify it.

The ICRC has explicitly expressed a desire not to enjoy the protection from this Convention for two main reasons: first because it is already protected through the Geneva Conventions, but secondly and mainly because, in order to maintain its image of impartiality and neutrality and to be able to act as a neutral intermediary, also in situations where UN troops are engaged in hostilities, it needs to be seen as separate and different, including from the UN.

The Convention is applicable not only in situations of armed conflict but also in situations of exceptional risk. It is not applicable, however, where a UN intervention is given a mandate of enforcement under Chapter VII of the Charter. International humanitarian law, however, applies in all situations where the Convention applies, including the latter where the Convention does not apply.

The Convention further specifies a series of acts regarded as breaches of the Convention, such as murder and kidnapping of personnel. States hosting a UN operation are obliged to guarantee the inviolability of personnel, premises and equipment assigned to an operation.

This 1994 Convention entered into force on 15 January 1999. Aid workers with close contractual relationships with the UN should not rely too heavily on the protections of the Convention at this time as there are potential contradictions in its terms and its scope of application remain uncertain and untested.

Extending Legal Protection

During its review in 1996, the 1980 UN Convention on Certain Conventional Weapons was strengthened with regard to Article 8, which originally provided for the protection of UN missions from the effects of mines and booby-traps. The revised version obliges each party to an armed conflict, in every area under its control, to provide protection against the effects of mines, booby-traps and other devices for missions of the ICRC, the National Red Cross or Red Crescent Societies or of their International Federation, and missions of other impartial humanitarian organisations.

Efforts continue to extend, by law, the level of protection, but especially also the scope of 'protected persons'. These are complicated, for example, by different interpretations of what constitutes 'humanitarian activity' and a 'humanitarian organisation', and by the multiplication of logos.

Annex 2

Annex 3 The UN Security Management System

Structure of Responsibility

The primary responsibility for the security of UN personnel and their dependants lies (as for all humanitarian personnel) with the host government. In some instances, the expectations that the UN has of the host government or the 'presumptive authorities' in this regard have been spelled out in more detail, for example, in an annex to the Memorandum of Understanding, beyond the clauses on 'Privileges and Immunities' of the latter document.

Within the UN system the Secretary General nominates a UN Security Coordinator. S/he and his/her support staff reside in New York (UNSECOORD) and are primarily responsible for the formulation of policy for all UN agencies, funds and programmes. In addition, individual UN agencies, such as UNHCR, WFP, UNICEF, also have an identified person or office responsible for the safety and security of the agency's personnel and assets. It is the function of this individual or office to liaise with UNSECOORD on policy issues, and to administer the security concerns that affect the specific agency.

At field level, one senior UN official is appointed by the Secretary General as the 'designated official' (DO) for security. This is often, but does not have to be, the Resident Coordinator or Humanitarian Coordinator. S/he will be responsible for the security of all UN staff and UN assets in a given country. The 'designated official' must set up a 'security management team' that brings together the heads or senior officials of the various UN organisations in-country. A smaller 'crisis management team' can sometimes also be constituted to assist the designated official. This would normally be at a more junior level than the Security Management Team (SMT) and would, conceptually, deal with the detailed management of a crisis, leaving the more senior SMT free to deal with its political ramifications. The 'designated official' can also be assisted by full-time 'field security officers', who can either be jointly funded by all UN agencies in a given location or can be agency-specific officers solely funded by a single agency. In either case they are to assist the DO/SMT in the management of security issues. Area security coordinators (ASC) are appointed in countries that are geographically so large that the DO cannot adequately discharge his/her security responsibilities. ASCs act as 'mini'-DOs for a smaller area and report to the DO. Finally, in larger cities, where there is a large but dispersed presence of UN staff, wardens can be appointed. The warden is required to be an information conduit to UN staff members living in his/her zone in the event of a loss of communications ability in the city.

Diagram 9: The UN Security Management Structure

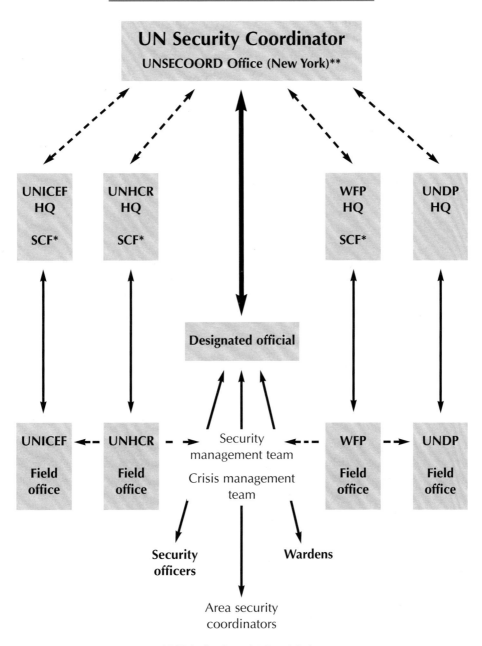

*SCF is the Security Focal Point
**UNSECOORD is the Office of the UN Security Coordinator

Country-specific Security Plan

This is the primary management tool at country level. The plan needs the approval of UNSECOORD. Currently the UN's response to different risk levels is structured according to a standard formula of five phases. The declaration of Phase 1 and 2 is at the discretion of the Designated Official, the declaration of Phase 3 and 4 requires authorisation from UNSECOORD and Phase 5 the authorisation of the Secretary General through UNSECOORD. Different parts of the country can be under different 'phases'.

Phase 1: precautionary; travel to the thus identified area only after prior clearance.

Phase 2: restricted movement; some staff members and their families to stay at home; essential staff to report for work; only essential travel authorised in and out of the country.

Phase 3: relocation of staff and/or their eligible dependants to a designated concentration site or to another part of the country, or outside the country.

Phase 4: programme suspension; evacuation of all internationally recruited staff except those involved in emergency humanitarian operations or security matters.

Phase 5: evacuation of the last remaining internationally recruited staff.

The UN also takes out a 'malicious accidents' insurance policy for its staff members.

Applicability

The UN 'security umbrella' covers all persons employed by the organisation and their recognised dependants. This includes locally recruited personnel, except for those paid by the hour. It also includes UN volunteers and transient consultants, officials or experts on mission for a UN organisation.

Locally recruited personnel and their dependants will not normally be evacuated, except when their security is endangered as a direct consequence of their employment by the UN. The 'malicious acts' insurance does not apply if an employee has acted in violation of the instructions of the designated official, except where the employee put his/her life at risk to save someone else.

The UN will seek to ensure that due process of law be observed in case of arrest or detention of its employees. This relates to the formulation of a formal charge, the right of visitation by the UN, and the right to medical assistance and legal council organised or supervised by the UN.

Non-UN Personnel

Some staff members of NGOs and inter-governmental organisations can benefit from the UN 'security umbrella'. This does not happen automatically, but requires the signing of a specific Memorandum of Understanding with the UN to this effect. The non-UN organisation is first 'sponsored' by a UN agency, then the MoU required is screened by the DoI and then has to be approved by the UN Security Coordinator in New York. Inquire into the details with your local UN office.

Note, however, a number of general characteristics of this arrangement:

1. The option only applies to organisations considered 'implementing partners' of the UN, in other words to organisations that have programme and project agreements with the UN. The MoU only applies for as long as the non-UN organisation is recognised as an 'implementing partner'. This may mean that it comes to an end when an agency no longer implements programmes or projects on behalf of a UN organisation. The arrangement applies to the national and international staff of the implementing partner. In crisis situations, and especially when it comes to evacuation, the UN's ability to do anything concrete for national staff may be limited.
2. Entering into such an agreement obliges the non-UN organisation to share security-related information with the UN, and to follow the security directives of the designated official.
3. UN specialist field security officers and area coordinators are usually funded on a cost-share basis by the various UN agencies in-country. Entering into a security arrangement with the UN implies that a non-UN organisation will participate in the cost-sharing arrangement. In case of evacuation, the cost of the evacuation will also be reimbursable to the UN.
4. The non-UN organisation remains responsible for risk and liability, and the UN will only assume limited liability in connection with travel on UN-provided aircraft.

The UN keeps the terms of this MoU under review so liaise regularly with the UN to keep yourself up-to-date.

Annex 3

Annex 4 Who is Responsible for Security at Field Level?

Models and Practice

Three ideal-type approaches among operational agencies are to regard security responsibility as:

- a general management responsibility among others, such as programme, personnel, finance management, etc;
- a specialist responsibility, located in a 'security officer';
- a combination of both with the security officer providing additional capacity and expertise to the managers.

In practice aid agencies, and NGOs in particular, not infrequently 'delegate' security responsibilities to people with other responsibilities, often the logistician, sometimes the administrator/office manager. Somewhat surprisingly these are the people sent to field security training courses, with no senior manager participating.

The rationale for this practice is not hard to see: risks and vulnerabilities are easily perceived with regard to vehicles and vehicle movements, cash and sites and site security. The logistician and/or the office manager are the staff members dealing with this, therefore they become a focal point for security. In addition, senior field managers tend to be totally overburdened and cannot add daily security management to their already difficult task. This GPR confirms that security management requires dedicated attention, and, in a fairly high risk environment, can become a full-time task. But it also indicates why such 'delegation' is problematic.

A Management Responsibility

The principle that security management, of staff and assets, is and remains the responsibility of the employing organisation and therefore of its senior managers, must be affirmed. At field level this means that the ultimate responsibility lies with the country representative whose authority can only be overridden by more senior managers at HQ.

A second principle is that all other managers, the deputy representative and sectoral or regional managers, as well as supervisors, also have a responsibility for security. This responsibility does not disappear when there is a designated security focal point or even specialist 'security officer'.

A logistician or administrator/office manager, as a mid-level manager, can therefore have delegated responsibility for security. But there are powerful arguments why they should not be the implicitly or explicitly 'designated focal point on security':

- Although telecoms, vehicles and movements, cash and site security and perhaps personnel issues come under their direct purview, these are only some of the areas of vulnerability and potential risk. They have in no way a comparative advantage, eg, with regard to sexual violence, abduction, civil unrest, political terrorism, or resentments and aggression resulting from programme matters.
- They are not typically the people who have responsibility for and access to the information to monitor the surrounding conflict, its dynamics and political economy. For that the agency director is normally best placed.
- They can experience contradictory pressures from their multiple tasks: as a logistician, the priority is to get the supplies to point X; as a security focal point, however, the same person has a different priority and should decide to delay the trucks because the situation is too unstable and risky; as an office manager, paying all the staff at the end of the month is desirable but from a security point of view it may be advisable to split the payroll and pay a third of the staff each on different dates to reduce the amount of cash kept in the office at any one time.
- Security being an additional function, the staff members are first and foremost a 'logistician' or 'administrator'. As such they have no authority over programme managers and programme staff who may be their peers or even superiors in the management hierarchy.

Being a full-time job and requiring certain expertise as well as a perspective not encumbered by other priorities and responsibilities, security management may be delegated to a staff member specifically recruited for that task. Already fairly common among the UN and the OSCE, this approach is gradually being introduced by NGOs in high-risk environments. A frequent problem here remains the common management mistake of 'responsibility without authority'.

Having a security officer separated from programme operations and senior management discussions and whose advice is only 'advice' and who can happily be ignored by all or by his/her superiors, is a waste of money and may give a false impression that you are 'managing' your security. For all practical purposes, as managers no longer see 'security' as their responsibility, it may even mean that your security is no longer 'managed'.

Annex 4

A Senior Management Team Task

The argument made here, therefore, is that, especially in more volatile and higher-risk environments, the third approach be adopted whereby security is dealt with by a senior management team that involves the country representative, programme and office management, the logistician and any full-time security officer and, if at all possible, competent national staff. Only such a team can bring in the relevant information from a variety of sources, weigh the various priorities and risks against each other, and ensure the required observance of decisions.

Annex 5 Private Security Companies

The subject of private security companies is sensitive in the aid world. Yet many aid agencies, at one time or another, have had recourse to private security companies, either international or national. This annex sets out some key questions, but does not pretend to offer a comprehensive review. Nor should its inclusion in this GPR be taken as a judgement for or against private security companies.

Prejudice and Principle

There are at least four possible reservations in principle against the use of private security companies:

Mercenaries

It is incorrect to confuse private security companies with mercenaries. The term private security companies encompasses as wide a range of actors as the term NGOs, and therefore similarly obscures more than it illuminates. Without claiming that this is a well-researched classification, it is important to distinguish between:

- **'Private armies':** armed personnel for hire for active battle operations are indeed 'mercenaries'. The most prominent example was Executive Outcomes (South Africa) which operated in Angola and Sierra Leone, for example.
- **'Military advisors':** these are private companies which may not deploy armed personnel themselves but which act as 'military advisors' for the armies of contracting governments and therefore get involved in operational army manoeuvres and/or in the training and reorganisation of armies or army units for such purposes. These are functions that have been regularly performed under the heading of official, bilateral 'military assistance', certainly during the Cold War, and that now can be privatised. An example is the role of Military Professional Resources Inc. (US) during the northern Balkans war with the forces of Croatia.
- **'Private security companies with non-offensive roles':** these do not engage in any of the above, but provide security skills and expertise to clients other than armed groups such as corporate business, diplomatic missions or aid agencies.

The distinction between these categories can, in practice, be fuzzy: involvement of a 'private security company' in 'security sector reform', for example, will involve retraining of police and army units, and as a term can cover positive retraining for greater discipline, respect for human rights and the rule of law, and greater accountability. But the phrase can also conceal training and equipping for more aggressive or repressive purposes.

Military and Police

Most staff in private security companies may currently be assumed to have a military or police background. But unless one is a principled pacifist, opposed not only to war but also to the existence of a well-disciplined police force, that in itself will not be a decisive factor. Most societies in the world recognise that there can be a legitimate use of force. Moreover, police and the military are likely to have a certain expertise and specialised skills with regard to security management. This should not be rejected a priori. In recent years ex-military personnel have also found new employment in many aid agencies, often in logistics and/or security management. Whereas there have been problems with individuals, these occur equally with other aid workers from a different background. In addition, there are examples of ex-aid workers who have gone on to work for private security companies. Reportedly at least one private security company has formally subscribed to the 'Red Cross/International NGO Code of Conduct'. One strand of opinion holds that former police may have a more appropriate preparation: they have been trained to deal with criminality, may have more investigative skills and may be more restrained with regard to using arms. But much can depend on individual personalities.

Ethics and Transparency

Your organisation may come to an acceptable working agreement with a private security company, but do you know what type of work the same company does for other clients? It is in principle conceivable that the same company – or if it is part of a larger holding, another subsidiary, perhaps trading under a different name – is involved in objectionable activities, for example, the production of landmines, the sale and export of weapons, the training of private militias for exploitative international corporations, etc. Similarly, the same company may be providing VIP protection to a government official whom you hold to be responsible for violent repressive actions or who is rumoured to be involved in illegal trade. In general it is very difficult to find out about such other 'services'. The structures of subsidiaries in holdings are, usually deliberately, complex and non-transparent. And a key trading principle of private security companies is 'confidentiality'. They may well not release the names of all their clients to you, nor provide details about the precise nature of the services they perform for other clients.

Several private security companies will argue that they are themselves very careful to operate ethically because they need to maintain a clean 'reputation'. That is correct, but your request for transparency does not fit well with the operating principle of 'confidentiality' on behalf of the client.

Another consideration is the background of the personnel in the company: have they ever been involved in illegal, criminal or abusive actions before joining the private company? This is not as simple a question as it may first appear: the first national police forces in Europe, set up in the nineteenth century, often recruited criminals since they knew how bandits and criminals operated. Similarly the armies of a number of states in a post-conflict situation may well contain soldiers who have committed atrocities and abuses but were given formal amnesty or were simply 'absorbed' into a new national army. And there will be teenagers who used to be child soldiers but are now trying to reintegrate into a 'normal' environment.

Privatisation of Security

The ineffectiveness of armies and police forces worldwide, including in so-called developed countries has created a growing market for private security companies. This is a worrying trend because these are for-profit companies. Basically they will only work for those who can pay for their services. This means that the 'rich' can buy increased security, whereas the 'poor' not only remain unprotected but also become comparatively easier targets for criminals. Spending on private security rather than on the reform and capacity-building of official law and order forces whose task is to provide general public security and protection reinforces this trend (Chapter 6). Also, in the same way as aid agencies undermine national capacities by drawing away the best staff, the proliferation of private security companies may undermine the quality of national police forces by drawing away their best personnel.

What Is It You Want?

Different private security companies (with non-offensive roles) offer different services. If you consider calling upon their services you need to ask yourself what you want and whether what they offer is appropriate for your type of organisation.

Annex 5

In general, the services on offer range from information and analysis, advice, training, the provision of personnel (experts/guards/intervention or quick reaction force) and project services to management services. The following examples are illustrative but not exhaustive.

Information and analysis can be what we have called in this GPR context assessment and threat assessment: an update on the overall political, economic and social developments in a country from a security point of view, and therefore a general appreciation of threats and risks. An advisory service can include a field-level security assessment of programme or project operations under consideration or it can also follow a 'security audit' of your current security management measures. Another type of 'advisory/management' service can be the development of overall standard operating procedures (SOP) to control risk, or a more specific component of your security plan such as the evacuation plan or measures to keep confidential information indeed confidential. They may advise/take the management decision that you should replace discretionary with mandatory procedures. Private companies can offer trained guards and specialised security equipment (for example, for site protection) and/or expert personnel to take over the management role for the security of your personnel and assets.

A number of private security companies also offer training for people operating in hostile environments. Journalists and aid workers are a new type of clientele for this kind of training. Training packages can be very diverse, ranging from general security awareness, to battlefield survival or hostage survival and rescue, with sometimes special sessions on topics such as surviving in extreme climates (hot/cold), counter-surveillance, post-traumatic stress disorder, route reconnaissance, map reading and navigation, or cultural sensitivity. It is up to you to be very clear about your specific training needs and priorities before you send people on a training course, or before negotiating a tailor-made training for you and your staff.

A key consideration in using private security companies, as with every hiring of outside expertise, is how to make it contribute to your in-house knowledge and expertise. How can you learn from them, and retain that knowledge and skill? The services offered by private for-profit companies, especially when they are used to working with corporate clients, may also carry quite a serious price tag. How do you invest so that your organisation gets the best value for money?

Match and Mismatch

Anecdotal evidence indicates that the experience of aid agencies with private security companies is mixed. Some have genuinely benefited from the specialised security skills that they provide, others have found that they tended to offer a 'one size fits all' approach to security management (generally towards the protection and deterrence strategies, rather than acceptance-oriented). What fits diplomatic missions or business corporations (and the UN?) is not necessarily appropriate for NGOs, with their decentralised mode of decision making, comparatively weak authority structures and discipline, charitable or humanitarian impulse and desire to be close to their target communities and intended beneficiaries. Security services and advice need to be adapted to their specific considerations and styles.

Selecting a Private Security Company

There are a number of questions that you may want to ask when considering using a private security company.

- If of international character, where are they registered, and/or are they registered and/or licensed also in the country where you want to use their services?
- What are they willing to tell you about their owners and shareholders and their affiliation with other companies or subsidiaries?
- What information are they willing to give about their clients and the services they have provided to different clients; do you get a selective sample or a fuller record?
- Whom of former or current clients could you get references from? (Other clients may not necessarily know more about the full range of activities of the company than you do!)
- What range of services do they offer?
- What precise service are you looking for?
- If they provide armed guards, are they properly licensed to carry arms and trained to use them?
- What is the background to their personnel, and what procedures do they have for screening their personnel before hiring them?
- Does the company subscribe to an internal or external code of practice? What does it say about:

- compliance with international and national laws and regulations;
- the clients they will not work with;
- the services they will not provide;
- the integrity of subcontractors they in turn may work with;
- the background of staff they will employ;
- relations with manufacturers/suppliers of security equipment/arms;
- the practice of 'commissions' or other inducements for information or services;
- the confidentiality surrounding clients and information about clients obtained in the course of service;
- procedures and actions following a suspected or reported breach of the ethical code?

Some Observations

The relationship between aid agencies and private security companies is clearly an uneasy one. It is up to the private security companies which want to market themselves as 'bona fide' and relevant to make clear their distinctions from 'private armies' and the like, and to put forward the guarantees they can offer about their quality and also their ethical integrity. It is also time aid organisations get together to review and evaluate their experiences with private security companies, and to formulate what they would consider the minimum ethical standards and the provision of security expertise appropriate for the aid world.

Annex 6 Insurance Cover

Insurance cover provides compensation, not protection!

Cost of Insurance and Non-insurance

Safety and security accidents and incidents can have major financial consequences for the aid worker concerned, for his/her family and for the agency. There are:

- immediate costs, such as for evacuation on medical grounds, bills for medical treatment, funeral expenses, etc, which can quickly run into very large sums of money;
- potential longer term costs, such as those resulting from permanent disability (for example, following the loss of one or two legs on a landmine); or the inability to obtain future insurance coverage when HIV positive.

Aid workers are often not briefed on the details of the insurance coverage the agency provides. Many aid agencies also do not have adequate insurance cover for war risk and malicious acts because of the high cost involved. This may be in breach of Health and Safety Regulations. Aid agencies are gradually paying more attention to this, stimulated, in part, by cases in which insurance companies refused to pay out or injured aid workers or the families of deceased aid workers sued the agency for compensation. Such direct compensation claims can bring small agencies to the brink of bankruptcy.

What to Inquire Into?

This annex is not based on a specialised examination of accident and war insurance policies and practices, but indicates some of the key issues that the individual aid worker and the security managers and/or agency headquarters need to consider. Aid workers are advised to obtain details from their organisation, but also to contact insurance companies and mortgage lenders and professional bodies.

What is the maximum coverage for:

- medical expenses;
- temporary partial disability (check the interpretation of 'temporary');
- temporary total disability (ditto);
- permanent partial disability;

- permanent total disability;
- loss of life?

Exclusion Clauses

Often insurance policies do not apply under certain conditions, and the details and interpretation of these exclusion clauses can be vitally important. Examples are:

- coverage only during work assignment (eg, while in Somalia, but not during a period of rest and relaxation in Nairobi);
- coverage only during working hours (eg, up to 18 hours, but not after or during weekends);
- coverage excludes war zones (what is the interpretation of 'war zone'?);
- coverage only if the agency has written guidelines;
- coverage only if the agency has written security guidelines which are demonstrably enforced (here the security manager may be held accountable);
- coverage only if the agency has security guidelines and provides security training;
- coverage only if the aid worker was following security guidelines (here the security manager will be held to account).

Other exclusion clauses can apply, for example, to staff on short-term contracts (may apply to consultants but does it also apply to international staff on a three-month assignment?) or to staff older than a certain age (often 59 years).

Invalidation of Other Insurance Policies

You need to crosscheck not only the extent of your accident and insurance coverage while working in risk areas, but also the potential impact of doing so on other existing insurance policies you have. Sometimes life assurance policies (such as those taken out with a mortgage) can become invalidated if you go and work in a high-risk area.

Beneficiaries of Life Assurance Policies

The whole question of insurance cover probably becomes even more important if there are dependants, typically a partner/spouse and children but perhaps also partly dependent elderly parents. You need to crosscheck not only the exclusion clauses, but also that they are clearly nominated as beneficiaries if you lose your life.

Cover After End of Contract

Journalists and aid workers injured or maimed in the course of their assignment may suffer the consequences long after their contracts have ended. They should question the applicability of insurance cover after the termination of their contract, and the moral but also tangible obligation that the agency acknowledges if there is no or inadequate insurance cover. An agency may choose to deal with this on a case-by-case basis, but that should not prevent it from spelling out some clear conditional parameters that will guide its final decision.

Insurance Premium Rates

Some insurance companies lower their premium rates for high risk areas, by as much as 30 per cent if the insured person can demonstrate that s/he has followed appropriate security training provided by a recognised/accredited agency. This has already been taken up by the journalist profession, but not to such an extent by the aid sector.

Insurance and National Staff

International aid agencies can be reluctant to address the issue of insurance cover for national staff as a matter of general policy. The most commonly used argument is that there are often large numbers of nationally recruited staff and the cost of international insurance cover for all would be prohibitive. Requests for compensation or financial assistance in the case of disease, injury or death are usually dealt with on a case-by-case basis. Although one can argue that all staff should be treated equally, the practical reality is that financial constraints exist and that aid agencies cannot fully insure large numbers of local people in conflict zones. That is no reason, however, to avoid the issue altogether. A country may be experiencing open conflict (eg, Sri Lanka) or violent crime (eg, Nigeria) and have a functioning national insurance sector that can be consulted. In other places (for instance, Afghanistan, Somalia, Chechnya) there will be an indigenous practice of 'compensation' payment, on which you can consult your national staff. In yet other places it is the practice for groups of relatives and friends to set up a common savings fund, and you can discuss with your national staff members the creation of such one 'insurance pot', with perhaps a lump sum of start-up capital from the organisation and monthly contributions from the participating employees.

Annex 6

Case Study: Insurance for a Kosovo Operation

An American aid organisation operating in Kosovo after the NATO campaign of early 1999 had full insurance. Its vehicles were insured through Swiss and Macedonia-based companies while all its staff and their personal assets were insured through a US-based company. Some national staff members lost all their personal belongings when their house, next to that of a Serb family which was set on fire through arson, also burned down. They were able to be fully compensated.

Resource:
See: Davidson, S and Neal, J (1998) *Under Cover? Insurance for Aid Workers* <www.peopleinaid.co.uk/undercover.htm>

The Humanitarian Practice Network – HPN
(formerly the Relief and Rehabilitation Network – RRN)

The Humanitarian Practice Network (HPN) is the new name for the Relief and Rehabilitation Network (RRN). As from 1 April 2000 the new **HPN** will continue the work of the former RRN in contributing to improved practice in the humanitarian field, but with several important changes.

The success of the RRN in producing objective, analytical and accessible material was confirmed by the conclusions of a recent independent external review (Sept–Nov 1999). The review also found that humanitarian practitioners are increasingly using its publications and that the Network compares very favourably with other professional information services. As a result of the review the purpose of the Network has been re-articulated to emphasise its role of stimulating critical analysis, advancing the professional learning and development of those engaged in and around humanitarian action, and improving practice.

Why the name change?
The use of the word 'humanitarian' in the **Humanitarian Practice Network (HPN)** is more in tune with today's way of thinking, and 'practice' reflects all that we do and who we target.

What else is changing?
Publishing will remain **HPN's** primary activity. Good Practice Reviews, published once a year as the flagship publication, will remain as management reference guides on a particular topic ' but with the further aim of being used as training manuals by specialist training organisations. Network Papers will be produced three times a year as a critical review of a specific thematic or sectoral topic, or an analytical and critical reflection of a particular approach in a specific country/region. The successor to the Newsletter will be published twice-yearly as a resource document with updates, practice notes and features.

The **HPN** *website* will become a key reference site for those in the humanitarian field, providing a resource gateway into the humanitarian sector. It will store the majority of past publications in English and French which can be downloaded for free. The value of the website will be enhanced by the number of organised web-links to key players in the sector, strengthening the thematic search function, creating a profile of masters and training courses relating to the humanitarian sector, and having a conference and educational/training courses announcement page. More opportunity for feedback will be possible through the enhanced website and, where authors agree, readers will be able to dialogue directly with them.

How do I join?
The **HPN** Newsletter is FREE to all on request. Full membership to the **HPN** costs only £20.00 per year (£10.00 for students) and entails automatic receipt of all **HPN** publications as they are produced, as well as a discount when ordering back copies. A number of FREE subscriptions are available to those actively involved in humanitarian assistance operations or in ongoing activities in countries experiencing complex political emergencies.

If you would like to subscribe to the **HPN**, visit our website <www.odihpn.org.uk> and subscribe on-line. Alternatively, contact the **HPN** via email at <hpn@odi.org.uk> or at the address on the inside cover of this GPR and the Network will mail you a copy of the latest newsletter, which contains a registration form.

The Humanitarian Practice Network is part
of the Humanitarian Policy Group at

Overseas Development Institute

Publications List
(June 2000)

Network Papers

HPN Network Papers are contributions on specific experiences or issues prepared either by **HPN** Members or contributing specialists.

Listed below are all **HPN** Network Papers produced between 1997 and 1999, with a selection of some of the earlier 'best-sellers' (1994-1996). For a full publications list, contact the **HPN** Administrator.

1994-1996 'Best-sellers'

7   *Code of Conduct for the International Red Cross and Red Crescent Movement and NGOs in Disaster Relief*   Ed. J. Borton (1993)

10 *Room for Improvement: the Management and Support of Relief Workers* by R. Macnair (1995)

12 *Dilemmas of 'Post'-Conflict Transition: Lessons from the Health Sector* by J. Macrae (1995)

13 *Getting On-Line in Emergencies: A Guide and Directory to the Internet for Agencies involved in Relief and Rehabilitation* by L. Aris et al (1995)

14 *The Impact of War and Atrocity on Civilian Populations: Basic Principles for NGO Interventions and a Critique of Psychosocial Trauma Projects* by D. Summerfield (1995)

15 *Cost-effectiveness Analysis: A Useful Tool for the Assessment and Evaluation of Relief Operations?* by A. Hallam (1996)

16 *The Joint Evaluation of Emergency Assistance to Rwanda: Study III Main Findings and Recommendations* Ed. J. Borton (1996)

1997-2000

19 *Human Rights and International Legal Standards: What Relief Workers Need to Know* by J. Darcy (1997)

20 *People in Aid Code of Best Practice in the Management and Support of Aid Personnel* Ed. S. Davidson (1997)

21 *Humanitarian Principles: The Southern Sudan Experience* by I. Levine (1997)

22 *The War Economy in Liberia: A Political Analysis by* P. Atkinson (1997)

23 *The Coordination of Humanitarian Action: the case of Sri Lanka* by K. Van Brabant (1997)

24 *Reproductive Health for Displaced Populations* by C. Palmer (1998)

25 *Humanitarian Action in Protraced Crises: The New Relief 'Agenda' and its Limits* by D. Hendrickson (1998)

26 *The Food Economy Approach: A Framework for Understanding Rural Livelihoods* byT. Boudreau (1998)

27 *Between Relief and Development: targeting food aid for disaster prevention in Ethiopia* by K. Sharp (1998)

28 *North Korea: The Politics of Food Aid* by J. Bennett (1999)

29 *Participatory Review in Chronic Instability: The Experience of the Ikafe Refugee Settlement Programme, Uganda* by K. Neefjes (1999)

30 *Protection in Practice: Field-Level Strategies for Protecting Civilians from Deliberate Harm* by D. Paul (1999)

31 *The Impact of Economic Sanctions on Health and Well-being* by R. Garfield (1999)

32 *Humanitarian Mine Action: The First Decade of a New Sector in Humanitarian Aid* by C. Horwood (2000)

Good Practice Reviews

HPN Good Practice Reviews are commissioned 'state-of-the-art' reviews on different sectors or activities within the humanitarian field. Prepared by recognised specialists, and subject to peer review, they are produced in a format that is readily accessible to field-based personnel.

1994

1   *Water and Sanitation in Emergencies* by A. Chalinder

2   *Emergency Supplementary Feeding Programmes* by J. Shoham

1996

3   *General Food Distribution in Emergencies: from Nutritional Needs to Political Priorities* by S. Jaspars & H. Young

1997

4   *Seed Provision During and After Emergencies* by the ODI Seeds and Biodiversity Programme

5   *Counting and Identification of Beneficiary Populations in Emergency Operations: Registration and its Alternatives* by J. Telford

1998

6   *Temporary Human Settlement Planning for Displaced Populations in Emergencies* by A. Chalinder

7   *EvaluatingHumanitarian Assistance Programmes in Complex Emergencies* by A. Hallam

2000

8   *Operational Security Management in Violent Environments* by K. Van Brabant (£14.95 + p&p)

Newsletters

HPN Newsletters provide a forum for brief reflections on current developments in the field, key policy issues, etc. Hard copies of the Newsletter are available FREE and an electronic version can be downloaded from the **HPN** website.

Placing a Publications Order

Network Papers	£5.00/3.50* + p&p
Good Practice Reviews	£10.00/7.50* + p&p
Newsletters	FREE

*A discount rate applies to **HPN** members who purchase back or additional copies of publications. Discounts are available for bulk orders. An additional charge is made for postage and packing.

Email: hpn@odi.org.uk Website: www.odihpn.org.uk